The Family Office

Boris Canessa • Jens Escher
Alexander Koeberle-Schmid
Peter Preller • Christoph Weber

The Family Office

A Practical Guide to Strategically and Operationally Managing Family Wealth

palgrave
macmillan

Boris Canessa
Düsseldorf, Germany

Jens Escher
Duisburg, Germany

Alexander Koeberle-Schmid
Köln, Germany

Peter Preller
Bad Homburg, Germany

Christoph Weber
Essen, Germany

ISBN 978-3-030-40380-5 ISBN 978-3-319-99085-9 (eBook)
https://doi.org/10.1007/978-3-319-99085-9

Library of Congress Control Number: 2018955893

Cover credit: Nednapa Chumjumpa / EyeEm

This Palgrave Macmillan imprint is published by the registered company Springer Nature Switzerland AG
The registered company address is: Gewerbestrasse 11, 6330 Cham, Switzerland

Translator's Preface

There is an old parable about the wise woman and a glass jar. She drops large stones into the jar until no more will fit, and then asks a child whether the container is full. "Yes, it is," says the child. So the wise woman adds in smaller rocks which tumble into the remaining spaces. When the child opines that now the jar is full, the wise woman pours in pebbles, then sand, and finally water. Each new material, smaller and finer than the one before, closes the ever-shrinking gaps until truly the jar can hold no more.

As I helped shepherd this book from a focus on the German-speaking world to a broader international outlook, I had that jar very much in mind. Each of the five authors is a specialist in a field crucial to the operation of a family office—law, family governance, leadership and succession and asset analysis and investment. Their chapters serve the same function as those big rocks, addressing the major weighty considerations that are involved with establishing and operating a family office.

The numerous interviews in this book are the smaller rocks, helping to fill the gaps that naturally arise between theory and practice. They contain insights and considerations gleaned from real experience working or advising a family office, building one from scratch, or being an owner of an established family office.

The new final chapter of this book delivers the pebbles. It reflects two specific questions posed to each interview partner: Firstly, what are potential traps that people face when looking to found or sustain a family office? Secondly, what is the future of the family office? The answers sometimes contradict each other, and that is fine. Real life contradicts itself sometimes as well, especially as you move firmly into the realm of your own specific needs and solutions.

And the sand and water of our parable? That fine-grained knowledge is to be provided by you and the generations that follow.

Königswinter, Germany Steven Sidore

Preface

The model of the family office dates back to medieval times. Its core function was embodied by the figure of the majordomo, the highest-ranking servant for a European house of nobility, entrusted to manage the house's domestic affairs. The first family office in the modern sense, the Morgan House, was founded in 1838 by captain of industry J.P. Morgan to serve his family. The office later took on the Vanderbilts, Guggenheims and DuPonts as clients, evolving into the first multi family office.

The real breakthrough for the family office came in the 1980s, a period of unprecedented wealth creation. Yet this had little to do with private jets, yachts, holiday villas and imposing oak-paneled offices. Disenchanted with the flaws inherent to commercial wealth management offerings, a growing number of ultra high net worth individuals and entrepreneurial families—first in the USA, then in Europe—simply began looking for alternatives. Many saw the wisdom in Morgan's choice to establish a separate, highly competent "deputy" between the family and its financial service providers. These new single family offices worked exclusively for their respective families to preserve and expand the accumulated wealth for the generations to come.

Financial service providers did not fail to grasp the potential of this trend as a potent business field for themselves. Wealth managers, larger auditing firms and tax accountancies began developing their own in-house family office-style service packages. Later, large financial institutions began offering packages of services divorced from their classic private banking or wealth management departments—the dawn of the commercial bank-bound multi family office. Over time some of those providers withdrew from the market, leading their former employees to found a wave of new, independent multi family office companies. These then served a clientele ranging from a handful of families to a high two-digit number of families, all very individually and hopefully free of conflict of interest.

The number of billionaires has grown sharply worldwide in recent years, with especially powerful growth observed in China. For the first time in documented history, 2017 counted more billionaires in Asia (637) than in the USA (563). Driven by this ongoing global creation of affluence, the ranks of single family offices have grown ceaselessly in recent years. At the same time, hundreds of multi family offices have also arisen around the world, especially in Latin America, the Middle East and Asia. With roughly $2.4 trillion expected to be passed on to the next generation in the coming two decades, many affluent families and wealthy individuals see real value in having a family office as a loyal partner and competent advisor. They rest easier knowing they have an organization working for them that can adapt to changing conditions and family dynamics and scale as the family and its wealth grow more complex.

This book approaches the almost dizzying array of family office solutions as its challenge and its mission. It was conceived as a forthcoming, transparent and above all else practically minded introduction for affluent families in the early stages of considering a family office. We, the five authors, are active practitioners within the family office sphere, and some of us are also member-owners of a family office. We try to write clearly and frankly about the advantages and disadvantages of single family offices and multi family offices, as well as classic bank-based wealth management without a family office. Our goal at all times is to demystify the topic and lend courage for families to get organized and undertake their first steps in this field.

The first edition of our book was written in German and aimed at the German-speaking family office market. While a few books had already been published on the topic, we felt collectively that those books were more aimed at decision-makers at existing family offices or family officers looking to deepen their technical knowledge. What was missing was an introductory book for those who had sensed the issue of 'conflicts of interests' in dealing with banks and other external consultants, yet lacked even the right questions to begin a serious exploration of setting up an institution of their own, or joining an existing one. The strong positive feedback we received showed that our approach was warranted.

This second edition has been revised and updated to reflect the broader international market. The material has been grouped into three informal sections:

Part I: Family Office Fundamentals (Chaps. 1–3),
Part II: Family Office Tasks and Strategies (Chaps. 4–9),
Part III: Family Office Governance (Chaps. 10–14).

Some chapters have been rewritten entirely, others supplemented to appeal outside Germany. Facts and figures have been refreshed. New trends on the market have been incorporated. Many new interviews were conducted with partners serving families from the Middle East, Africa, the US, Canada, Mexico and Europe. We would like to thank all those family members and family officers who spoke frankly and openly about their individual family offices and their approach. We collected our observations together in this book because we believe that sharing knowledge benefits both the field and the families in it. We are grateful that our many interview partners chose to join in this mission.

Special thanks go to Steven Sidore of In-Tense Translation for preparing this manuscript. Mr. Sidore did much more than simply translate the German version into English; he edited, restructured, re-wrote and drafted new chapters to break them out of their 'German' mindset and ensure that they would speak to a broad audience. He also supported and transcribed the book's many interviews. Without him, this book would not have been published in this format.

Our thanks also go out to Palgrave Macmillan for agreeing to publish this second international edition, and to our editors Ms. Tula Weis and Mr. Joseph Johnson for their steady support. We also thank Ms. Stefanie Winter from Springer Gabler who published the first edition of this book.

And of course our thanks go out to you, our readers, for putting your trust in our insights. We believe this work will educate without overloading—and open the door for you to start asking the right questions of your own advisors and planning a solid foundation for this and future generations. For this, we wish you all the best.

Düsseldorf, Germany	Boris Canessa
Duisburg, Germany	Jens Escher
Köln, Germany	Alexander Koeberle-Schmid
Bad Homburg, Germany	Peter Preller
Essen, Germany	Christoph Weber

Contents

About the Authors

Boris Canessa is a part of a large industrial family whose many branches now cover over 200 members in many different nations worldwide. In 2005 he and a number of his relatives founded a single family office to offer comprehensive consulting to family members. Since then he has served as the chairman of the family office's advisory board. Boris Canessa is also member of the board at the German Association of Independent Family Offices (VuFO).

Jens Escher, LL.M. (attorney at law/tax adviser/certified tax attorney) is a salary partner at the international law firm Taylor Wessing in Düsseldorf (Private Client/Tax). He focuses on consulting for corporations, high net worth private clients and their family offices in the areas of succession/asset structuring/foundations. He is also an honorary professor at the University of Leipzig in the field of tax law and a lecturer in the field of "Corporate Succession, Inheritance & Wealth Management" at JurGrad GmbH (University of Münster).

Alexander Koeberle-Schmid holds the titles of Diplom-Kaufmann, Mediator (BM®) as well as Succession and Executive Coach (ICF). He studied at the WHU—Otto Beisheim School of Management, earning his doctorate there on the topic of "Family Business Governance." As an expert in family business succession, family constitutions, boards of directors, governance and family offices, he has advised many different families in Europe, Asia and the Middle East.

Alexander Koeberle-Schmid supports family-run companies and family offices as an independent member of their board of directors, publishes regularly on the topic of family-run businesses, family business governance and family offices, is a popular speaker and media expert on issues related to this field (quoted e. g. in Frankfurter Allgemeine Zeitung, Wall Street Journal, Manager Magazin). He is a lecturer in the field of Strategy, Family Business Governance and Mid-Sized Companies at EBS Universität für Wirtschaft and Recht and the FHDW Fachhochschule der Wirtschaft in Germany.

Peter Preller, LL.M. has served since October 2011 as the senior client consultant at HQ Trust GmbH in Bad Homburg, the multi family office for the Harald Quandt family, offering comprehensive consulting for complex client assets. He has over 16 years of professional experience in the fields of family office and asset management, with a focus on consulting and support for large private portfolios, family associations and foundations. Mr. Preller was named partner in 2012. Prior to 2011 he worked as a client advisor at UBS Sauerborn, a unit of UBS Deutschland AG. His initial professional experience came at FERI Family Office AG, first as an analyst focused on capital market analysis and hedge fund research in the Research department and then starting in 2003 as a Junior Client Advisor at the Sauerborn Trust AG multi family office. Peter Preller, born in 1976, holds a graduate degree in Business administration and holds an executive MBA in "Private Wealth Management," earning a Master of Laws (LL. M.). In 2008 he became a Certified Corporate Succession Consultant (zentUma e. V.). Since 2014 he has been an instructor in the Master's program in "Corporate Succession, Inheritance and Wealth Management" at the University of Münster.

Christoph Weber is managing director and co-founder of the WSH Family Office, Düsseldorf. After studying economics and training as a banker, Christoph Weber worked in various managerial positions in the central private client unit at Commerzbank, and then helped establish and lead the family office of the private banking house Trinkaus & Burkhardt in Düsseldorf. In 1999, Weber joined with two mid-sized family-run firms to found the WSH Deutsche Vermögenstreuhand in Düsseldorf. He also served as the managing director of the new organization, which was structured as a classic family office for the founding families and a small circle of select entrepreneurial families. His consulting was focused on strategic asset allocation, comprehensive financial planning and management of large private portfolios. He has published numerous articles on these topics in industry journals. Christoph Weber frequently supports academic projects on research topics in fields related to family offices and family governance. He is also chairman of the board at the German Association of Independent Family Offices (VuFO).

List of Figures

List of Tables

1

What is a Family Office?

Boris Canessa, Christoph Weber,
and Alexander Koeberle-Schmid

The basic concept of a family office is simple: an entrepreneurial family establishes a financial back office dedicated exclusively to the management of its wealth. Historically, the first families to build out this model were ultra high net worth industrial giants with names such as Morgan, Vanderbilt, Dupont and Guggenheim. The employees of these new organizations were tasked with attending to the external financial interests of the family, at a level of professionalism matching or exceeding that found in the family's own operating business. Over time, those employees would come to handle all reporting, supervising and controlling tasks for the family and its members. This was the original form of the family office, which today would be called a 'single family office.'

The defining characteristic of the family office is its freedom from conflict of interest: It pursues no commercial interests of its own and its entire staff are employees of the family. This fundamental requirement serves as the foundation and cornerstone of the trust that a family must have if the family office is to fulfill its primary objective—the preservation and development of wealth—and its extended mission of fostering long-term cohesiveness in the family. It also applies, with some modifications, in the more complex form of the family office, the so-called 'multi family office.'

1.1 Why a Family Office Makes Sense

Today's ultra high net worth families are increasingly questioning the wisdom of engaging external commercial organizations to manage their wealth. Numerous academic studies have shown that dissatisfaction among bank

B. Canessa et al., *The Family Office*, https://doi.org/10.1007/978-3-319-99085-9_1

customers is at record levels. Perhaps more notably, the mass media has also picked up on the strong anger among customers, with a flurry of articles in recent years about the rising tide of complaints and lawsuits against wealth managers related to losses in securities trading. Politicians, sensing a fertile ground to connect with voters, have not shied away from criticizing banks and their investment products.

This widespread negative coverage reflects a broad-spectrum dissatisfaction among affluent parties with the consulting services of banks and financial service providers. The financial crisis that emerged in 2007 further illuminated government's seeming inability to master the rapid pace of change in this field and led many wealthy parties to re-evaluate their options. In fact, poor experiences have bred a fundamental disinclination in many wealthy individuals to shares in "bank funds" and other volatile asset classes.

Practical Example: Experiences of a Single Family Office Client

Our family office really opened our eyes! For many years, my four children and I were private wealth management clients of a large bank. Each of us had a somewhat larger portfolio under management. Given our long history together and the extensive range of consultation it offered, we trusted the bank.

At some later point, the employees of our newly founded family office took over these discussions for us. What we learned is that the bank was charging each member of our small family a different set of fees. This was quite unprofessional of them, since the services were always the same. But what really irked us was learning that even the lowest set of those fees was still more than 50% higher than customary market prices!

A different member of the family then informed his bank he was considering terminating his contract and joining our family office. When he asked whether a modified set of fees could be explored, they dropped those fees massively without any further negotiation. Another member of the family had received notification of the fee structure in writing from his bank. When the family office then controlled the numbers, it found that a variety of fees were missing from the list—and that the real accrued fees were over two-and-a-half times higher than listed.

These experiences taught us as a family that it benefits all of us to bundle our interests and knowledge onto one shared family office. I mean, each of us can do with our fortune as we please. But we don't need to all make the same mistakes, and this lets us share and learn from one another.

Wealth Management by a Family Office?

Wealthy families are increasingly asking whether there are different, more effective structures for managing their wealth. Entrepreneurs and entrepreneurial families in particular are looking for suitable alternatives for successful asset investment and a full range of consulting on asset-related questions. At its core, a new type of wealth manager is being sought. The family office appears to offer a solution.

Before exploring the question of if and how a family office can meet the specific needs of high net worth families, it makes sense to first flesh out the definition of what one is. Easier said than done, unfortunately, as there is no uniform, globally accepted definition of a family office. One reason for this is that family offices can be set up in a wide variety of ways and pursue a wide range of core missions. Sara S. Hamilton, founder of the Family Office Exchange, sees the family office as a central resource that develops custom strategies tailored to a family's specific needs. Family offices can serve as a controlling instance for costs and streamline the use of external strategic consultants. In her view, the concept of the family office is rooted deeply in traditions and activities that have withstood the passage of time.

In his book "Family Office in Private Wealth Management," Peter Schaubach, a professor specialized in family offices, defines family offices as an "organizational unit established by a family or individual with a large portfolio of complex assets to grow that wealth more effectively; it achieves this by bundling the strategic, tactical and operative services related to the configuration, coordination and mobilization of financial, social and human assets, harnessing long-term advantages that help create value" (Schaubach 2011, p. 63).

Christian von Bechtolsheim and Andreas Rhein, both family office experts, writing in their publication "Management of Complex Family Assets," underscore the central importance of engaging a family officer free from any conflicts of interest: "The decisive factor is a family officer who serves as a trustee in the interests of the wealthy party. Starting from a position of freedom from conflicts of interest, he can steer the overall portfolio to meet the specific needs and objectives of the client. This independence is another essential characteristic and differentiation criterion for family offices" (von Bechtolsheim and Rhein 2009, p. 371f). Unlike the representatives of a bank, the family officer is working solely in the interest of the wealthy individual. He has no underlying mission to sell any specific investment product. The book "The New Family Office" by Lisa Gray, a renowned family office consultant, builds on this point:

> They must transform their identities from investment management consultants into wealth optimization consultants, realizing that the wealth optimization consulting model provides the basis for long-term competitive superiority. (...) educating investment management consultants in such wealth management disciplines as compensation plans, retirement plans, alternative investment strategies, asset protection, estate and gift tax codes and charitable planning. (Gray 2004, p. 3)

Synthesizing these various definitions, we arrive at the following description: a family office is a self-contained organizational unit belonging to one or more families or individuals with a large portfolio of complex assets. It exists to organize the management of that wealth by bundling assets and streamlining services for better long-term growth. The active consulting that the family office provides to its individual members or family as a whole must always be free of conflicts of interest.

1.2 Reasons for Founding a Family Office

With this basic understanding of the family office—one that will be enhanced considerably in the chapters to follow—we can now turn to the considerations and situations that can potentially drive a wealthy family to establish a family office. One important caveat in advance: Every wealthy family looks back on its own unique past and out onto its own current self-identity and situation. The potential paths that lead to the creation of a family office are just as distinctive and varied. In many cases, the sale of the family's company has put the family into unfamiliar territory.

The sale of the family's company can have the following impacts:

- **A sudden rise in current assets,** typically in the form of (low-return) liquidity. A family in this position can feel a certain (subjective) pressure to invest the assets more professionally and effectively, or to apply it to further entrepreneurial goals.
- **The loss of the professional management team** that had previously, if indirectly, also handled strategic questions related to the investment of private assets and which had guaranteed the family a certain threshold of financial expertise and a collegial exchange of ideas.
- **The loss of the clerical staff** that had always handled the many different administrative tasks with efficiency and professionalism.

(*continued*)

(continued)

- **Constant overtures from private banks, wealth managers and other (typically sales-oriented) capital market experts** competing for a mandate to manage the assets. The language, approach and thought processes on the part of these experts is often entirely different from the way the wealthy family is used to being addressed. This can produce an inner sense of pressure to "do something sensible."
- **Loss of identity.** Up until the sale, the family's self-identity was tied up in its entrepreneurial nature and with the company itself. Cohesiveness, pride and the family's sense of self were based on that business success. After the sale of the firm, the desire can often arise to engage in a new set of entrepreneurial activities.
- There is precious **little time** to become accustomed to the new state of things and to accommodate to the new normal.

These and other changes leave the family feeling suddenly at risk of falling apart as a family (and in particular as a "business-owning" family). In addition, the loss of the mission to lead and support the company can leave a certain void, particularly among the family members active in the company. To counteract this dissolution of the family and to provide a new entrepreneurial goal to its members, a family office is often founded to serve as a shared anchor and "new family firm." In many cases a new family constitution reflecting the modified situation is also composed. Following the sale of the company, the family leader faces distinctive challenges: His or her gravitas and leadership skills are crucial to keeping the family and the fortune intact and helping define a new vision of their future together.

The leader of a small family (in the first or second generation) may well be able to induce the creation of family office structures on her own, especially if the family is used to accepting the suggestions ("instructions") of the family leader uncritically. Timing matters, however. There is often not much time to try to counteract the centrifugal forces that set in after a cash event.

When considering a family office, the family leader should take into consideration the fundamentally changed character of its asset portfolio. After all, leading a company and managing a private fortune are two very different endeavors. During the initial stages in particular, the primary focus should be on creating new structures that are free from conflicts of interest and competent networks that help the wealthy party structure, diversify and invest the assets optimally. A single family office or a multi family office free of conflicts of interest are potential options.

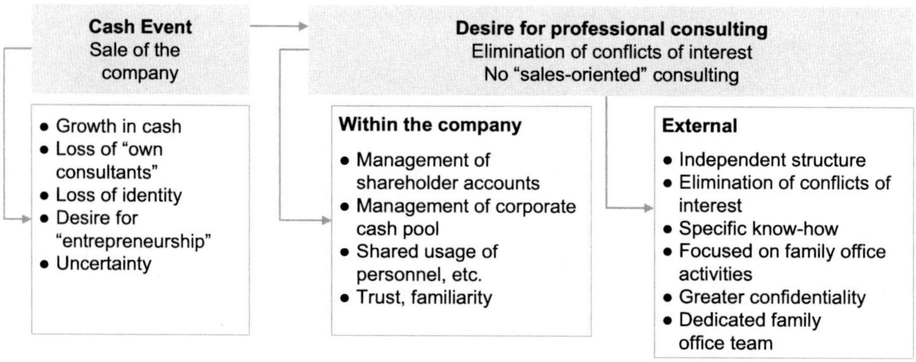

Fig. 1.1 Common reasons for founding or joining a family office

The process is more complicated if the family leader must convince a larger number of shareholders about the benefits of founding a family office and/or if an extended family is to be integrated. In such a situation it is recommended that the 'opinion crafting' work be started even before the official date of the cash event, meaning before the money flows into private shareholder accounts and countless wealth managers begin "wooing" the beneficiaries (see Fig. 1.1).

Professional, Risk-Appropriate Consulting for Investable Wealth
There are also other reasons why a family might potentially desire the benefits of a family office. Developments within the family business can potentially heighten the appeal of a dedicated but stand-alone wealth management institution, such as when the divestment of individual company units and the acquisition of (minority) shares in other companies sets the stage for a diversified family holding. Because each subsidiary of the holding has its own executive structure, the corporate executives often experience a reduced workload. Their attention must instead swing to a rising wave of portfolio management and risk diversification tasks and identifying synergies, as well as tax issues and questions of asset management and supervision. The liquidity from the divestments and new acquisitions must also be professionally invested within the holding structures. In such situations, the holding companies sometimes develop into comprehensive family offices, frequently with a focus on the private equity field.

1.3 Expectations of the Family Office

At this point we have spent some time discussing the background and attractiveness of a family office, but little discussing the concrete tasks or potential structures of a family office. While the latter topic will be explored in detail in Chap. 2, we can now delve into the nuts and bolts of what a family can expect from their family office.

1.3.1 Professional Wealth Management

A family office is created primarily to establish a greater degree of professionalism and positive results in wealth management. In some cases, this occurs through active management of stock portfolios by the wealthy party. The family office then supports in direct, affordable and transparent capital investment, delivering benchmarks for objective comparisons with other managers. With time, the family office tailors its wealth management methods to fit the needs of the specific family, to the advantage of all of its clients.

For many family offices, the actual trading in securities, buying and selling of stocks, bonds, raw materials, and derivatives is often just one small part of its wealth management program. In fact, some family offices do not personally handle such portfolios at all, instead concentrating exclusively on picking external wealth managers and negotiating advantageous wealth management contracts and fee structures. In this way, family offices lay the groundwork for more effective forecasting and better performance by all participants.

Of even greater priority for many wealth holders is avoiding a major loss of assets. This concern is understandable, as a significant destruction of wealth or a personal bankruptcy on the part of even one single family member can potentially do more than just threaten the cohesion of the family. Such events can put irreconcilable strains on the continued existence of the family-run company itself. A family office is an effective tool in this regard, as it inherently involves an intensive, professional audit of all contracts and investments. Coupled with a competent and comprehensive review of statuses and relationships, significant risks can be identified and addressed before they ever occur. The structural changes typically suggested by the family office, including for example the founding of limited liability investment trusts, are an effective hedge against such irrecoverable losses. Some may downplay the potential for grievous losses or bankruptcy among a family member, calling such scenarios absurd or scaremongering. A family office should not, however, operate on a provision basis, as this approach by definition encourages it to serve its own interests. Its activities should be solely oriented toward the interests of the family. Uniform and consistent asset reporting by the family office, stretching across all asset classes and managers and conducted on an ongoing basis, is a tremendous aid to knowledgeable, data-driven decision making.

A family office also assumes responsibility for archiving contracts and documentation. It can then serve as a convenient, lower-cost contact for tax-related questions and information, while also maintaining the paper trail that is essential to reclaiming damages in the event of misconduct by one of the managers. A family office not only encourages this model of advanced asset management—it often improves performance significantly, while streamlining costs at the same time.

1.3.2 Promoting Family Unity

Beyond this, the family office offers the wealthy family counselling on questions of family governance and internal cooperation. While it may not be clear at the time of founding, a family office also eventually can play an important role in reinforcing a family's shared sense of identity. The family office coordinates and promotes not just the flow of information within the family, but also serves in some cases as the coordinator and first point of contact in the establishment of a family constitution and organizing the ownership and management transition.

In addition, it can serve in a mediating role if conflicting opinions arise within the family (see Fig. 1.2). Yet there are limits to how much the family office can actually mediate family conflicts. What the family office can do is raise such discussions to a more objective and professional level, helping to separate emotion from factual issues during discussions within the family. But

Fig. 1.2 Potential considerations when founding or joining of a family office

its potential as a lightning rod, mediator or judge in such family arguments is highly limited.

When family contracts (including wills, marriage contracts and medical power of attorney notices) are composed or revised, the family office can also function as a discreet and neutral partner with the freedom to ask difficult questions. It also handles the filing, administration and routine upkeep of any generated documents. In this way, a family office strengthens the sense of association within the founding family and makes an active contribution to forging an "entrepreneurial spirit" and shared sense of entrepreneurial responsibility, especially among the younger generation.

1.3.3 Other Benefits

A family office can also relieve the family of time-intensive issues beyond mere wealth management. One example: in its role as a family secretary, the family office can also coordinate and even take over services typically known as "concierge" or "lifestyle management" issues, such as booking plane flights and organizing moves. In many cases it can also manage insurance policies (health and life insurance, general liability insurance), employee contracts and even the processing of payments (including private transactions). Tasks such as cataloging art collections, supporting in the acquisition of private real estate and secretarial services are often offered as side services by family offices.

The press often tries to prop up such services as the central purpose of family offices. Such reports are the reason why family offices are often perceived by the wider public to be "event planners for the extravagances of the super-rich"—and not as highly professional wealth consultants who, in a role that is free of conflicts of interest, can effectively serve the interests and needs of successful owners of mid-sized businesses.

In reality, the ability of a family office to offer such services on a large scale is limited. For one, the personnel structure of a family office is not typically suited for these types of lifestyle services. Beyond this, the framework conditions (defining of costs and fees and proper staffing levels) for such services are not normally taken into consideration during the founding or selection of a family office. They are, as the name suggestions, a convenience, but not the main mission.

As Mark H. Daniell, a family officer, and Sara S. Hamilton, founder of the Family Office Exchange, write in "Family Legacy and Leadership":

> Wealth can be a door to a far more fulfilling life for individual family members. It can also provide the foundation for a positive and lasting legacy for the family as a whole. However, without a clear philosophy of wealth, financial advance can trigger conflict and heighten feelings of regret or guilt among inheritors. By defining a philosophy of wealth clearly, potential negative consequences can be avoided. (Daniell and Hamilton 2010, p. 19)

Practical Tip: Use of a Family Office

Think early about the economic benefits, the benefit of family unity, and other benefits a family office can provide for you and your family, and what concrete financial expectations you hold. Those will help dictate the responsibilities of your family office.

Bibliography

von Bechtolsheim C, Rhein A (2009) Management komplexer Familienvermögen – Organisation. Strategie, Umsetzung, 2nd edn. Gabler, Wiesbaden

Daniell MH, Hamilton S (2010) Family legacy and leadership – Preserving true family wealth in challenging times, 1st edn. Wiley, Singapore

Gray L (2004) The new family office – Innovative strategies for consulting to the affluent. Linnius, London

Schaubach P (2011) Family Office im Privaten Wealth Management – Konzeption und empirische Untersuchung aus Sicht der Vermögensinhaber, 4th edn. Uhlenbruch, Bad Soden

2

How is a Family Office Structured?

Christoph Weber, Boris Canessa,
and Alexander Koeberle-Schmid

Unlike a bank or consultancy, a family office should be crafted precisely to the needs of the family. Because of this, a seemingly limitless range of varieties are possible, on a spectrum from fully independent to those that resemble a family office but are not (yet) independent from the operating business.

This chapter explores the various stations along this spectrum. On one end are 'family office-like' functions handled internally by the operating business; on the other end are classic single and even multi family offices. An overview of the various strengths, weaknesses, risks and opportunities inherent to each of these approaches is then discussed.

2.1 The Development of the Family Office: From Part of a Firm to a Separate Entity

Some families chose to leave a significant portion of the profits within their company. The shareholder assets are accumulated or "pooled" into shareholder accounts, which are invested as a block to achieve better returns or diversification. In the beginning, these investments are typically managed by the chief financial officer or an administrator, all on behalf of the family shareholders.

These employees (regardless of whether executives or back-office staff) often only have limited professional experience in the field of strategic, tactical and operative asset allocation, the selection of managers and the due diligence process. Beyond this, they are only rarely specialists in private asset controlling (with knowledge of the standard benchmarks of that field) or experts for income tax questions and inheritance planning. If the family members live in

B. Canessa et al., *The Family Office*, https://doi.org/10.1007/978-3-319-99085-9_2

different corners of the globe, then even experienced company executives will quickly reach the limit of their competences.

This situation holds numerous significant risks for all involved. First, the cohesiveness of the family and the collaboration between firm and family relies on a bond of trust between the company's executive team and the family leaders. If family members have the justified impression that "the firm" is causing damages to their private affairs, then that trust will disappear quickly. Emotional and legal fights with claims for compensation can cause lasting erosion to the family's unity, the reputation of the patriarch and the solidarity between the shareholders and the company.

Practical Example: From the Experience of a Family Officer

One of our clients was (and remains) a passive shareholder in a family company. Previously he had allowed the Finance department of the company to provide advice on various private wealth questions. He followed that advice blindly and felt well taken care of, as the patriarch of the family was ultimately keeping an eye on all this work. Two years ago it came out that the company had advised him incorrectly on the assessment of a highly specific taxation situation—leading to damages in the millions, to be paid from his private accounts. Professional advisors would never have made the mistake. We hardly need to describe the client's mood when he found out about the disaster! Fortunately the damages were over 10 years in the past, and all responsible parties, including the patriarch himself, were already in retirement. The previous private asset consulting structures within the firm had been dissolved a few years earlier, and since then we've been providing the consulting to the clients. When all was said and done, there was no one left for him to direct his rage at. We shudder to think of how things would have gone if the client had learned about these damages just a few years earlier. Tending to the needs of a private person is an entirely different affair from managing a corporate bottom line and requires an entirely different set of specialized knowledge.

The employees of a family business organizing the wealth are fundamentally aware that they are ill equipped to tend to the private interests of the family members in a comprehensive and professional manner. So those employees end up living in fear of causing a major loss of assets. Neither the company executives nor the family members themselves for that matter can feel truly comfortable in this situation.

Other structures are needed to provide the family with the support and care they need. After all, a family office is much more than just a "consulting firm for capital investments." The family office is a regular partner and consultant in highly sensitive matters, such as last wills and testaments and powers of attorney; it is involved in ownership succession and family governance issues; it also coordinates all steps needed for private tax filings and handles a majority of the private payment transactions, and much more. In many cases the family members being supported are understandably reluctant to involve executives from the company in their personal affairs; the executives for their part are also rarely eager to get mixed up in emotional and/or private topics.

For this reason, the company's executive ranks should encourage and support the establishment of professional structures for the management of the family owners assets. Once built up as a separate unit, these structures represent a family office, whether called one or not. These family offices are either developed as departments within the company or are spun off from the company into their own firms. It is less common that they be immediately formed as their own stand-alone organizational structures. Over time, they typically evolve from a department of a company into a separate subsidiary of the company and then into an independent unit. During this genesis, it is essential that the leaders from the company are the ones to initiate and support the process—and that they regard a family office that arises this way as part of the company.

Benefits of integrating the family office into the operating company:

- The **interests** of the shareholders can be **more easily harmonized** with the interests of the company. A cooperation forms between company and family office. Company and family values can be reconciled, with the family office serving as the communicator and defender. Measures by the shareholder organization (shareholder meetings, integration/grooming of the junior generation, family secretarial services, etc.) and the management of the family office itself serve to bring the owners interests and the corporate interests into sync.
- **No capital is "withdrawn" from the company,** but rather it remains available for investment and acquisitions to the company. Through its subordinated family office, the company has knowledge of the owning family's financial situation and can factor this more effectively into its strategic assessments and investments and into the advice it provides the family.
- **Synergies can be established between the family office and company,** such as in shared use of technical equipment (IT systems, facilities) and personnel resources (such as temporary vacation staffing). Beneficial synergies can also arise through the bundling of purchasing power (investment portfolio fees) and the pooling of know-how within both family office and company.

In older and larger families, the majority of family members are unlikely to be still active in the company. Few family members are likely to have pursued the training or careers necessary to work in the area of capital market investments and private wealth management. Over the course of years, family members will have built up appreciable sums of investable assets but often feel overwhelmed with the effort of asset management.

Nuclear families in particular tend to transfer all responsibility for wealth management to "relatively competent" individual family members (perhaps a brother-in-law who is a lawyer or tax advisor), or trust Father to handle it, simply because he always has in the past. These persons are often hopelessly overburdened. Yet fearing a loss of respect, or that old errors might be uncovered, they frequently refuse to admit it. Larger business-owning families can have an extremely attractive pool of wealth. If everyone engages in their own separate wealth management, then they are also simultaneously splitting up those cumulative assets.

There are consequences of splitting up the assets, including:

- **Loss of purchasing power:** Each family member is cared for by the Sales department at wealth management firms and banks, because their investable assets rank below the "institutional" level.
- **Loss of know-how:** Without shared structures, the individual members of the family cannot learn from each other's successes (and failures). A common family office allows that wisdom to be shared.
- **Better quality through bundling of power:** Bundling of interests (and assets) can justify the funding of a more intensive due diligence process, which provides deeper insights and better conditions for decision making.

In larger family associations, family members can bundle their interests by engaging or hiring shared consultants and managers, such as a controller to select external wealth managers and review the various wealth management mandates. The focus often initially falls to purchasing power and streamlining of costs, as well as harnessing the acquired expertise.

Family members quickly recognize the benefits that come through the bundling of their interests and establish their own comprehensive consultation structures. The jump to a full family office is sometimes the product of a long, ongoing process, but just as often comes abruptly, such as when younger family members propose forming their own family office structures in the aftermath of a graduation or wedding. Poor experiences, such as a severe erosion of wealth by a family member due to bad decisions, can also spur the founding of a family office.

2.2 Structures and Models of Family Office

An organization can legitimately be called a family office at the point when investable capital held by the entrepreneurial family is managed by a team of employees dedicated exclusively to the family and which can care for them without any conflict of interest.

The original form of the family office is and remains the single family office, whose sole owner and client is the founding family. That model has been expanded and adapted into a number of other 'multi family office' forms. A survey of the different models is helpful for establishing a rough overview (see Fig. 2.1).

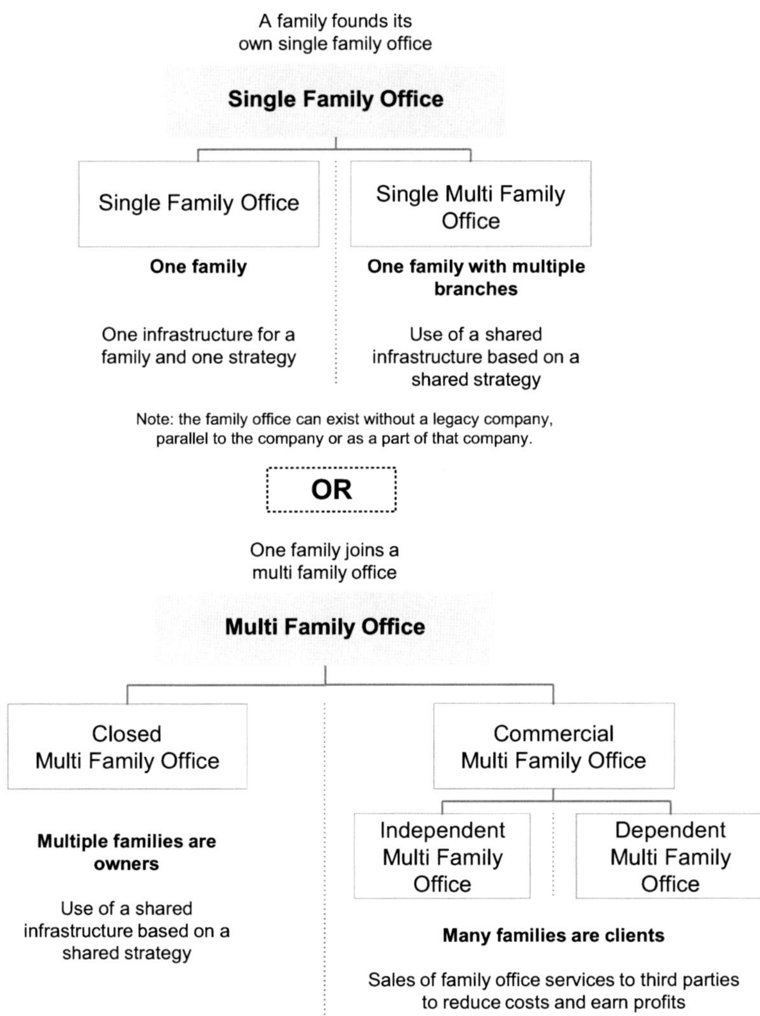

Fig. 2.1 Overview of different structures of family offices

2.2.1 What a Family Office Can Offer: Tasks and Structures

Each category of family office, and each individual family office as well, differs based on the specific services it offers. There are a variety of factors that dictate which tasks the family office will handle or not handle: the goals of the wealthy individual and family; whether a legacy company exists alongside the family office; whether the family office is some type of unit within such a company; or whether the family office is the sole common element binding the family together. Important parameters include the size of the assets, questions of how much time the wealthy parties are willing to commit to the family office, its legal anchors and tax considerations.

Many other factors could be mentioned as well. The point is that the services offered by a family office must be individually conceived and thus the structure must be individually developed. No two family offices are exactly alike. A single family office might only offer highly specific services, such as wealth management, reporting and controlling as well as convenience services. For other services, it solicits external consultants, such as for legal and tax consulting, family governance, estate planning and coaching (see also Fig. 2.2). A detailed exploration of the different services offered by family offices will come in the various chapters on the responsibilities of the family office (starting with Part II, Chap. 4).

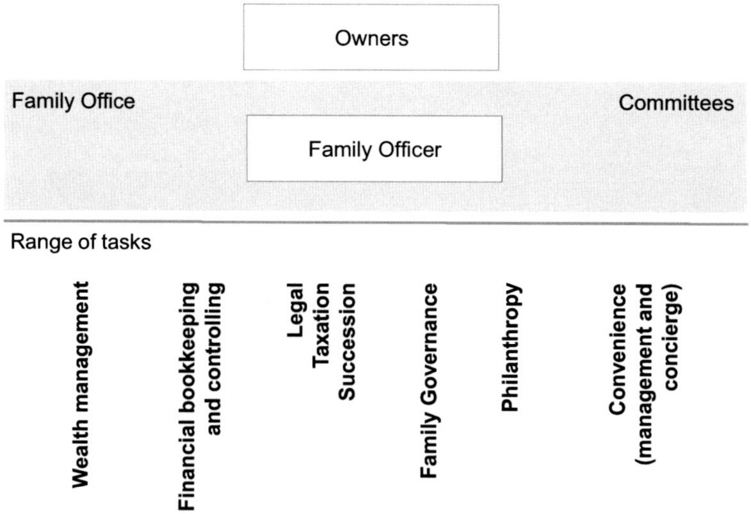

Fig. 2.2 Tasks and governance of a family office

In terms of the structural design, the question of services offered goes hand in hand with the question of ownership (see Fig. 2.2). In a single family office, this is the family, potentially with multiple branches. For a multi family office the owners can be either various families or banks and other independent persons who merely provide their services to the wealthy families. In terms of the family office itself, the governance question must always also be asked: who will lead the family office and which other committees, such as an advisory council, will be implemented? Appropriate management systems must naturally also be found, as well as mechanisms to address tax and legal issues. Each of these topics will be explored in the various capitals on the structure of a family office (starting with part III, Chap. 10).

The following list gives an overview of the most important tasks, functions, and responsibilities that a family office can handle on the family's behalf:

- The family office as a **strategic consultant**: The family office supports and advises the family on the development of a sustainably oriented strategy for the allocation and management of its wealth.
- The family office as a **manager of wealth managers**: The family office represents the extended arm of the family in the implementation of its asset strategy.
- The family office as **controller**: The family office reports back to the family on a regular basis about the development of the overall asset portfolio, as well as the individual asset classes and investments—all in the form, depth of detail and timing desired by the members. This is important for identifying investments that are not thriving and allowing for optimizing or remedial steps. It controls the work of the commissioned contractual partners, such as banks, wealth managers, real estate managers and other financial service providers.
- The family office as **informational gatekeeper**: Inherent to the management of a complex wealth portfolio is a flood of information and data from the various service providers and tax accountants that must be processed and assessed. The family office is responsible for serving as the first stop for this data, analyzing it, breaking it down into manageable (i.e. reportable) chunks and where necessary proposing countermeasures based on the information. It can then present it to the family in a concise form, with the key facts and recommended follow-up actions.
- The family office as **authorized representative**: Inherent to the management of a private fortune are various operative activities to be performed by the contracted service providers. Monitoring and managing those third-party vendors is a challenging task, and one that many families are gladly willing to delegate. The family office thus has the assignment of serving as the family's representative in dealings with the banks, wealth managers, real estate managers and all others who work for the family or who will do so. This includes reviewing offers, negotiating contracts, controlling completed work and monitoring costs.

(continued)

(continued)

- The family office as **tax, law and succession consultant**: If these services are not commissioned from external specialists, the family office can supply tax and legal advice related to investment issues as well as ownership and other legal matters. The family office can also support the family in handing over ownership and responsibility to the next generation and can support in dealing with conflicts.
- The family as **family governance** and **philanthropy expert**: Families typically develop a family constitution and pursue family governance measures with the aid of an external specialized consultant. Where the family office plays a crucial role is actually putting those strategies into practice. It coordinates the various family activities, such as shareholder meetings and family weekends, and is responsible for organizing the family's educational program aimed at helping the next generation become responsible owners. If a philanthropic foundation is in place, it is also typically heavily involved in coordinating that organization's activities.
- The family office as a **concierge**: Sometimes the family office provides support for issues related to the personal life of the family members. Depending on the family's budget and needs, these services can either be very narrow or very vast.

2.2.2 Models for a Single Family Office

There is currently a wide range of different models for wealth management handled internally within the family. Depending on their size and structure, they may bear more or less resemblance to an institutional family office. In some cases, the line of demarcation between the corresponding department at the operating company is difficult to see. One can clearly speak about a single family office when a family establishes a staff and technical infrastructure completely separated from the company, both organizationally and physically, and dedicated solely to the management of the family's private assets (see Fig. 2.1).

The line becomes a bit fuzzier when trying to delineate between private wealth controlling for the family when it is handled by employees of the company (such as the secretary and chief financial officer), performed alongside their normal corporate tasks, and a situation where the patriarch of the company is managing the wealth directly from his desk, with the help of his corporate staff. The question of status as a single family office also arises when a father and son recruit a secretary and form a small family office in what used to be the granny flat on the family's property.

In summary: The more professional the structure of the units, the better the likelihood they can create an investment and management strategy for long-term management of the family's assets; as the organization grows towards a level where it can reasonably base its wealth management on that strategy, one can increasingly and more confidently talk about a single family office. Within this constellation, the single family office typically handles all legal and taxation issues, which may also be tied up in corporate holdings. In many cases the office is also responsible for philanthropic engagement and serves as a hub for all family governance issues, like family activities and family education.

The single family office that serves just one family, typically a nuclear family, is the "purest" form of a family office. The owner and clients are one single family. One special variant of the single family office, and hence a bridge to the multi family office model, is a "single multi family office" (see Fig. 2.1), which is owned not just by one single family in the narrower sense, but rather manages the assets of multiple branches of the family. This set-up differs from a classic multi family office insofar as the single multi family office does not take any clients from outside the family.

2.2.3 Models for a Multi Family Office

As already mentioned, the market for family office services has grown exponentially in recent years, with a dizzying array of different provider structures. For a family unwilling to accept the expense and complexity involved with founding their own office, or which is looking for a new multi family office, it can be difficult to differentiate between the individual service providers. Adding to the confusion, the provider market does not break down cleanly in terms of the different models for family office services. With that said, there are certain characteristics that can be used to distinguish between the different providers, and there are some commonalities that can be used to aggregate them into groups. No judgement should be attached to these categorizations. They are solely intended to allow for a differentiated discussion of how the classic multi family office (see Fig. 2.3) differs:

- from not-for-profit multi family offices (typically a closed multi family office),
- from companies that are legally independent but where the family office is run as a commercial business (independent multi family office),
- and from providers that are a department or subsidiary of a financial services provider (dependent multi family office), such as a bank or financial auditing firm.

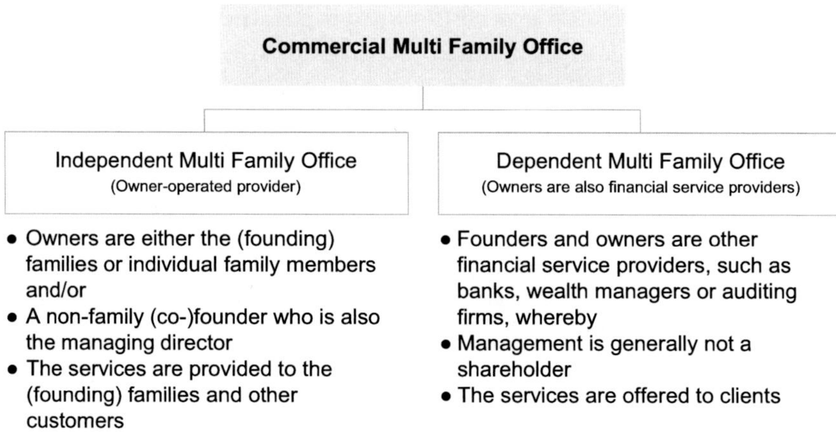

Fig. 2.3 Topography of the multi family office landscape

A family office that belongs to multiple families is typically called a classic independent multi family office (see Fig. 2.1). Sometimes they are owner-operated, in which case its services are exclusively offered to its owners. This does not rule out the possibilities that it will accept other families as shareholders at some later point, and they would then be able to use its services. There are also closed multi family offices whose families opt to engage an external CEO, including a share in ownership after a certain probationary period. "Closed" here refers to the fact that the family office does not routinely and actively seek new clients, as a commercially oriented family office must do.

Engaging an external manager as a co-owner does bring with it the risk that an "outsider," someone potentially lacking emotional ties to the family, will nevertheless have influence on the strategic orientation of the family office. On the other hand, that same situation can also cultivate an executive whose bonds to the company and his co-owners grow strong and deep, encouraging him to stay with the family office for the long run.

Commercial multi family offices deliver their services to other families and clients as well, not just the owner of the family office. In this configuration, however, the family or bank that owns the family office runs it as a commercial enterprise, meaning its mission includes maximizing of shareholder value. Intentional differentiation is made here between independent and dependent (affiliated) family offices (see Fig. 2.1 and especially Fig. 2.3). This latter version accepts families who are not (co)-owners of the family office, but only as pure clients.

A commercial, dependent family office would be a subsidiary or separate financial division of a financial services provider. Practically speaking, "dependent" multi family offices are usually owned by banks, wealth managers and financial auditing firms. A commercial, independent family office typically emerges when executives leave the private wealth department of a bank and open their own family office business, so as to offer their services without being bound to any specific bank. The families they serve have a purely client status.

The structures of the multi family office depend greatly on the ownership model. A small, independent organization is naturally very different than the Family Office unit of a bank. The tasks and services that a family office offers can vary greatly and are generally managed through a services contract that specifies the specific scope, nature and costs for the family office packet. Some family offices thus focus solely on asset reporting and controlling, while others promise a full spectrum of services. More details on the possibilities here are explored starting with Chap. 4.

For some families, the crucial factor is what position they will hold within the family office. One family may only be open to situations where they have not only a contractual relationship with the family office, but also a shareholder status so that they can help steer corporate policy. Yet such situations can be rare; there are far fewer family office companies willing to offer a share of ownership alongside a pure client status. Where such opportunities do exist, they are rarely in the public eye. These relationships are usually only brokered through private contacts.

2.2.4 Potential Conflicts of Interest at a Commercial, Dependent Multi Family Office

When joining a multi family office run by third-party ("non-family") owners, the interests of the families receiving consultation, such as favorable terms in the company's policies, can deviate from those of the manager as a commercial actor. Commercial family offices are intended to earn a profit, while the supported families have an interest in keeping their consultation costs as low as possible. The classic multi family office variant, which supports the families without focusing on its profitability as a family office, is excluded from this consideration.

For a dependent commercial multi family office to offer the greatest possible added value for the family being supported, it is essential that potential conflicts of interest between the parties be kept as minor as possible. The family office's profit optimization goals cannot be allowed to come at the cost of the family. The multi family office should be able to demonstrate extensive experience in the areas targeted by the family, or at the very least should offer strong uniform coverage of all asset classes. Beyond this, the program of family office services should represent their core business, and not side services.

It should be assumed, at least initially, that any bank-bound multi family office will serve as a platform for the sale of the house's own products and financial services. What makes this tolerable in some situations is the unparalleled international network and broad experience in a variety of asset classes that only large banks can offer. Beyond this, such banks frequently have their own research and macroeconomic departments. There are certainly a number of financial institutions capable of performing the tightrope walk between service as a professional, largely neutral family office and as representatives of their own economic interests.

It can also be presumed that wealth managers offering their clients family office services are looking to drive their own portfolio management business and gain an advantage over their competitors. On the other hand, for families who expect their family office to be primarily responsible for the management of their security portfolio, the bundled expertise of a joint strategic consultant/executing wealth manager may be worth the risks.

A financial auditor or legal consultancy will generally concentrate on accounting, tax and legal tasks. Yet they are also very well positioned to consult on fields that are closed to most family offices for professional licensing reasons, meaning external consultants must be brought in. Beyond this, the professional ethos of financial audits, tax accountants and lawyers does fit well with the core idea of a family office as an objective manager of the interests of the client family.

Practical Tip: Take Tasks and Structure into Account

When considering founding your own family office or joining an existing multi family one, give consideration to the type of family office (single vs. multi family office), the potential tasks and structural options. The following chapters will provide greater detail on the individual tasks and structures.

From the United Kingdom: "I think, for me, if I had capital at that level, I'd find it empowering."

Interview with Simon Foster

This wide-ranging interview touches on many of the themes in this book, especially the value of transparency, the involvement of family members in the family office itself, convenience services and philanthropy.

This interview was conducted by Dr. Alexander Koeberle-Schmid.

Your family office is based in the UK, but the family itself has a different background, correct?
Simon Foster: The T.Y. Danjuma Family Office was created in 2010 to represent a high net-worth Nigerian family. The family are well-known entrepreneurs in Africa, and the patriarch of the family is a noted African industrialist working in the fields of shipping, oil and gas—lots of heavy-lifting industries.

So who actually owns the family office?
SF: Well, the interesting point for us: we always advocate having a family office which is owned by the family. And I think that's the right way to do it because it

Simon M. Foster *is Chief Executive Officer at the TY Danjuma Family Office, which he joined in 2011. Between 2011 and May 2017 Simon acted as CFO for the family office. He qualified as an accountant with Ernst & Young and has over 20 years of post-qualification experience in international investment environments. He is an experienced Family Office executive and has in excess of 17 years' experience acting in Director, Company Secretary, CFO and CEO capacities for diverse international family offices, investment vehicles and their portfolio companies from bases in the UK and Bermuda.*

Simon has twice been the architect for the initial creation of family office/private client investment structures. In addition to his role within the TY Danjuma Family Office he sits on numerous boards and acts as Chairman of the Family Office Council—a Family Office industry body. Simon is a qualified accountant and holds both the UK ACA and Canadian CA accounting designations in addition to a BA (Hons) in Accounting and Finance. He also has extensive corporate finance and shareholder exit experience including IPOs, trade sales, mergers and acquisitions, structured finance and restructuring programs. He is also an individually chartered member of the Chartered Institute of Securities and Investment.

eliminates the conflict of interest. Everybody who works in it, including myself, are employees of the family. We know which side of the table we sit on and there's no conflict of interest between the family office and the family.

I think when looking at family office architectures, there's very often a difference between family offices depending on whether the family is still in business or if they're a financial family solely with a pool of wealth to manage. In the case of my family office, the family is still highly industrious in Africa, there's still the family operating businesses, and that's the core of what they do.

What the family office does is offer a number of services, part of which is investing the liquid wealth of the family.

So what is the structure of the family who owns the businesses and the family office, and are they heavily involved in the family office?

SF: We work for a number of generations of the family, each of whom tend to have ownership stakes. The family office itself is owned by the first and second generation of the family. At this point we are providing services to the first, second and third generation of the family.

What I like about our structure—and from a governance perspective, something I highly advocate—is that the family members are extremely closely involved with the family office. We have a number of the family members who are employees of the family office. They act in a senior capacity in the family office. The family office is their day job.

From my perspective, this means the family is heavily embedded in the day-to-day decision-making taken by the family office, be it investment, be it advisory, be it anything. We're highly wedded together.

In formal ways as well?

SF: Yes, it starts with our board structure. Our board is composed of five directors. The patriarch of the family is our chairman. Two next-generation members of the family are directors. And then we've got one executive director, which is me, and one non-executive director. One of the family members is a non-executive director as well.

So I think from a balance of family involvement it works really well from a compliance and governance perspective that we're wedded so closely together. And the degrees of separation and involvement between the family office and the family is quite low and I think that works really well for adding value to the family.

Is your family office, and the investment in relation to the businesses the family owns, an instrument of the overall wealth diversification?

SF: Yes. There are degrees of interaction and degrees of repost against each other between the operating businesses and everything else the family does.

One of the things we did structurally which I'm really proud of and I think was very smart was using a private fund to manage family wealth.

We created a Singapore-based "UCITS-compliant" fund and we use that as the master liquid wealth portfolio. We use a regulated fund manager in Singapore to manage that and we act as sub-advisor to the fund manager.

But what that has meant though is that we've created a very, very flexible investment management structure. So that means that we can act as a fund manager to related-party entities as well. We manage a bit of money for family-operating businesses, a bit of money for the family charitable organization, various family trust funds, various family members, various family businesses.

This has allowed us to provide our liquid wealth management services across the gamut of the other things that the family are involved in.

Does this affect your approach to transparency?

SF: We are huge fans of transparency. We think more enhanced transparency is coming to the family office sector. I think there's a global thrust around it.

So we see big industrial fund managers in America giving back the external AUM and saying: "We're a family office now," and I think what that creates is a situation where family offices in some environments are becoming dark pools of capital that the regulator knows very little about. Because of that, at some point the regulators are going to start stepping into the fray and look for more understanding of what's going on in the family office world.

How do you work to counter this?

SF: We are extremely transparent. If we were regulated, if we were publicly traded, it would have absolutely no impact on our reporting standards because we already meet or exceed the best-of-breed practices in those environments.

One of the things that we thought was important was using jurisdictions which work well from an 'OECD White List' perspective—highly transparent countries with very, very strong reporting structures. And for various reasons we thought the UK was a really good fit for that.

So, for us, one of the key governance planks was being involved in a country where there's transparency. From a governance perspective that means we file accounts every year at Companies House and we follow western-world governance principles in our operation.

Does that mean you follow UK company law across the board?

SF: We do. We follow the Walker Report, we have non-executive directors and I think that it's a knock-on effect for every asset class and the governance of every asset class. So what we've tended to do is this: for every different asset class we have a company which fits that asset class and then we deal with governance for that by having a board of directors, and that board of directors is typically composed of family members and professional staff so that we insure we have balance between the family and the investment team around it.

And also we also have investment management committees where appropriate. Just to make sure we cover the right voices from a governance perspective.

From an internal reporting standpoint, that is a lot of moving pieces. How do you convey this information to the family?
SF: In terms of reporting for the family, it's horses for courses, you know. Some people want to consume that level of detail of information, some people would rather have dashboard wealth reporting, with two pages to show me everything that's going on. And we try to cater a little bit to both.

Can you tell us about the key aspects to your financial risk management?
SF: We do lots of things. One of the things we've done is we've tried to use best-of-breed reporting, best-of-breed governance from regulated and publicly traded entities.

So, in terms of risk management, we look at several things. One I think of the most important things that we've done is that we've created strategic asset allocations for both the fund, the property portfolio, private equity, everything that we do. We're created a written mandate that describes exactly the process and our limits around that.

Certainly within the fund we look for our approach to be along the lines of the way a pension fund would do it. And I think that's really fitting with our conservative wealth protection mandate, with limits in portfolio construction between, say, bond investment, equity investments, commodity investments, alternative investments, etc., and limits on the amount we can invest in it. So they're trying to capture how much risk we can take on within the fund.

We furthermore have limits within the bond portion of the portfolio that describes the investment-grade bonds vs. non-investment grade bonds and we also have sub-categories about ratings of bonds, etc.

So from a governance perspective, we are quite strapped down. But I think that's important, because I think our investment thesis in a way is part of our contractual involvement with the family. It describes what we're going to deliver and it also establishes the rules of what we're able to do with the pools of wealth that we manage.

Compliance is an issue all around the world. What role does it play in your family office?
SF: It's interesting—I think intriguingly, one of the things that was a really good decision for us came very early in 2010 when the family office was very new and we hired a compliance officer. So we have an in-house compliance

officer, which is fairly unusual for a single family office. But I think it's worked out really well.

We have mandates, we have rules as we were talking about earlier from a compliance perspective and I think our compliance officer makes sure that we are staying within that from an investment/decision making perspective.

The regulatory backdrop keeps changing and one of her main duties is to keep an eye on that regulatory backdrop, to keep us up to speed with it and help us understand where there are things that are changing in places where we really need to do more.

Part of the role panned out a little differently than I would have expected it to. And I think a lot of what our compliance officer does is what I would call "outward-bound compliance." Because we represent an emerging-economy family—I think if you're an emerging economy family you are held to a higher standard than European family offices or American family offices would be.

And because the family is African, as with most emerging economy families, there's a degree of political exposure, and which certainly fits the bill with us, and so that means we're in constant dialog with our bank, the financial service providers maintaining and making sure that we have good in-house KYC documentation. It's been absolutely vital. And the compliance functions, one of the major roles has been maintaining dialog with our financial counterparties and making sure everyone continues to understand who we are, what we are and what we do.

Let's move on to family governance. What measures do you do on the family governance side to increase family cohesion?

SF: I think one of the things that has worked quite well for us strategically has been using a set of UK companies to host the family office. What we've basically done is we've created the family office company with family members as shareholders. So while there's no formal family council, when we hold AGMs for the family office—and because various family members are board members as well—when we hold directors meetings, what that means is that the various individual family members are meeting around a table to talk about the operations of the family office.

What I really like about that is we've used company law and company governance to embed family interaction and family governance as well.

How have you achieved this?

SF: It's actually quite a simple and elegant solution to an issue that resonates with many families. I think by having all family members as shareholders in the family office, that formally means that when you have an AGM, everyone has a right to speak. And that creates some nice natural cohesion about debating where the family office fits in the investment matters of the family.

And also I think the directorship and approach has also worked really well for us, in that our board is heavily involved and has a heavy concentration of family members in it, all of whom are directors. So I think in a way our corporate governance actually turns into family governance as well.

Do you also offer convenience services for the family—anything from booking hotels or vacations to searching for the right schools for the next generation?

SF: I kind of think with most families and most family offices the mandate changes over time. We've been going since 2010 and I think what we actually do now has changed quite dramatically.

From a formal standpoint, we don't actually offer concierge services like booking trips and those kind of things in our mandate. But over the years we have grown into a property manager for the family and we have sort of turned into managing various family members' investments. So things that are not formally under our mandate, where people have individual holdings, we quite often become involved in that.

But I think some family offices tend to shy away from concierge services and we don't hold it out as something we do. But quite often we do become involved in things just because we're trusted advisors to the family. So if an individual was looking to start a business, or looking to build a structure for a member of their family, we will quite often be asked to comment on it or be involved.

And who pays the fees or your salary, then? Is this paid by all family members, or does it reflect who asks for what in terms of advisory service—how much they invest and so on?

SF: You hit on a really good point, because when you talk about making recommendations about family offices, I think one of the things that people miss is: what's the funding strategy for the family office?

Our funding strategy is actually quite simple: the heart of what we do is acting as a captive, in-house fund manager to the family for liquid wealth and property portfolio.

So we are run as a company. We have a revenue line. And we generate that revenue line by charging management fees to the property portfolio and to the investment portfolio, and that's what actually pays for the salary, keeps the lights on, keeps the fridge going in the office.

And because we're funded by charging investment fees, any ancillary services that we provide to the family are essentially covered in the already-in-place funding strategy.

So we don't itemize time and materials billed for stuff. We're already remunerated by the investment management fees that we charge.

You also mentioned that the family pursues a foundation and philanthropic activities. Can you talk a little about that?
SF: That is a separate entity from the family office in this environment. Several years ago, the patriarch of the family created a charitable foundation in Nigeria. Makes perfect sense, because he is Nigerian. He's passionate about Nigeria.

And that basically acts as the charitable arm to the family's activities. Its core focus is on women's rights, education, and river blindness. That's not formally under the remit of the family office. It's a sister entity, even if there is a degree of overlap in that family officers, as people who have gained trust through time, and various members of the family act as trustees in the foundation or directors of family businesses.

Thank you for this fascinating discussion. To wrap things up: Can you give us three recommendations you would give a family thinking about building or founding their own family office?
SF: Sure. My first view is this: I think in most case where I've met people who are talking about building a family office, my very strongly felt advice would be to do so. And my point around that is this: most families I meet with that have the wealth and the knowledge to do that—most of them have had operating businesses, maybe even operating empires, and they've had the confidence to go out and build these empires.

Why would they lack the confidence to actually manage the end product of those financial empires? The family office is just a business. There's no mystery or mystique around it. And I think, for me, if I had capital at that level, I'd find it empowering. You know, having this entity that's focused on helping me do what I need to do with the financial power of the family.

The other thing I'd say following that vein as well: the beauty of a family office is that it can be anything you want it to be. It can manage liquid wealth, it can manage property wealth, it can assess succession planning, it can manage operating companies. It's a bespoke company designed to meet the needs of the specific family and I find the arguments against having one to be relatively thin when you think about the benefits.

The other advice I would also give to people starting this up is: it's a strange world. I've seen situations where family offices have become fashionable. People want family offices because everybody's got family offices. And it's perceived as what you do.

And if I was a wealthy family building one, I'd take it back a step. And I actually do a real user-needs analysis of what comprises the family wealth, what they're actually involved in, what they actually have, what they don't have, and what needs managing.

So I think it's important that you get the right architecture in to build the family office, because you can end up with something that is not well built to fit your needs. So, to me, the art around that is effectively understanding exactly where you fit, understanding your tax exposures, understanding your assets and entities and then building something rational around that. I think people leap in too quickly without having done the groundwork.

3

What are the Fundamental Success Factors for a Family Office?

Boris Canessa, Christoph Weber,
and Alexander Koeberle-Schmid

High net worth individuals considering a family office face an early, fundamental choice. One path calls for founding their own single family office dedicated solely to caring for their family. The alternative is joining an existing multi family office, established by another family or external third parties to serve the needs of multiple families.

There are of course many factors in this decision. One that causes perhaps the most uncertainty: how much money does a family need to justify opening their own single family office? And along the same lines: what volume of assets is better managed by a multi family office operated by a third party? We won't keep you in suspense: There is no one-size-fits-all answer. A few considerations may however help clarify the options.

3.1 Founding a Single Family Office: How Much Money is Needed?

3.1.1 Analysis of Costs and Required Services

A single family office should be led by a highly qualified expert in capital markets, willing to apply that knowledge on behalf of the wealthy family. The directors of a family office should ideally have previous executive experience in private banking or as financial managers for capital investments at a pension fund. In many cases these are former partners at a tax consultancy or wealth management firm with capital investment responsibilities. The crème de la crème can

B. Canessa et al., *The Family Office*, https://doi.org/10.1007/978-3-319-99085-9_3

command a hefty salary, so payroll costs are a major cost factor when planning a potential budget. What that salary is buying, however, is the services of a candidate far better qualified than the family itself to address questions related to capital markets. It would make little commercial sense to delegate such a crucial responsibility to anything less.

Global statistics about the salary structures for family office managers are spotty. Sulger, Buel & Company polled 25 British single family offices about their salary structures. David Bain collated the results in "Campden Wealth," writing that single family offices in London paid their executives between €179,000 and €465,000. Bonus payments then totaled another 20 to 50% of the base salary. Other management functions came with annual salaries between €95,000 and €310,000, including bonus payments of between 15–20%. The study also noted that salaries in Switzerland tended to be somewhat higher and those in the USA significantly higher. The Campden Research study "The Global Family Office Report" (2015) found that family office executives in Europe earned approx. €300,000.

An executive with the relevant qualifications will likely need (at least) one or two assistants to help with asset accounting, due diligence processes and other recurring tasks in the family office. These assistants should be qualified enough to represent the CEO during periods of vacation or sick leave. The family office team will also require one or two secretaries. Beyond personnel costs, a single family office can be expected to accrue expenses related to maintaining an office, including materials. Travel costs, standard upkeep costs for the IT infrastructure, depreciation on furniture etc. must also be expected.

Table 3.1 gives a very rough overview of the cost structure. Larger investments or activities abroad increase not only travel costs, but also potentially personnel costs, as employees with a more specialized profile are needed. An extensive

Table 3.1 Costs of a family office

Cost category (in thousand EUR)	**Very small structure**	**Medium structure**	**Your estimate**
1 to 2 executives	200	600	
1 to 3 assistants	60	220	
1 to 2 secretaries	35	130	
Rent (including running costs)	40	70	
Technology (phones, IT)	30	70	
Other office costs, depreciation on furnishings, travel, legal and tax consulting for specialized questions, mediation, coaching	65	150	
Misc.			
Total	**430**	**1240**	

spectrum of responsibilities also brings with it higher personnel requirements, and with it rising personnel costs. In all, the costs for a CEO can range significantly higher if deep specialized knowledge is needed in the fields of direct investments, foreign investments or other highly specialized fields.

Synergies with existing resources from a legacy company (such as office space, secretarial services and IT infrastructure) can potentially be used to defray expenses. The location of the family office also impacts its expected costs (rents and salaries tend to be higher in London, Tokyo and San Francisco than in Dresden, Germany or Winnipeg, Canada).

Practical Tip: Schedule of Costs

Be clear about the scope and nature of the single family office you are planning. This will then form the basis for a precise schedule of costs. Real-life experience in the business world teaches that costs frequently often overrun their original budgets, but the estimates nevertheless provide important guidance.

The costs indicated above are all direct costs. Family offices can also expect to accrue other wealth management fees, typically a percentage of the assets under management. These fees must also be calculated against expected annual returns. If those costs appear unreasonably high, then it is reasonable to question whether the benefits of a family office truly outweigh the costs (see Table 3.2).

The aforementioned asset volumes involve investable wealth that is not tied up in the family's legacy company and for which the family office founder has full authority. This is important, as it is not the task of the family office to control the family's operating business or to replace its structures. It is instead entrusted with caring for the family's "free" interests and asset items,

Table 3.2 Expected costs for a family office

Impact of cost burden	430 k EUR overall costs for the family office	1240 k EUR overall costs for the family office	Your estimate
Cost burden = 0.2% results in	218 mn. EUR assets	620 mn. EUR assets	
Cost burden = 0.4% results in	108 mn. EUR assets	310 mn. EUR assets	
Cost burden = 0.6% results in	72 mn. EUR assets	207 mn. EUR assets	
Target cost burden = ___%			

meaning those not bound to the company. Even a simple cost framework makes clear that any answer to the question of how big a net worth is needed for a single family office relies very strongly on how extensive the structures of the family office will need to be—and what overall operating costs the family office is likely to accrue. Beyond this, the estimated usage of a single family office is also crucial, as it reflects which magnitude of costs is likely be perceived as appropriate by its owners.

It is important to remember that initial successes during the early life of the family office often push questions of cost into the background. This changes after several years, however, as the novelty wears off and the tedium of daily business sets in. Because the structures and responsibilities of different single family offices often vary greatly, the levels of cost that are perceived as acceptable also diverge significantly. With this in mind, Sandy Loder, founder of AH Loder Advisers, reports: "According to a survey carried out by Campden Research in 2011, the actual cost of running a family office is around 63 basis points of assets under management" (in Archer and Hauser 2015, p. 73). The same 2015 survey by Campden Research revealed a cost basis of approx. 80 basis points of internal cost for the family office and an additional 19 basis points for costs related to external consultants (see Moodby et al. 2015, p. 42).

3.1.2 Motivation and Commitment by Employees in Relation to Size of Wealth

There is another factor of perhaps even greater importance than cost when founding a family office or joining a multi family office: motivation and commitment on the part of the employees. As with any service business, the employees are a family office's most important asset. Those employees must have an unusual passion for their work and be ready to come to the office highly motivated to produce top results—for days, weeks, months and years on end.

This then ultimately leads back to the question of the "minimum net worth" required for a single family office. Do the available investable assets offer enough of a challenge to keep the former director of a private banking department satisfied in the long term? Will the former financial head of a pension fund and her team of three to five hand-picked employees find sufficient interest in these tasks for the long run? Assets that comprise a few real estate items in the owner's hometown and two securities portfolios of €20 mn. each (with 70% invested in bonds) may not provide much fascination and challenge for a highly qualified team. There are no clear answers here, but one can safely assert that as asset portfolios grow significantly larger, more complex and internationally positioned, they also grow more motivating and interesting for a high-carat team.

If the family's wealth is highly focused in one asset class, then even a smaller net worth could potentially justify the establishment of a dedicated team. Imagine a portfolio comprised primarily of a dozen pieces of real estate in the owner's hometown, each half-funded with external leverage; while the value of this portfolio may fall under €50 mn., it may be reasonable to found one's own small real estate management firm to handle it properly. In many cases businesses of this kind ultimately serve as a bridge on the family's journey to a more comprehensive family office.

We hope that we have established that there is no clear and universally applicable net worth above which the founding of one's own single family office is justified. Nevertheless, when exploring the perspectives listed above (cost base for structure, long-term motivation of team), a common rule of thumb holds that assets totaling approx. €250 mn. should be sufficient to justify a single family office structure.

Similar minimum sizes are discussed in academic works on this field. Family office experts Farkas-Richling, Fischer and Richter, writing in "Private Banking and Family Office" from 2012, note that a family should generally begin considering their own family office after achieving a net worth of over €100 mn. Only approx. 25% of single family offices actually manage wealth totaling less than €300 mn. (see Farkas-Richling et al. 2012, p. 242).

Kirby Rosplock, a family office researcher and consultant, similarly states in "The Complete Family Office Handbook" that very different minimum asset values can be expected: "Once again, the debate continues in the field about what amount justifies the creation of a family office; generally, however, family wealth experts such as Barbara Hauser estimate that a family should have $200 to $300 million in assets to warrant establishing a single family office. Remember, however, this is a general rule of thumb, not a hard and fast base range" (Rosplock 2014, p. 8).

Yet some authors name significantly different minimum figures as well. For example, Kathryn McCarthy, a consultant to families and family offices, finds: "The operating cost to build out a fully functional family office typically require a minimum in the range of $500 million to $1 billion" (Archer and Hauser 2015, p. 13). Ian Macdonald and Mark McMullen, also family office experts, see things differently: "Although the Security and Exchange Commission refers to $100 m investable assets as a minimum for a single family office, other commentators believe that $30 m is a more appropriate minimum" (Archer and Hauser 2015, p. 13). And Richard C. Wilson, who runs the Family Office

Club, warns in his book "The Family Office Book—Investing Capital for the Ultra-Affluent": "I want to dispel a myth: Many industry studies will tell you that you need $100 million to $250 million or more to set up your own single family office solution. … I don't believe that is true. Due to technology and the ability to leverage taxation and risk management experts and consultants, I have found some successful single family offices with 'only' $30 million to $50 million in assets" (Wilson 2014, p. 10).

3.1.3 Successful Scenarios for Single Family Offices Managing Smaller Fortunes

As previously stated, there is no clear "minimum net worth" for a single family office. Smaller fortunes can also potentially justify a family office structure, presuming several prerequisites are met (see Fig. 3.1).

First, the high net worth individual must be prepared to be heavily involved in the family office over a long time horizon. Deep knowledge on economic topics and capital market issues is required—or at least the readiness to acquire deep knowledge of these fields.

A study by Kirby Rosplock found that seven in ten family offices are led by a family member, usually a charismatic executive personality with good relationships and influences within the family. They then succeed in motivating the entire family (or individual members) to make joint investments in the (shared) family office. There are two primary benefits to this personal involvement by a member of the family: first, it reduces payroll costs for the family office; second, it simplifies communication, since the wealthy individual is already present for all decision-making processes (see also Rosplock 2014, p. 235).

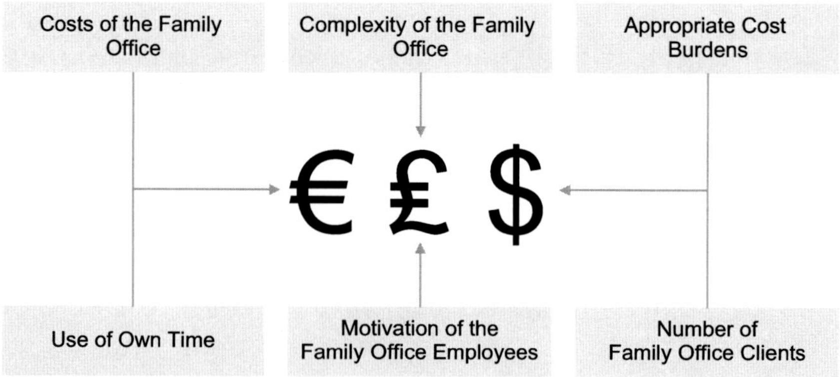

Fig. 3.1 Factors influencing the necessary volume of resources when founding a single family office

If this constellation is selected, then a consistent program of outsourcing should be pursued, as noted by Richard C. Wilson in "The Family Office Book—Investing Capital for the Ultra Affluent" (see Wilson 2014, p. 23). Many multi family offices offer their reporting services to third parties as well, and these can also be outsourced if the family establishes its own family office. Tax and legal issues can be handed off to external practices. Wealth management can (and should) also be primarily outsourced. The family constitution or family charter can also be formulated with guidance from external specialists. Convenience services can also be bought externally. To make it simple, the only thing you would need is a list of preferred, trusted advisors for the different fields.

The core task for the family office in this scenario is restricted to the coordination of various external consultants, the execution or coordination of external due diligence processes and the archiving of all relevant bills and receipts. This represents an affordable model for a single family office, as well as for the efficient and effective management of a (relatively) small fortune. Even so, the affluent individual should consider whether the management of x mn. euros in current assets will be enough to keep himself and two or three employees passionate for their task five days a week, eight hours a day. From this perspective, that "x" should probably be closer to €100 mn. than €30 mn.

3.2 Success Factors for a Single Family Office

Once a single family or a family with multiple branches has enough cumulative wealth and a corps of highly motivated employees, the lure of a single (multi) family office may be strong. The following recommendations may be helpful in that process:

- **Don't attempt too much at once:** Your future single family office can only justify its own existence by providing services significantly better than those of the competition. This is a high bar to clear. It's unrealistic to expect that it will achieve that level of quality in multiple areas "right out of the gate"—yet that is perhaps the single most common reason why family offices fail. Too much is attempted in the euphoria of the founding phase, heightening the disappointment later when some services fail to better the offerings from the competition. This can quickly lead to disillusionment, which in turn can lead to the dissolution or sale of the new family office. When founding a single family office, one should initially focus on a few core competencies and then only add in other services over time.

- **Defining central services:** This includes reporting across all asset classes, all portfolios and real estate or private equity investments, all in a consistent and comprehensible form. Reporting is used to make data-driven decisions in asset investment. Efficient management of bills, receipts and in particular contracts is an integral component of this.
- **Select between two and maximally four asset classes:** These are the asset classes that matter most to the family. The family office itself should eventually handle these, although in many cases a new single family office will solely coordinate all services related to them. "Coordinate" may mean that the family office intensively controls and monitors the work of consultants for the first few years before subsequently taking these tasks onto itself. To avoid overtaxing itself, other asset classes should only be added in at the family office over the course of time.
- **Pick loyal and experienced employees:** The central element of any single family office is naturally its employees, who work exclusively in the interest of the family members. What is needed here are consultants experienced in selecting partners and negotiating wealth management mandates, and in particular in the negotiation of fees, and who know how to position the investments legally to be as tax optimized as possible. The family office should be strong not just in strategic development, but also and in particular through the implementation of successful action steps. The selection of the finest employees should be the focus of all the initial activities. The candidates should have deep and widely based experiences in the practical implementation of the goals set by the founders. They should also work well together personally, with room to bond fully as a team.
- **Ensure freedom from conflicts of interest in the team:** Trust-centered collaboration with the family office relies critically on the idea that employees are focused solely on the interests of the family members. Poorly conceived bonuses (such as bonuses that encourage "daring" investment strategies or apply only for certain asset classes) can threaten this trust. An overly hasty integration of wealth management into the office can also lead to conflicts of interest. After all, in-house staff will likely find it difficult to report on their own that their wealth management efforts have been anything but successful, let alone "wealth eroding." It is human nature for them to always put their own wealth management efforts in a good light.

Practical Tip: Formulate Vision and Core Values

Work together with your family and, if one already exists, your family office to formulate a set of vision and core values for your family office. Record them in writing and post them someplace visible in the office. They offer an aspirational reminder to both family members and family office employees about the ultimate goal of their work.

The following questions should be answered during the conceptual design of your family office:

- Which services will be central to the family office, which will be fringe activities and which aptitudes on the part of the employees are required to achieve this?
- Should the family office manage the wealth itself, and if yes: which asset classes should it cover?
- Should the family office be able to influence the operating company, or does it exist parallel but independent from it?
- How can freedom from conflict of interest be ensured?
- Who may receive consulting (and who may not)—i.e. should the family office remain a single family office for the long term?
- Where should the family office stand in ten years, and how should it justify its existence in the long term?

Formulating written answers to these questions and success factors can help you concentrate on the truly essential. This helps you avoid losing sight of the large, long-term goals.

3.3 Founding a Closed Multi Family Office

In a closed multi family office, two or more families share elements of their family office (keeping in mind that there are also commercial multi family offices which will not be the focus in this chapter; see Figs. 2.1 and 2.3). Typically these are individuals who are dissatisfied with the private banking services offered by their banks, wealth managers or other financial service providers. They are ready to create their own financial back office to handle all oversight aspects related to asset management, or share an existing one.

There are several benefits to a closed multi family office compared with a single family office, the most obvious being the opportunity to share costs. The catch is that no one family can dictate the organizational, technical and personnel structure of the company entirely on their own. Even decisions on which consulting tasks will be offered are subject to co-determination with the other founding families.

There are a variety of reasons why families might elect to accept the compromises associated with a closed multi family office. For example, an entrepreneur who lacks the time to care for his wealth on his own is unlikely to find the time needed to construct a healthy single family office. Insofar as the wealthy individual cannot entrust another family member with that setup process, pursuing collaboration with an existing closed multi family office is thus probably a wise choice. It ensures that the interests of the affluent individual and his family will be managed in a targeted, comprehensive and efficient way. In particular, when an entrepreneur or lead employee reaches the point when it is time to start handing off his management tasks on a regular basis to young talent, the family office opens up a parallel structure to explore new, entrepreneurial ideas.

The choice to join a closed multi family office does not inherently have to be carved in stone. If the family later determines that their own family office structures would offer more benefits than initially surmised, or if the collaboration with the closed multi family office leads one member of the family to develop a deeper interest in that organizational structure, then the family can work to develop their own single family office. There are a number of ways to approach this: they can build their own organization from scratch or undertake a "rolling" adoption of employees of the closed multi family office into their own single family office. Families are advised to include stipulations allowing such approaches in their contract with the closed multi family office, even if they initially have no intention to pursue this course.

The bottom line: The more similar the needs of the individual families and the orientation of their asset allocations, the simpler this reconciliation process will be. And the more stable, sustainable and ultimately economically successful the positioning of the closed multi family office for its founding families.

3.3.1 Fundamental Decisions When Founding a Closed Multi Family Office

The first central task for the founding families is establishing a joint conceptual family office strategy for the closed multi family office, and then to push binding ratification (see Fig. 3.2). It contains the guidelines for the establishment of the office at the operative level. Families can then use that document to set a course to achieve the optimal long-term functionality of the family office and to prevent the office's daily work from being impeded by disagreements about structural questions within the founding families.

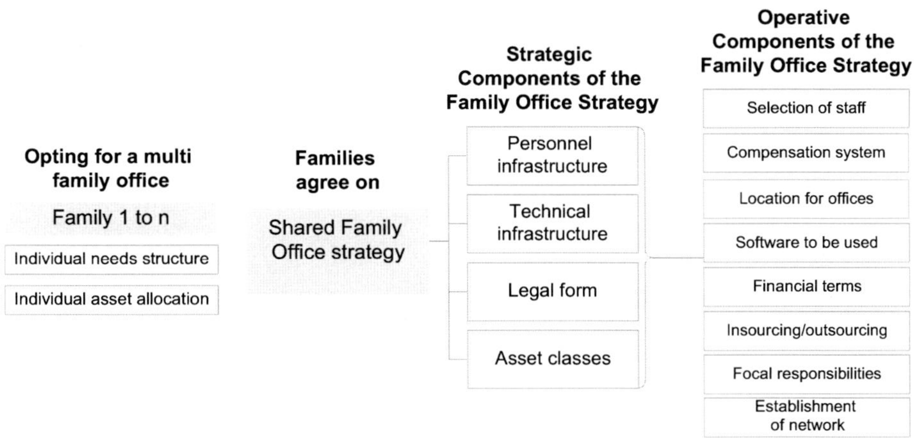

Fig. 3.2 Founding and development of a strategy for the closed multi family office

Another important decision made at the start relates to the selection of the legal form of the company. This choice should reflect not just corporate law, but also, and even more importantly, tax liability issues. And one should take into consideration the ownership structure of the classic multi family office and the number of families that will join. In addition, regulatory law also increasingly plays a role here (see Chap. 10).

Once the legal framework has been established, the next decision is which asset classes the closed multi family office should cover through strategic consulting and oversight. The broader the closed multi family office's coverage across all asset classes, the better its ability to preserve and grow the wealth entrusted to it. In particular when individual families wish to set different focuses for their asset allocation, a closed multi family office oriented toward diversification can react flexibly. It offers competent support in all matters from bonds to stock purchases, without losing sight of the bird's eye view.

The technical and personnel infrastructure then depends on the spectrum of asset classes that the closed multi family office is expected to support. The greater the diversity that the family office wishes to offer beyond individual asset classes, the greater the challenges for reporting (and in turn: the stricter the specifications for reporting software).

A globally minded all-round talent must be engaged to headhunt the personnel for the coordination and information channeling tasks, as well as specialists capable of delivering detailed, up-to-date information about their respective individual asset classes.

Once the founding families have made the basic decisions and codified these in a corporate strategy, the operative implementation phase can begin. The same measures must be undertaken as they would in any newly founded business.

Practical Tip: Before Founding a Closed Multi Family Office

If multiple families are interested in founding a closed multi family office together, the community of families must first sit down and discuss their motives, expectations and objectives. Presuming they see eye-to-eye here, they should then collaborate on a family office strategy. This includes aspects such as the legal form, personnel and technical infrastructure and questions of which asset classes should be explored for investments. An external specialist and moderator should be engaged to help guide the discussion.

3.3.2 Responsibilities of the Managing Director of a Closed Multi Family Office

The first step to founding a closed multi family office and the definition of the family office strategy is the hiring of a CEO. This figure's responsibilities go well beyond the selection of the personnel, technology and the organization of workflows and the future economic leadership of the office. The CEO serves as the extended arm of the families, as a special trusted party and deputy whether dealing with internal or external matters.

This person should possess broad and deep specialist qualifications and extensive professional leadership experience in the finance industry. Very strong interpersonal skills are also required—including aptitude at picking and leading employees based not only on their expertise but also how they will fit with the team and for their ability to interact effectively with the owner families. This position of trust requires a strong sense of responsibility, personal engagement and empathy—paired with a generous dose of self-confidence and poise to meet the leaders of the family at eye level. At the same time, this person must be prepared to step forward as a representative of the families, impressing upon the financial world the strength of its position and fighting like a lion for the interests of the families, if need be.

The CEO has the task of building up the closed multi family office as a company and establishing all necessary operational structures. Ideally, she will already have a history of entrepreneurial activity. Otherwise, the family leaders should use their own entrepreneurial insights to assist her in the early phases. Those early days in particular should be used for intense dialog between the families and the CEO. If the participants can afford the time, they should meet quarterly during that first year.

It is also sensible for the representatives of the founding families to form an advisory and/or investment council to ensure that lines of communication are open between the family office and the families on issues beyond just wealth management, and that questions about the leadership of the office can be posed on a regular basis.

Practical Tip: Joining a Closed Multi Family Office

For better or worse, families who wish to join an existing classic multi family office are spared the costs and efforts of founding the office and deciding its orientation. Their challenge instead comes in reviewing its policies and vision closely for potential negative impacts on their asset management. The relationship with a family office should be a partnership for life, across generations. For this reason, a switch between multi family offices should be avoided at all costs. This makes it all the more important to make the right choice the first time.

3.3.3 Issues When Developing towards a Commercial Multi Family Office

When developing the strategy for their closed multi family office, one very important question that families must pose themselves is whether the character of a closed multi family office should be retained (multiple families are owners of their multi family office), or whether the company should also offer certain services to third parties (see Figs. 2.1 and 2.3 for a comparison of the forms of single family offices and forms of multi family offices). These parties would not become shareholders in the family office, but rather exclusively clients. The closed multi family office would then be considered a full-fledged commercial multi family office.

Like a single family office, the closed multi family office is normally financed based on the 'cost coverage' principle. In other words, annual budget planning involves forecasting the running costs for maintaining the office, which are then spread among the owning families. Each family makes an advance payment for the current year based on that budget. At the beginning of the next year, the budget is compared against actual costs and any overpayment or underpayment is reconciled. An office set up in this way does not make a profit. It solely covers its operating costs.

This means there are few options to subsidize the maintenance of the family office by generating alternate revenue streams. To relieve themselves of a portion of the costs of running the closed multi family office, they offer their services to other families and take on external mandates. They become, in other words, a commercial multi family office. The stronger the commercial nature of the business, the greater the vigilance that the founding families must maintain against potential conflicts of interest.

With that said, profit expectations related to the sale of classic family office services should not be overly high. One must presume that the contracting families will show the same cost sensitivity as the founding family, meaning margins will tend to be very low.

The situation is quite different if significantly higher margin services, such as wealth management, the establishment of a mutual fund or the identification of capital investments, are being sold. This brings with it the risk of conflict of interest, however, and can potentially lead to blurring of the original character of the closed multi family office in favor of a purely commercial wealth management service.

3.3.4 Specific Issues Related to Commercial Multi Family Offices

Nowadays any former multi-level marketing firm can call itself a "family office" or start offering related services on its website. Those firms typically lack the experience needed to handle the breadth and width of these complex assignments. Beyond this, many do not possess the specialized expertise and professional infrastructure to perform this work effectively. Providers of this type have always been strongly sales oriented. A service provider is not a family office just because it calls itself one.

But even for serious, authentic commercial multi family office providers, a meticulous review should be made as to whether the services they offer meet the family's requirements. If you need comprehensive strategic consulting—i.e. across all asset classes—and comprehensive controlling for its implementation, companies that are specialized solely in individual asset classes (such as only in securities or real estate) will not offer any additional value.

If the family has a diverse set of international connections, then a commercial multi family office that is well networked and internationally oriented is needed; in this example, a small office centered only on investment and contacts in the French speaking world might well be the wrong partner. A large commercial multi family office tied to a major international bank might instead be a better choice, as it will have the necessary resources and contacts to make the joint endeavor a success.

3.3.5 Reporting: An Important Task for the Multi Family Office

It has been noted several times that transparent and detailed reporting represents a significant added value on the part of a family office. Numerous software packages are now available on the market for this purpose; each one is marketed based on its own special focus, but very few are capable of delivering satisfactory reporting of the total asset situation. The main benefit of such programs is the interface they create to the tax accountant or mandated bank, facilitating data transfer between those establishments and the family office. What should be avoided, particularly for large, complex asset portfolios, are hand-crafted Excel solutions. These are vulnerable to errors and are hard to maintain, which leads to unnecessarily high financial planning costs.

Here too it is important to look back to the remuneration model for the closed multi family office. Many affluent individuals prefer to have a family office financed solely by fees from the families it serves. If a multi family office is also paid by third parties (such as in the form of commissions) or otherwise benefits from the implementation of its investment recommendations, then conflicts of interest can emerge. With that said: any client of a multi family office who expects unflinching "remuneration purity" should be prepared to pay appropriately upfront for the office's work. It ultimately doesn't help the family to demand fee cuts from the multi family office if they leave the organization unable to maintain the professional, cost-intensive infrastructure necessary to handle the family's complex needs. The economic stability and independence of a family office are the most important foundational pieces for establishing a reliable partnership that is free from conflicts of interest.

Practical Tip: The Family Office's Services Should Be Derived from Actual Goals and Expectations

The family should come together at the start to formulate a set of goals and expectations for the family office. Those can then be translated into concrete terms in a written needs profile. The services that your family office should offer can then be derived directly from that document.

3.4 Success Factors for a Multi Family Office

Not only the establishment and operation of a closed multi family office, but also a commercial multi family office, especially when it is an independent multi family office, is intended to produce benefits for the families beyond those of the classic financial services offered by banks and wealth managers. This added value derives from the many functions and responsibilities of a multi family office in its relationship with the families, with parallels to the executive structure of a mid-sized business. The multi family office does not replace past or future financial service providers such as banks, wealth managers and insurance agents. They will continue to be tasked with carrying out the family's investment strategy at the operative level. It instead positions itself between the families and the executing partners by representing the interests of the families and controlling and overseeing the work of the service providers (see Fig. 3.3). The same applies for the relationship between the multi family office and the family's tax accountant, lawyer or family governance consultant. The multi family office will ideally not seek to replace that figure, but rather to engage in a lively transfer of information, with ongoing harmonization on all relevant matters.

This comprehensive program of functions and activities sets a high bar for any multi family office's organization, structure and ethics. Regardless of whether a multi family office works as a commercial multi family office or a closed multi family office: it must be ensured from the start that all its actions

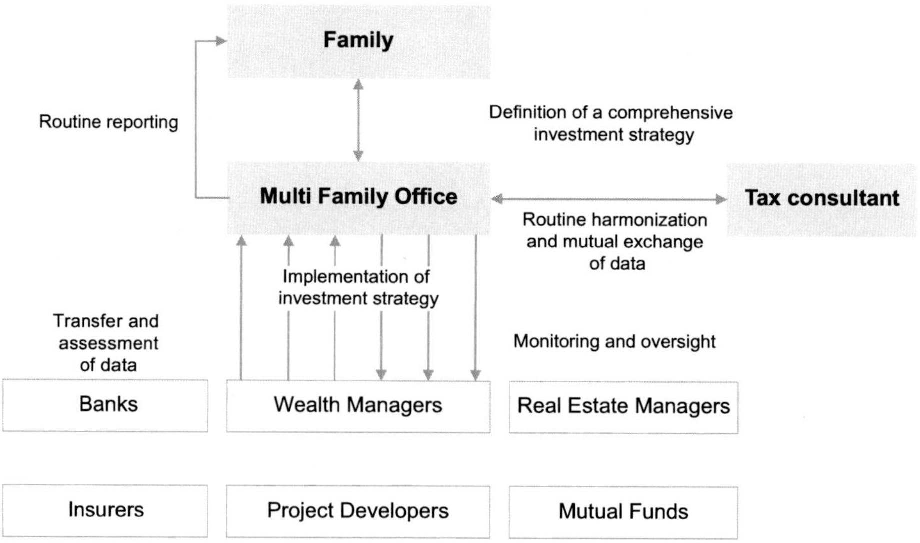

Fig. 3.3 Positioning of a multi family office for wealth management

and employees are oriented toward the interests and benefits of the families. Economic self-interest on the part of the multi family office must always be suppressed where it is counter to the interests of the family. This demands a high degree of loyalty and identification with the families on the part of its executives and employees.

If the normal consulting fees by the multi family office are to be supplemented with commissions for the selling of investment products, this increases the potential for conflicts of interest. This can be an acceptable risk if the multi family office is 100% transparent about its cost structure, detailing all supplemental income items and passing on savings where appropriate.

The more complex the family's asset portfolio, the greater the level of professionalism that the multi family office must have. Established multi family offices have the advantage that they already have a professional staff and technical infrastructure in place. The company's employees will almost always display strong specialist qualifications and long years of experience in their respective economic working fields.

The challenge for multi family offices is less in applying its technical expertise successfully and more in understanding the (often unspoken) expectations and objectives of the families. A successful multi family office must have more than just a strong sense of empathy: A notable level of commitment and dedication and the ability to buy in completely on the family's goals are a given. The trickier factor is a willingness to serve as an honest and self-confident sparring partner, willing to question even established wisdom to promote the family's interests.

The technical and personal qualifications of the multi family office's employees also matter in terms of the added value that they can produce for the families. At the heart of this effort is reporting, which is central to the quality of the advice and care. It fulfills two essential tasks: On the one hand, it provides the family officer with all the data he needs to assess investments and identify mistakes early on. It is also helpful for ongoing controlling of the costs and services from the contracted service providers. Furthermore it also allows the family office to monitor that the defined asset allocation policies have been rigorously observed.

Reporting also increases transparency for the families. The entrepreneur will be accustomed to receiving data on a regular basis from his Controlling department or auditor, and to wielding that data to assess the economic health of his firm, identify vulnerabilities or inefficiencies and decide on measures to keep the company on track. The multi family office should help the families with the management of their own fortune through transparent, meaningful reporting.

The economic stability of the multi family office as an independent operation is also very important. The multi family office should work with an income structure that allows it to finance the costs of operation sustainably for the long run. Each family should make its contribution at a volume that reflects the intensity with which it uses the office's services.

The further the multi family office moves away from the pure cost coverage principle, the stronger its profit orientation. The greater the commercial orientation, the greater the risks it must take to maximize profits. A family should review the economic solidity of any multi family office before agreeing to join it.

By commissioning a multi family office to manage its own wealth, the family can derive various advantages for itself and the generations to follow. The most important prerequisites for this are explored in the chapters to follow. Yet the same primary concept we started with still applies: freedom from conflict of interest by the family office is essential.

Checklist of Considerations When Founding or Selecting a Family Office

There is no one-size-fits-all model for a family office. The benefit a family can derive from its family office stands in direct correlation to whether that family office is positioned to fulfill the family's real wants and needs.

The following checklist touches on a variety of important criteria that a family may want to consider when assessing the range of services offered by (multi) family offices. This is only a partial list and should always be supplemented with questions related to the family's specific needs (Table 3.3).

Table 3.3 Family office checklist

Single family office or multi family office?	**Yes**	**No**
Is there reasonable justification for the family to found its own single family office?		
Is the prospective budget for a family office in line with the volume of assets under management, or would any potential cost savings and improved performance fall far below the level needed to compensate for setup and maintenance expenses?		
Are the investable assets sufficiently large to keep the family office team busy and interested in their assignment?		
Does the family have sufficient free time to handle the founding of this new enterprise?		
Is there some other pressing reason, either related to the family or its operating business, for the family to establish its own single family office?		

(continued)

Table 3.3 (continued)

Which services should be outsourced? Would the family be better off handing everything over to the care of a multi family office?		
Are there existing family offices that cover all (or most) of the services the family desires and which would accept the family as a new client?		
Are there companies or vendors that can provide the services the family desires in a professional and affordable manner (tax consulting, wealth management, reporting, real estate management, family governance, succession, mediation)?		
Are there services the family requires that cannot be offered by a multi family office and which might thus justify the founding of a single family office?		
Size, complexity and sectoral/regional structure of the wealth	**Yes**	**No**
Has a special event (such as the sale of the company) left the family's assets primarily in cash? Will the family office bear primary responsibility for investing those assets based on a long-term, diversified strategy?		
The family office should be highly experienced at developing strategies for private wealth management that extend across many asset classes.		
The family office should have experience in all asset classes, in asset allocation and in the assessment of the economic landscape.		
The family office should assign a high-level executive with outstanding coordination skills and global thinking to work with the family on strategic development.		
The family office should be open to partnerships with external service providers and wealth managers, especially for peripheral services that cannot be provided with the same professionalism using its own structures.		
Does the family and its wealth have an extensive international character, or should the investment be based on an internationally oriented investment strategy?		
The family office should have broad experience in capital investments in the relevant countries.		
The family office should have experts highly experienced in dealing with the specific complex legal and tax questions that arise when working internationally.		
The family office should possess an international network of specialists, including attorneys and tax consultants, and arrange for local back office partners where appropriate.		

(*continued*)

Table 3.3 (continued)

Is a strategy of broad diversification desired across all asset classes?		
The family office should have a strong degree of specialist knowledge and experience in all asset classes.		
The family office should possess a broad network of specialists in the individual asset classes with the experience to deliver expert analysis on individual investments and/or support the implementation of the investment strategy. They must also of course have a willingness to collaborate on this effort.		
The family office should deliver reporting that provides both a transparent overview of overall wealth portfolio and a detailed assessment of each individual asset class.		
The family office should have branches in relevant foreign countries to support with investments where needed or should be open to fixed partnerships with service providers there as needed.		
Freedom from conflict of interest	**Yes**	**No**
Does the family insist on its family office not benefiting economically through the development or implementation of the investment strategy (i.e. commissions for recommending specific investments)?		
The family office should base its financing purely on fees charged to the families it serves.		
The family office should not accept any (commission) payments by third parties (including wealth managers, agents, mutual fund companies).		
The family office should not run an operative business in any field where it is also responsible for controlling the partners of the family (such as banks or wealth managers).		
Is the family willing to accept that its family office will receive supplemental remuneration by third parties (provisions)?		
The family office should be absolutely transparent about any (commission) payments it has received before giving investment advice to the family.		
The family office should inform the family regularly about the composition of the overall remuneration that it receives from the family, including any commissions it has withheld.		
The family office should regularly provide information to the family by divulging its operating numbers, to demonstrate that it is economically stable without relying on payments by third parties to survive.		
The family accepts that some conflicts of interest are inevitable within the family office. Any such conflicts of interest are to be balanced out by its broader expertise and more extensive internal structures.		

(*continued*)

Table 3.3 (continued)

Operative tasks	**Yes**	**No**
Within the context of implementation of its investment strategy, does the family expects its family office to identify capital investment opportunities and/or actively manage its securities portfolio(s)?		
The family office should be licensed for its jurisdiction to handle capital investment responsibilities.		
The family office should be licensed with the appropriate authorities for its jurisdiction for the active management of the family's securities-based assets.		
A single family office would eliminate these steps, reducing time and expense.		
Informational requirements	**Yes**	**No**
Does the family expect customized reporting, harmonized to the various levels of knowledge and informational need of its individual members?		
The family office should provide custom reports (in terms of structure and content) to the individual members of the family.		
The family office should deliver short, transparent overviews (executive summaries) or more heavily detailed analyses upon request to the individual members of the family for use in decision making.		
The family office should where desired collate and store all documents necessary for tax returns and make these available as needed to the tax accountants.		
Does the family wish to be informed about developments at regular intervals either electronically, by phone or personally?		
The family office should be able to create the desired reporting at any preferred interval (daily, weekly, quarterly), including on short notice.		
The family office should be able to work with whichever form of communication the client family prefers, presuming it is given sufficient warning.		
Involvement	**Yes**	**No**
Would the leader of the family like to assume an executive-like position in the management of the family assets?		
The family office should be able to establish a communications infrastructure with the family such that harmonization between the leader of the family and the family office is possible for any operative questions (establishment of a "red phone").		

(*continued*)

Table 3.3 (continued)

The family office should if needed be able to offer the family leader a flexible, dedicated position in the family office.		
The family office should work on the basis of a clear strategy developed by the family and should know which family members can influence or even determine the implementation of the family strategy in the family office, and through which bodies.		
The family should know which family members are authorized to access which information about other family members (asset figures, pre-nuptials…).		
The family should know which family members can make investment decisions for other family members.		
The family should know which family members are liable for losses, should they occur.		
The family office should have a clear procedure on who decides about the admission of new family members as shareholders of the family office, adjustments to the fee structure and all other governance aspects.		
Does the leader of the family solely wish to be involved with decisions at the strategic level and otherwise views herself as serving as a form of unofficial supervisory board?		
The family office should handle operative management tasks, from an HR, communications (executive reports, decision documents) and regulatory standpoint.		
The family office should fulfill the family's need for transparent reporting (overview of the transactions conducted by the family office).		
The family office should work on the basis of a clear strategy developed by the family and should know which family members can influence or even determine the implementation of the family strategy in the family office, and through which bodies.		
Ownership structure	**Yes**	**No**
Does the family insist on (co-)owning the family office, so as to have influence on its (business) policies?		
The family office should fundamentally be oriented toward being able to take in new shareholders in an uncomplicated manner.		
The family office should in this situation not be oriented toward maximizing profits, but rather solely covering its own costs, to avoid divergent profit expectations that could cause conflict within the ownership circle.		
The family should concretely review the option of founding its own family office.		

From Germany: "A family office will sink or swim based on the qualifications and aptitudes of its personnel."

Interview with Klaus Kuder

This interview touches on differences between single and multi family offices, family governance structures and typical mistakes when founding a family office.

This interview was conducted by Peter Preller.

Mr. Kuder, you are considered one of the pioneers of the German family office scene. Long before the concept had become popular, you were already working as a managing director setting up and leading a bank-bound family office and went on to coordinate the fusion of three multi family offices. You then served as chairman for that large new organization. In 2014 you founded your own multi family office, Kuder Familypartner GmbH. What moved you to take that step?

Klaus Kuder: My idea was to offer families a service that combined the desire for their own discrete, individual single family office with the wider spectrum of options and greater reach of a multi family office. What I had repeatedly found in the past was that single family offices tended to concentrate on specific areas, usually based on the structure of their assets or the specific dynamics

---

Klaus Kuder *first encountered the world of family offices in 1994, during a stint in New York as a consultant and administrator for private wealth management at Deutsche Bank. He held that position through the end of 1998, when a client invited him to oversee the comprehensive restructuring of that client's portfolio. In 1999, Kuder became the founding director of the Deutsche Family Office GmbH, the family office product from Deutsche Bank in Germany. It was the predecessor firm to the Wilhelm von Finck Deutsche Family Office AG and the Deutsche Oppenheim Family Office AG, for whom he served as chairman of their respective boards. Klaus Kuder left the Group in 2014. Today he is managing director and partner at Kuder Familypartner GmbH, which he founded in November 2014 as a provider of consulting services to notable entrepreneurial families. He sees in his firm a unique service that combines the benefits of a single family office with the advantages inherent to a wider multi family office. Klaus Kuder is a founding member of the German Association of Independent Family Offices.*

at play within the family. Yet there are risks in becoming overly specialized, namely the threat of missing out on opportunities that don't appear at first glance to fit within the family's scope of interests. My idea is to bridge this gap. By working together closely with multiple families, we formulate ideas and approaches that can potentially be of interest for the other clients. This leads not only to a broader pool of expertise, but also opportunities to join in on business and investment ideas that leverage the economies of scale to the benefit of the families. In fact, the interplay between multiple clients quite often awakens a set of impulses and considerations that simply don't exist in single family offices, or at the very least which potentially cannot be articulated in quite the same way when taken in the context of a single wealthy family. This connection between proximity and individuality, paired with a broader reach and independence, is at the heart of my company's concept.

Based on your experience, what is the difference between the services offered by bank-bound and by bank-independent family office structures?

KK: The key factors are positioning and the business concept. A family office stands for comprehensive consulting that is not captive to any product. This is all the more important if the family office owner is known for a specific product or service, such as a bank, fund manager, tax advisor or attorney. In this case, the family office must be structured to complement those strengths if it is to be viable for the long term. Historically, banks in particular have frequently encountered problems in finding a sustainable and credible balance between their banking and their family office services. UBS, Berenberg, Lampe and the houses of Hardy, Grunelius and Hauck & Aufhäuser are just a few examples where the family office concept has failed over time due to a lack of clear delineation from their classic banking business. They eventually squandered the trust of their family office clients and, ultimately, the managers at their parent firms.

You have to set a clear accent: What does the family officer stand for, and what does the bank stand for? The points of difference and overlap must be clear and transparent. Otherwise it becomes difficult to credibly establish the independence that one would expect from a family office. In a pure family office, the consultants are in my opinion focused solely on the needs of ownership, regardless of which topics or asset classes are being reviewed.

Beyond this, differences can also be observed in terms of which services are offered for a given family office, such as real estate management, controlling and consulting on controlling, finance, tax, legal and wealth management.

What special challenges did your company face when it was first founded, and which ones do you anticipate as it matures?

KK: The business model and philosophy are of central importance. As already mentioned, I decided to put the focus for my company on comprehensive consulting, by which in this case I mean: generalist. From the start, I eliminated the potential conflicts of interests related to supplementary specialized services. Otherwise special challenges invariably arise that, unless handled quickly and with tremendous discipline, can lead to existential conflicts of interest. Beyond this, the desired business model must be harmonized with the regulatory requirements. That's an aspect that shouldn't ever be underestimated.

What challenges do you see for the future?

KK: Whatever the type of growth, it is essential that the focus remains on the client. Ultimately, we as family officers are obligated to the well-being of our clients and are compensated for this service. Families expect that their advisors will keep up to the minute on the latest developments in a wide range of important, relevant themes. For example, a growing number of investors are expressing anxiety about their ability to preserve their wealth at all, a reflection of the increasingly failing trust in the stability of cash value and in our currencies. In the past, factors like the Cold War or hyperinflation caused a deep-seated sense of unease; today it is terror, blackmail, etc. While the family office cannot deliver a quick answer to these fundamental questions, its most basic purpose is in fact to work together with the client to investigate, prioritize and act in an effective manner.

What are the biggest mistakes that one might make during the founding phase of a single or multi family office, and what considerations can help avoid them?

KK: There's a clear tip in this regard: Before you move to actually found anything, you need to be clear on those things for which your family office will really be responsible. This means formulating three to five objectives for the family office to pursue. It sounds simple, but it's not. You'll quickly find that it's much simpler to put 20 to 30 wishes to paper than narrowing it down. But in my view, that's the wrong approach because you're bound to get bogged down. If you try to balance too many plates at once, it's highly likely that a few are going to fall and break. So while it's a simple piece of advice, it's also a crucial one. Whether the family office should focus, for example, on private equity investments or perhaps instead on bookkeeping and asset reporting will have a major impact on how that family office is structured, in terms of personnel and technical infrastructure. Along the same lines: trite as it sounds, the family office must keep an open line to all participating family members, not just the leader of the family. The children may have other points of interest and expectations of the family office. These must absolutely be accounted for if each family member is to identify with the family office and is to enjoy the greatest degree of acceptance possible. This is especially important because the family office, if well managed, can make a significant long-term contribution to cohesiveness within the family.

How do you avoid potential conflicts of interest between the families?
KK: There should be clear rules of engagement and the greatest possible degree of transparency. This is important not just when managing the interactions between multiple clients, but also within an individual family office mandate, including a single family office. A lack of transparency leads to mistrust. Mistrust destroys acceptance of the family office and robs it of the foundation it needs to do business. And nobody should want that.

What role should family governance play in the range of services a family office offers?
KK: Questions of family governance form a decisive point and in essence serve as the foundation for a whole range of other topics. The family office is part of governance and can help keep the family and its wealth together. If it's handled poorly, it can also lead to greater splintering. What is the relationship between the family and family office? Who controls it? What role do family members play in the steering of the family office? How is the family office positioned vis-à-vis the family's operating business? What overlaps exist, and which of these are desirable and/or undesirable? These are just a few of the aspects that play a role in governance. When a family office has been positioned effectively, it can serve as an anchor for the family and as a point of identification. Otherwise in the long term it becomes a foreign body, with neither acceptance nor trust. That makes a big difference in large or old family clans in particular, where centrifugal forces tend to grow bigger and stronger with each generation; that force pulling the family apart needs to be managed and the sense of unity must be preserved within the family.

What would you recommend families think about when they are contemplating the founding of a single family office, or joining a multi family office?
KK: Beyond the business model and the formulation of goals and desires for the family office, recruiting also plays a major role. The aptitude of the family officer often ends up deciding the success or failure of the family office. Training, experience and qualifications are important. Just as important is empathy on the part of the advisor and his or her ability to engage with the family. This may sound simple but it isn't, because decisions aren't always made on a rational basis. Even this simple example shows that the selection process for a suitable family officer must follow certain rules. The fit at a personal level can, in borderline cases, prove significantly more important than their expertise on paper.

Let's assume that a family has the type of asset volumes that lend themselves to economic operation of a single family office of its own. What criteria would indicate to you that they would be better served founding a separate single family office, and when would you recommend joining a multi family office?
KK: The question that the family must first answer is: Do we have the will and desire to create our own structure, including the management and monitoring that go with it? If you're creating your own organization, there must be a strong willingness to delegate tasks to external service providers. With that said, having your own family office can also promote greater closeness, individuality and discretion.

What factors matter in assessing the human resources of a family office?
KK: HR decisions—qualitatively and quantitatively—should reflect the tasks and the services the family wants their family office to handle directly on its own. Beyond this, the complexity of the family also impacts the personnel structure.

What role does the size of the portfolio to be managed play, as well as the number of family (households) and asset classes to be managed?
KK: The size of the wealth to be managed is not necessarily the decisive variable. A large pool of wealth in the billions can be structured simply, such as if a large portion is in just one stock or is tied to the family's operative business. The number of family members requiring support and the asset classes are more likely instead to impact the technical and HR constellation of the family office.

Should a family office retain its own experts for this, or buy in that expertise from third parties?
KK: I would fundamentally recommend that services be purchased on the market where possible, as this is better and more affordable and not in conflict with internal goals. Services tailored to the family and sensitive issues by contrast are generally better handled internally.

By your reckoning, what are the minimum requirements for IT structure (hardware and software)?
KK: This depends on which IT and personnel structure is required based on the physical office layout. I would break it down as follows: The first tier involves system reliability and stability within a secured environment. Next come issues such as individualized software solutions, interfaces to other programs, including real estate management and bank and portfolio management software. The third tier then involves mobile solutions to allow access to one's own asset data at any time. This is a requirement that I've increasingly been hearing about, formulated in particular by younger family members.

One can imagine that the provision of sensitive asset data to external sources brings with it very specific requirements for data protection and compliance.

What costs would you expect to be associated with operating or joining a mid-sized, privately held family office? Is there a direct correlation between the costs and the size of the assets being managed?
KK: Costs vary greatly and are hard to generalize. With a minimum set-up of one to three persons (senior executive, junior executive, assistant) and a stable IT infrastructure, costs of between €500,000 and €1 mn. per year can be expected, depending on competency, experience and seniority. If specialized knowledge or special experience is required, then costs can rise significantly above that mark. In any case, it can be said that personnel costs always represent the largest cost point in the overall budget for a family office. But as mentioned: A family office will sink or swim based on the qualifications and aptitudes of its personnel.

Bibliography

Archer C, Hauser BR (2015) Family offices. Globe Business Publishing, London
Farkas-Richling D, Fischer TR, Richter A Eds, (2012) Private banking und family office, 2. Edition. Schäffer-Poeschel, Stuttgart
Moody N, Tasman-Jonex J, Finnigan M (2015) Campden Research/UBS – The global family office report 2015. London
Rosplock K (2014) The complete family office handbook – A guide for affluent families and the advisors who serve them. Wiley, Hoboken
Wilson RC (2014) The single family office: creating, operating & managing investments of a single family office, 1st edn. CreateSpace, Lexington

4

Structures for Managing Wealth

Peter Preller

Few things can come to define an entrepreneurial family more than the company it owns and the associated affluence that it has built up over years and even generations. Multiple members of the family will typically have served in the company's employ, and the institution itself can anchor the family through good times and bad. The company and the riches it has generated must be understood as more than just symbols of the family's distinct history; they are also the family's enduring economic lifeblood. There are many potential challenges to preserving wealth over an extended period so that it can be passed to future generations. The following highlights a few of the key considerations in this effort.

4.1 Family Wealth Management

Debt levels for participants in developed economies are currently hovering at record levels. In the Euro Zone, total debt (as a percentage of GDP) for national governments, their households and non-financial companies totals 230%. The same figure for Japan stands at an inconceivable 367%. The 245% measured for the United States is, against its backdrop of comparably better demographic development, actually considered moderate (*Datastream Thomson Reuters, accessed 6/15/2015, HQ Trust GmbH, Bad Homburg, analysis the author's own*).

These levels arose during decades of overwhelming peace and before the trend towards graying societies had become clear. The dual problems of unfavorable demographics and mountains of debt are now exacerbating each

B. Canessa et al., *The Family Office*, https://doi.org/10.1007/978-3-319-99085-9_4

other. Japan's population is expected to sink from its current level of 127 mn. citizens (2005) to just 100 mn. by 2050 and ultimately around 64 mn. in 2100 (*Wikipedia, accessed 8/13/2015*).

Government debt and debts from private households and companies have a deflationary impact. This starts with delayed consumption and eventually translates into reduced economic activity. A large portion of government debt was applied to economically infeasible projects. In addition, government policies incentivized private investors to allocate money for projects that were clearly and predictably economically infeasible: in the USA, the government-nourished real estate bubble that ran through 2007; in Germany, the IPOs for Deutsche Telekom in 1996, 1999 and 2000 and, after German reunification, poorly considered allocations for East German real estate using tax incentives. In retrospect, the timing of these episodes was almost comically poor.

The central banks initiated a program of countermeasures for these issues, reasoning that an inflation of debt might be less "painful" than deflationary debt relief through national insolvencies and the collapse of debtors. Their efforts included policies such as 'quantitative easing' to artificially depress interest levels below national economic growth rates by buying bonds and other assets; their hope was to combine these measures with inflationary tools to then re-establish a moderately acceptable debt level. Central banks are powerful institutions, and in the age of paper money, their "firepower" should not be underestimated. They can instantly create money if they so desire, and beyond that have the option of issuing bonds for all state debts and other investments. Yet viewed objectively, these measures and similar ones to come are a bit like open heart surgery—invasive and promising only a decidedly unclear outcome.

Yet there are also positive trends: Globally speaking, there have never been as many new scientists and engineers as now, and networking and innovation are growing strongly. Human creativity should never be underestimated and might yet find a way to allay our many environmental problems. The X-factor here is education. It is the key to solving challenges and building affluence.

Given this environment, families that have sold a business and families still operating their legacy business each face a number of difficult questions related to the wealth they have accumulated inside and outside the company:

- How can our wealth be preserved and expanded?
- What objectives do I wish to pursue with this wealth (personally or as part of a family)?
- How should our wealth be invested?
- What steps should be taken to implement our strategy?
- What is a suitable structure to achieve these goals?

The potential answers run the spectrum from outsourcing all area of wealth management (including asset allocation, manager selection, wealth reporting and controlling, selection of custodian banks, tax consultants, etc.) to handling all elements in-house. In many cases, the starting point will reflect the family's economic roots. Where a family has a history in a given industry, investments in that area will typically be managed internally by the family office, with other classes then outsourced.

4.1.1 Vision and Mission of the Family Office

From the start, the family should clarify internally how actively it wishes to be involved in the structuring and later in the active business operations. Is it important that some family member always be incorporated into the daily workings of the family office? Or would the family prefer to limit itself to questions of long-term strategic orientation and routine informational sessions such as the annual shareholder meeting?

One primary function of such meetings is indeed reviewing the costs structures for the various elements involved in operating the office. The family office and its infrastructure, regardless of whether run by the family or by a third party, represent one such tier. Costs related to fees for external banks, auditors, tax advisors, asset managers, financial controllers and reporting experts are another. Beyond these, cost blocks proportional to the size of the overall portfolio should also be expected, regardless of whether the portfolio is managed by the family office or external asset managers. In negotiating with custodian banks and wealth managers, family officers can try to leverage the buying power of larger portfolios into reduced fees by percentage.

The family or family leader should clarify how much of this work they wish to handle on their own and how much should be outsourced. Their choices will also help define staffing needs. Is someone in the family willing and qualified to assume this sort of position? Corporate governance is another significant long-term contributor to the success or failure of any family office. How much is a family capable of assessing on its own, and what will it wish to decide for itself in the future? It matters greatly which persons are actively involved, as their attitude will set the tone for the corporate culture. Just like in any other company, values are conveyed internally and externally through the comportment of management: Character, qualification and experience must stand in harmony with the family interests.

A single family office has the freedom to operate based on its own precise individual goals, while multi family offices are better positioned to harness the economy of scale. The greatest potential for volume-based cost savings are in asset controlling and reporting as well as an asset management, where IT infrastructures, software and capital market analyses can generally be shared by multiple families even as they pursue their own highly individual needs.

This also impacts the selection of a suitable company structure for the operative family office and for its control and oversight committees. In many cases advisory boards are formed to support the family. The aforementioned questions must logically also be addressed by this committee as well. It should be remembered that it is easy to establish structures once, but more difficult to streamline those structures once in place. Careful consideration should be given in advance whether more complex structures could lead to undesirable dependencies on advisors, a situation referred to in academic circles as part of the "Principal Agent theory." The impulse also applies when assigning mandates to external service providers.

From an asset allocation standpoint, one of the first questions to address is whether the company itself should be counted as an asset in the analysis. Seen objectively, the company fundamentally represents a proprietary capital investment whose risks are comparable with those of an equities-based investment. Yet the risks associated with the company often 'feel' smaller than those for a publicly traded corporation. This is only perception, however, usually reflecting that the entrepreneur has learned to be comfortable assessing market challenges, the specifics of the industry and company-specific questions, i.e. managing risk.

For publicly traded companies, investors without large packages of shares are limited to voting at the shareholder's meeting. If any given shareholder of a large corporation disagrees with management's chosen strategy, their only real channel to express that discomfort is to sell their shares. Fundamental risks such as inflation (rising prices) and deflation (falling prices) are always comparable for the shareholder and the entrepreneur. One's own active company should thus always be taken into consideration.

4.1.2 Yield Requirements and Targets

What yield requirements are in place? Are there running expenses? Running expenses are ultimately to be viewed as a liability. Are there other liabilities as well? Should the wealth be preserved in real terms, meaning in step with inflation? In other words, should the buying power for that wealth remain just as high in the future as it is now?

This question is often answered with a yes, as people typically wish to retain the same material standard of living as today (same purchasing power), especially if the company might potentially be sold and they might have more time for the "nicer" things in life. For wealth to be preserved in real terms, it must be invested. Implicit in this is an important point: Families that have already achieved a high degree of wealth need to act to preserve that affluence. The goal is not to grow the wealth through methods that expose them to greater levels of risk than they currently face.

The question then turns to a suitable inflation rate, meaning: given the individual "basket of goods" of importance to the investor, how quickly are prices rising for those goods? Pinning down a practical answer can be extremely difficult. It's instead more effective to determine how much money the individual or family intends to withdraw each year.

Practical Example: Potential Withdrawal Amounts

Yield requirements of 6.5% p.a. might adhere to the following model:

Presumed inflation 1.5%
Withdrawal: 2.0%
Costs: 1.0%
Taxes*: 2.0% (*simplified: approx. 30%)
Yield requirement: 6.5%

If annual value growth of 6.5% is achieved, then 2% can be withdrawn without degrading the real value based on these sample inflation figures. If no withdrawal is made, then the wealth would grow in real terms by that amount. Note that this represents an ambitious yield target, especially against the current background of extremely low capital market yields.

4.1.3 A Survey of Asset Classes

Depending on their particular strategy for achieving the desired yields, investment managers can choose between a variety of different asset classes. While the nomenclature isn't quite uniform here, one can make a rough differentiation between "stock-like" investments and "bond-like" investments. All asset classes and sub-asset classes ultimately fit roughly into these two categories. Gold is an exception, as it represents its own distinct asset class.

"Stock-like" investments involve equity capital in the extended sense, for example:

- Stocks (equity shares in publicly traded firms); stock sub-asset classes: regions, industries…
- Private equity (equity shares in privately held firms); private equity asset sub-classes: regions or styles such as buy-out or venture capital
- Hedge funds (using stock-like instruments)
- Real estate holdings with leveraged financing (direct investment)

"Bond-like" investments involve equity capital in the extended sense, for example:

- Bonds (standardized and saleable debt securities with a fixed interest rate)
- Bond sub-asset classes: investment grade bonds, high yield bonds, emerging market bonds, private debt (non-publicly traded loan debt and private loans)
- Hedge funds (using bond-like instruments)
- 100% equity financed real estate holdings (without leverage)

Stocks, private equity and real estate offer ongoing (rising) yields over extended periods of time, including dividends; bonds also offer yields (unlike equity investments), such as through interest income. Because the yields are fixed, however, they are categorized as "annuities."

Why are hedge funds and real estate categorized as falling within both of the overarching asset classes? Hedge funds can, depending on their structure, evince a more stock-like or a more bond-like character. Hedge funds offer tremendous freedom in the implementation of their strategy. They seek to leverage inefficient pricing of individual investments, or even entire investment classes, to their owner's benefit. This can for example involve pricing differences between individual stocks: Imagine that an investor buys stock A and sells holdings in stock B. The investor is predicting that stock A will rise and intends to sell for a profit when it reaches some higher level. At the same time, the investor is predicting that stock B will fall and intends to turn a profit by buying back the stock when its price is lower. There are strategies for all conceivable markets, including raw materials, foreign currencies, bonds, stocks, etc. In many cases managers take out lines of credit to leverage economies of scale in situations where only minimal percentage differences in valuation are present. This approach brings with it exposure to the real risk inherent to these funds: total loss of value.

Asset managers have the goal of achieving absolute positive value growth in all market phases, regardless of whether the markets are rising or falling. The financial crisis that ran from 2007–2009 exploded the projections and reputations of many managers, leading to disappointment among their investors. Hedge funds can nevertheless be sensibly taken as part of a portfolio. After all, good managers can minimize losses even in times of crisis and achieve positive numbers in growing markets, which in the long term produces attractive results.

These differences are, for the purposes of this text, hair-splittingly fine. What matters is that hedge funds can be used in different ways within the portfolio construction, such as for diversification and reduction of portfolio fluctuation. Hedge funds generate capital gains, not current income.

4.1.4 Asset Class: Real Estate

Real estate offers a long-term, rising stream of rental income. Differences within the class become clear during a financial or economic crisis. Real estate that is financed with equity only is crisis-proof, even when empty—at least in principle. Real estate financed primarily with leverage is vulnerable to crises, because loans must still be serviced even when falling rental income and market prices sink. The forced sales that often occur in this situation usually produce 'bad' prices for the seller. Given the divergent nature of these situations, "Real Estate" as an asset class is actually classified as part of both groups.

The simplicity of real estate as an asset class makes it relatively easy to tax, and in the past it has been an especially popular target for cash-strapped legislatures.

A few historical examples from Germany:

- **Rent controls** in the 1920s: Landlords were forbidden from increasing rents, despite the high rate of inflation. As a result, the property owners found themselves faced with (still rising) investment costs, but a rapidly shrinking rental income that soon covered no more than a fraction of their expenses. Beyond the general economic misery, this particular step led to the impoverishment of a large swath of the middle class during the 1920s.
- The **"House Interest Tax,"** an income tax on residential property, was enforced from 1924 to 1943.
- The **Equalization of Burdens Tax** was put into place starting in 1948, whereby property owners were assessed a land charge that was then recorded in the title register.
- The latest example of legislative intervention is the **Rental Prices Brake**, notably introduced in cities such as Berlin.

4.1.5 Asset Class: Gold

Gold cannot be arbitrarily replicated, and as such cannot simply be created by a central bank. As a result, gold cannot be devalued in the same way as paper money and retains its purchasing power. Gold is the sole investment that offers long-term protection against deflation and inflation. It must however be mentioned that this only applies over very long periods of time. For this reason, gold is frequently called a "crisis currency."

The global acceptance of gold represents another benefit. Three important aspects speak against gold as a long-term investment. First, gold offers no compound interest; at best, it appreciates as capital. Stocks by contrast produce roughly 33% of their overall yield long-term as dividends (*Datastream*

Thomson Reuters, accessed 7/29/2015, author's calculations), putting gold at a massive disadvantage. Second, history teaches that ownership of gold can be legally abolished during times of crisis (as was the case in the USA from 1933 to 1974), reducing its de facto protection against crisis. Third, preservation of capital is only ensured over very long periods of time. In the short or medium term, fluctuations in the price of gold can make this impossible. For this reason, differentiation must be made between liquidity reserves in gold, such as coins, and a long-term investment in gold.

4.1.6 Home Currency

The proposed 6.5% p.a. yield target contains a component called "withdrawals." Withdrawals are generally booked in investor's home currency, which corresponds to the prevalent currency in the country or region in which the family primarily lives. Care must be given that investments intended to produce current returns for withdrawal should be invested in the home currency.

Fluctuations in investments in the home currency, such as the Euro, are significantly lower than for investments in foreign currencies. Currency fluctuations can significantly overshadow current returns—a devaluation of the (foreign) investment currency can easily "eat up" any income from the interest voucher. For this kind of investment, differentiation must be made between the investment and the investment currency. Insofar as the opinions about currency trends are not unanimous, currency hedges should be implemented.

These same considerations also apply to hedge fund investments if they are placed within a larger portfolio as investments to reduce fluctuation and produce the greatest degree of stable yields possible. In concrete terms, this means that in many cases it is sensible to make hedge funds investments with safeguards against currency fluctuation. The hedge fund portion of the wealth should be designed to avoid excessive currency fluctuations, positive or negative alike. These decisions should be made early on during strategic planning.

4.1.7 Yield and Risk

How do the various basic investment classes behave during different phases of deflation and inflation? Which assets are likeliest at bare minimum to preserve wealth that has been accrued in some cases over generations? Because we are working in an age of paper money, analysis tends to focus more heavily on inflationary risks than deflationary ones. Yet realistically, a deep and lasting

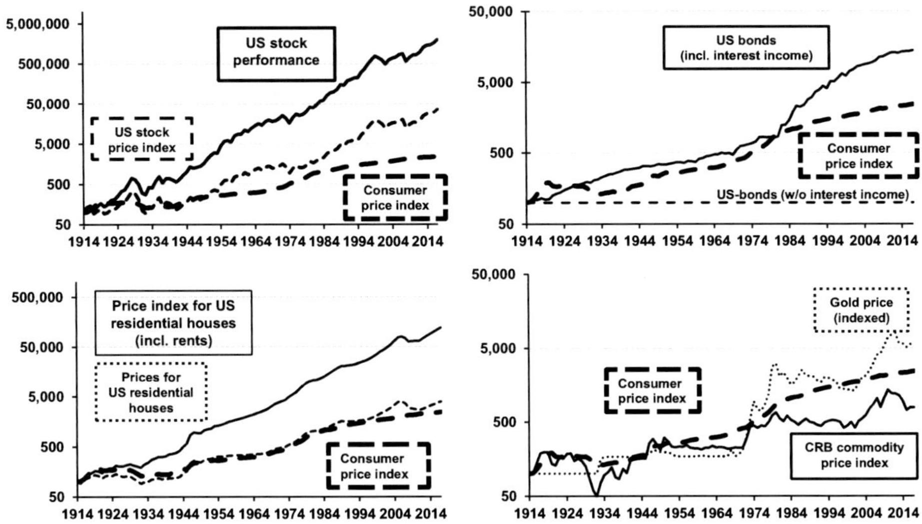

Fig. 4.1 Long-term outlook for capital markets (Source: *Datastream, HQ Trust GmbH*)

deflation could only occur at this point if the central bank wished for it to be so or was weakened too far to sufficiently fight it.

Moving clockwise from the upper left, the graphs in Fig. 4.1 show the extended historical price trends for American stocks, real estate, gold and government bonds respectively. Real estate has been an effective way to preserve wealth in real terms—even without the reinvestment of rental income (dotted line). If rental income is into account, then significant real wealth growth was observed (solid line). For investments in US annuities, wealth is only preserved if all interest income is completely reinvested. Since 1914, this would have delivered a 140× increase (*HQ Trust GmbH, Bad Homburg, author's analysis*) of the wealth. Without reinvestment of interest income, the capital would not have been effectively protected (dotted line).

Bonds have actually even suffered long phases of value degradation: From 1940 to 1981, a portfolio of investments in US government bonds lost 56% of their real value (i.e. accounting for inflation) and were stagnant from 45 years in total (from 1940 to 1985). This is not difficult to imagine, given the current interest rates. Bonds currently have a 30-year rally behind them. Starting in 1981, former US central bank president Paul Volker raised rates within just a few months from 10% to 19%, throttling inflation overnight (which had preciously reached 15%); interest rates have fallen in the decades since then to today's current record lows. This is the moment in Fig. 4.1 when US annuity significantly moved away from the performance of the consumer price index.

At the same time, global debt rose to nearly unprecedented high levels, of the sort seen previously only in the aftermath of the Second World War.

In light of today's rates, it can thus virtually be ruled out that bonds will ever again represent the levels of value they once did. Quite the contrary: Bonds will very likely continue to be considered a very safe instrument but among the poorest performers in real terms. As such, bonds must be viewed as the least suitable asset for long-term capital preservation, especially if the interest income is withdrawn.

Stocks are the best instrument for preserving wealth, even when dividends are not reinvested. A program of consistent reinvestment of dividends can lead to as much as a 15,000× growth (*HQ Trust GmbH, Bad Homburg, author's analysis*).

Gold by contrast provides protection only along very long time frames, and with severe fluctuation. The strong price trend for gold in the past ten years is ultimately well above the inflationary curve.

Stocks are, in the long term, the yield-heaviest investment, although they have one key disadvantage in the short term: price swings can be massive. With the luxury of a medium-term outlook, this is not a major issue. But severe drops in share prices can trigger strong uncertainty in investors, which represents a significant limiting factor for this type of investment.

A global portfolio of stocks would have lost 56% from its high in 2007 to its low point in 2009. Dividends dropped by approx. 30% in that period, meaning ongoing yields from a global portfolio of stocks dropped by that same percentage. This is a crucial and in some cases unacceptable risk, especially if (the family's) income is being generated from investment of the wealth (see Fig. 4.2).

This leads directly to one of the most important questions that an investor or family must ask itself—one that truly demands an honest answer: How much risk can be sustained, both financially and emotionally? Poor judgement here can lead to the complete destruction of the wealth, especially if a forced sale in reaction to share prices collapsing in a crisis then locks in those losses.

4.1.8 Movement of the Investment Classes

When constructing a portfolio risk strategy, consideration must be given to the movements within the asset classes in relation to one another. Each asset class has its own distinct characteristics and trend dynamics. This can be helpful during portfolio construction, as these insights can help structure portfolios with less volatility.

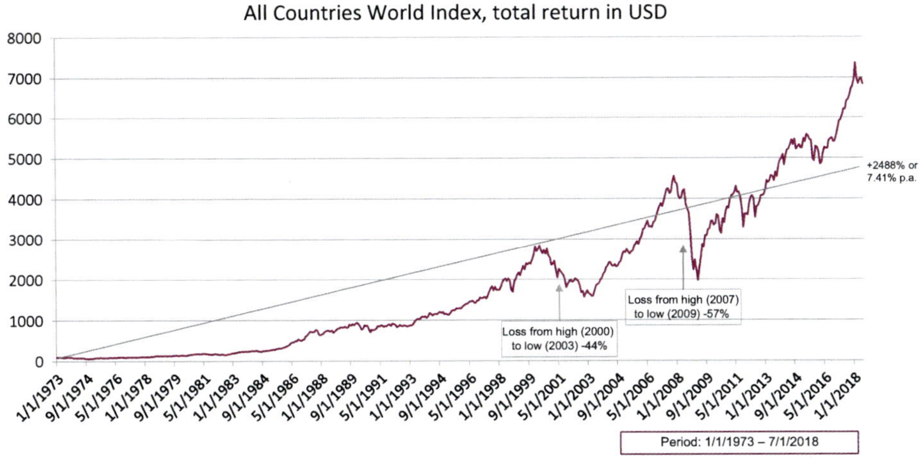

Fig. 4.2 Global stock prices since 1988 (Source: *Datastream, HQ Trust GmbH, author's calculation*)

- A correlation of −1 means that the rates are moving in precise counterpoint.
- A correlation of +1 means that the rates are moving in precise synchronization.
- Example: Stocks and bonds with a correlation of −1

A portfolio is constructed from stocks and bonds: If the value trend for the stocks is negative, then the value trend for the bonds will be positive, although not necessarily at the same intensities. This mirrored movement means that a drop in value of stocks is partially or entirely counterweighted by a growth in value of bonds.

It is helpful to understand historical correlations. Concrete correlative prognoses, by contrast, tend to be unreliable. Even so, it is possible to make some observations about the two selected key asset classes, stocks and bonds: Since 1998 stocks and bonds have moved in synchronicity. When stock prices fall, then interest rates fall as well (see also Fig. 4.3).

The described correlation is illogical from an economics standpoint, as falling investment yields and falling interest rates should in theory boost stock prices. Yet because the analysis of a company (reflected in its stock price) discounts its future earnings due to the low interest rates, the company's current value is increased.

A simplified example: The sum of future profits for a share totals 1000. This is discounted at an interest rate of 5%, representing a cash value (the company's value) of 200. Were that interest rate to stand at 2%, then the company's

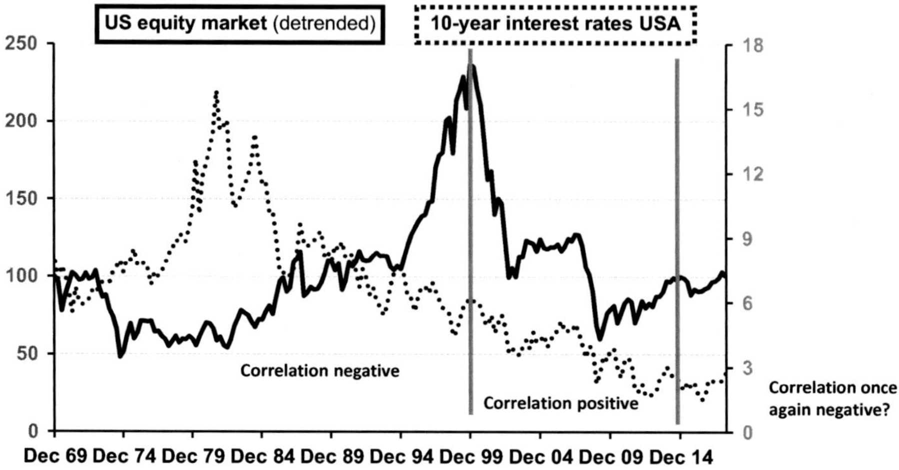

Fig. 4.3 Correlation between stocks and bonds since 1995 (Source: *Datastream, HQ Trust GmbH*)

value would be 5000. (The calculation has been simplified for the purposes of this example). As interest rates fall, the current discounted value rises based on the cash value formula for perpetual payments: Cash value = annual long-term yield/interest rate.

The phenomenon may reflect a fundamental loss of trust in long-term global economic growth since the bursting of the American hedge fund Long-Term Capital Management and the Russia bank default of 1998. Investors concluded that stock markets fall as interest rates drop. It then follows that falling interest rates are a result of poor economic growth, combined with low inflation rates, and that for this reason the prospects for success by companies must also be estimated as poor. This aspect merits mention because since the overturning of this relationship (correlation) in 1998, it has been quite easy to construct mixed stock/bond portfolios that are relatively well shielded from volatility. It may be reasonably questioned whether this characteristic that reduces the risk of volatility will continue to be effective in light of the extremely low interest rates, and if not, whether huge challenges await. In mixed stock/bond portfolios, this produces an undesirably high level of fluctuation.

To forecast portfolio behavior in periods of crisis, a select asset structure can be assessed using scenarios based on historical data. Calculations and scenario analyses of this type can also be expanded to include expected characteristics. These evaluations provide a useful instrument when formulating long-term target allocation. As shown above, the focus will be on difficult periods for capital markets and gaining the family's approval for the proposed asset structure—a necessary first step to formulating a suitable long-term target structure.

4.1.9 Liquidity and Illiquidity of the Overall Portfolio

There are a variety of risks that must be taken into account when investing wealth. The family office, whether a single or multi family office, must be aware of and manage those risks or else outsource management responsibility. From the family's viewpoint, the topic of liquidity and illiquidity are important ones here (see Fig. 4.4).

How liquid or illiquid is the overall portfolio? How high may the illiquid portion of the assets become? Illiquidity represents a risk if unexpected events lead to a need for cash, such as during a succession event when estate taxes must be paid. Liquid assets increase flexibility to acquire discounted assets during times of crisis. At the same time, the danger exists that investment assets will need to be sold at a disadvantageous time. Illiquid assets such as private equity have a "disciplining" character in those situations, as they force the prospective seller to solicit real pricing from the market, and the results are often so low that the potential sale is then abandoned. The dynamic is different when a sale must be made. This scenario can also arise when external capital, meaning a financial leverage, has been used. The creditor can determine when the loan will be called in, and this typically occurs during stormy periods of crisis.

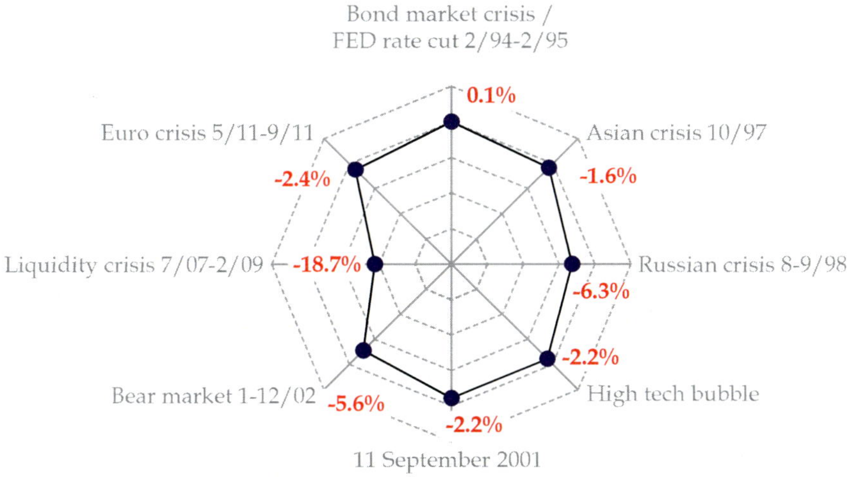

Fig. 4.4 Portfolio behavior in periods of crises (Source: *HQ Trust GmbH*)

4.1.10 Asset Allocation

An example involving stocks and bonds helps illuminate which decisions lead to which results. This helps make it easier to assess performance in the individual investments (see Fig. 4.5).

Long-term asset allocation, meaning the division of monies into various asset classes, has a very strong impact on overall long-term results. A time frame of ten years or more is foreseen. In simple terms, the question is whether a family should invest long-term at levels such as 80% stocks/20% bonds, or vice versa. This decision represents the so-called "strategic asset allocation."

It reflects the long-term goals, personal risk tolerance, spending behavior and yield expectations for the investments. The target specifications can diverge greatly, which can lead to problems in difficult markets or financial crises, since risk tolerance is a personal matter. It is not at all unusual for tension to arise even within a single family. If no suitable orientation of the assets is established, during periods of crisis the yield requirements may exceed the actual current yields and/or the desired liquidity and fungibility may be lost.

It is relatively simple to determine one's own yield requirements, as expenses can be tallied up using a personal inventory of net assets. Quantifying expected yields is considerably more difficult and less certain, although in general long-

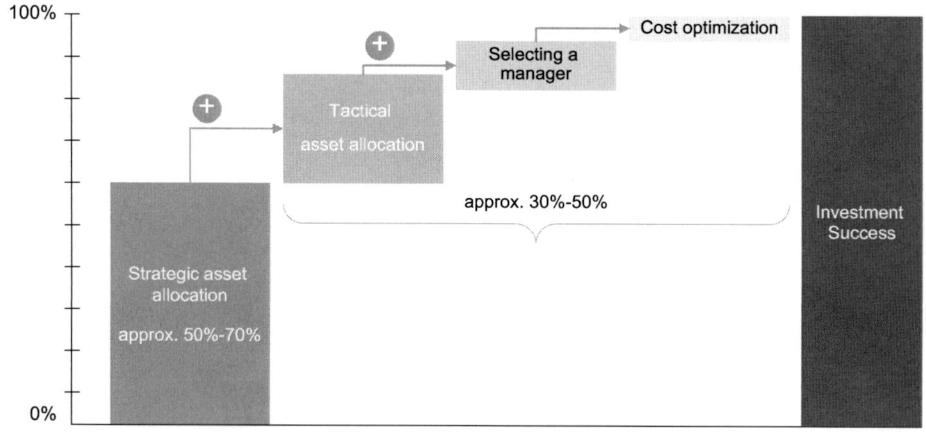

Fig. 4.5 Value contribution from asset allocation (Source: *Fundamentals: Gary P. Brinson, L. Randolph Hood and Gilbert L. Beebower, Determinants of Portfolio Performance, The Financial Analysts Journal, July/August 1986; Randolph L. Hood, Determinants of Portfolio Performance – 20 Years Later, The Financial Analysts Journal, September/October 2005, HQ Trust GmbH*)

term yield expectations can be defined with more certainty than short term ones. This can be attributed in particular to short-term events or shocks that cannot be foreseen, but which in the long term—from a wealth investment standpoint—have little impact.

While strategic asset allocation accounts for the market yields from the respective markets—known as the "beta"—the field of tactical asset allocation endeavors to achieve greater yields ("alpha") through deviations from the long-term allocation. In the short and medium term, emphasis is added or removed at the level of the investment classes and equity asset classes. For example, a tactical allocation decision might take the form of putting special weight on European shares within the securities asset class. This either causes the entire asset class to be more heavily weighted or for the extra emphasis to draw away from other stock regions. For bonds, for example, different types of ratings and durations can be selected.

Tactical asset allocation is based on short-term models that explore not only valuation models, but also flows in and out of an asset class, as well as sentiment indicators that measure the mood of market participants (from very positive to negative) toward specific investments. These indicators serve as contrarian indicators. Very positive sentiment among market participants is evaluated as a sales signal, while highly negative sentiments are seen as a buy signal.

Picking a manager, and in particular the art of finding precisely the right match for the family's investing sentiments, is another crucial task. It necessitates a set of review and selection processes known collectively as 'due diligence,' typically conducted at both the quantitative and qualitative levels. The manager's performance is evaluated based on her history of results, filtered through a set of probing questions such as these:

- What demonstrable price trend can be documented for the broadest possible time horizon?
- From a capital markets viewpoint, which especially difficult periods were successfully navigated?
- How does the manager's performance stack up to that of the competition?
- What was the value driver behind the strategy?

The qualitative due diligence encompasses questions that cannot be derived from the figures alone:

- How does the investment process work?
- Do the statements and the historical performance match the presented investment process?

- What is the structure of the manager's operation?
- Does the manager work in a stable environment or team?
- Which remuneration structure does the management use?
- Does the manager also invest his or her own money in his funds or strategies?
- Which fee rules are in place?
- How much does the management cost?

The simplest variant in terms of asset allocation involves placing the individual's assets in a global stock index fund and a global bonds market index fund. The specific split, as explained above, will then ultimately reflect the investor's risk threshold.

At the opposite end of the complexity spectrum: an ambitious family office undertaking its own comprehensive analyses of asset and sub-asset classes and then framing both the strategic and tactical allocation. It then picks managers and administrators and even key investments, initiates the transactions and performs asset controlling and reporting across all sections of the portfolio.

These two radically different examples show that an affluent individual must determine how much time and energy he or she is willing to dedicate to these themes, and whether he or she is in a position to add value to the process. If outsourcing is chosen, then this same consideration also applies to a stock manager.

These two examples are extremes on a spectrum. In practical terms most families choose a personalized solution in the middle, one that orients itself toward existing familial and business structures. The thematic explorations to this point merely serve as conceptual boundary points for the following considerations.

4.1.11 Diversified Portfolio

In very simplified terms, an evaluation that is currently high generally tends to result in lower future returns. If a company or real estate is 'bought high,' it can often be presumed that future returns will be below-average in relation to the purchase price. Excepting, of course, situations where the growth prospects are also notably strong. The price of an investment does not necessarily reflect its value. For example, experienced analysts know to look for indicators of overly optimistic Return on Investment (ROI) expectations when a majority of investors are very positive towards a specific investment.

One example of this kind of false assessment of future return prospects came between 1998 and 2000, in the returns expectations of many investors in high-tech shares, which were in fact significantly overpriced. In early 2000, the high-tech shares (from the NASDAQ index) produced dividend yields of approx. 0.2% p.a., with a risk-free interest rate of 6.5% p.a. The ongoing returns from a high-tech stock portfolio were hence just 3% of the alternative money market. Put another way: The interest rate for a money market investment was 32× greater than that of the high-tech shares.

The high-shares (as listed in the NASDAQ Composite Index) went on to lose up to 75% of their value; it would take until 2014 before they re-attained those 2000 index levels. The development of Germany's Neuer Market ("New Market") was even more drastic. The Neuer Market Index of the 50 largest tech stocks was launched in 1997, and by spring 2000 had climbed to a market capitalization of over 100 bn EUR, only then to fall by approx. 95%. The index was dissolved in 2004. (*Datastream Thomson Reuters, accessed 8/15/2015, HQ Trust GmbH, Bad Homburg, author's analysis*).

Looking at today's ratings, the group of fixed rate investments (bonds) clearly represent the poorest prospects for success. In the future, target return levels such as the previously discussed 6.5% p.a. (see section on "Yield Requirements and Targets") are highly unlikely to be achieved through an allocation involving 50% stocks and 50% bonds. This can be attributed at least in part to the fact that a 50% share of bonds would, based on today's levels, provide almost no return.

In the opinion of HQ Trust, this traditional allocation corresponds to long-term return expectations of approx. 3.2% p.a., with 11% volatility. The targeted return of 6.5% mentioned in the example on page 63 would not be achieved, although the portfolio would be liquid. Only by including illiquid investments such as real estate, private debt and private equity can the returns target potentially be achieved. Those long-term returns expectations are, based on analysis of HQ Trust, at 6.5% p.a. with volatility of 11% (see also Fig. 4.6, *HQ Trust GmbH, Bad Homburg, author's analysis*).

The question arises whether the family would reach consensus on this type of allocation. Bonds, generally regarded as "safe," are weighted extremely low with just 5%, while the share of illiquid assets, including private equity, real estate and private data, appears very high.

The composition always inherently reflects the investors' sensibilities. Each asset class is evaluated based on its attractiveness, liquidity or illiquidity and other cash flows, and the ongoing portfolio is then adjusted to reflect the requirements.

So what is the best way to formulate a long-term allocation? The assessment of the investment types can for example be conducted using three criteria: first

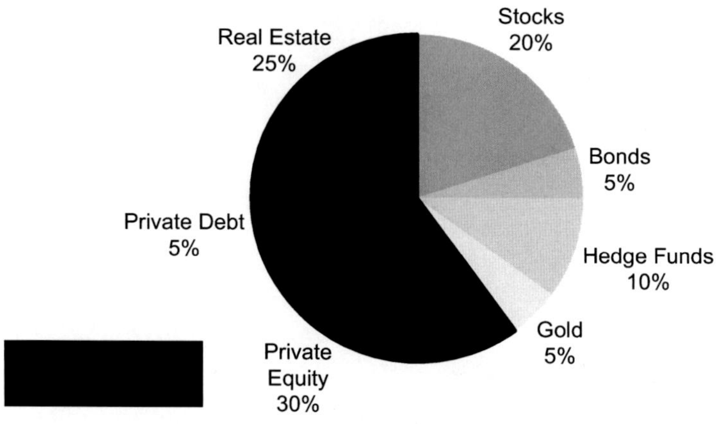

Fig. 4.6 Diversified portfolio accounting for illiquid investments (Source: *HQ Trust GmbH*)

the investors' own history, second the other segments within the same asset class, and third by the other asset classes:

1st dimension: Current stock evaluation vs long-term stock evaluation average
2nd dimension: Current stock evaluation/Europe vs. stock evaluation/USA
3rd dimension: Stock evaluation compared with bond evaluation

One evaluatory benchmark could, for example, come through the price-to-earnings ratio (P/E). This common tool expresses the share price as a multiple of the earnings per share. P/E is generally considered to be a leading indicator, meaning it typically works with profit forecasts. A bonds P/E, expressed in 100/interest in percent, can add a third dimension of comparisons between bonds and the investment class. Interest rates of 2% thus produce a bonds P/E of 50.

Over the long-term, investors in the stock market should become familiar with the so-called Shiller PE ratio. This indicator was developed by Nobel Prize winner Robert Shiller and is defined as price divided by the average of ten years of earnings (moving average), adjusted for inflation. Because the time frame of ten years encompasses various market cycles and thus various profit levels, this benchmark is considered a helpful tool in determining the long-term profit that can be expected from a company. Its explanatory power (as expressed by the R^2 [R squared] statistical measure) is very high, and its insights have proven an effective method for understanding stock performance in the past.

For bonds, by contrast, yields are simply and directly based on the current interest rates for the corresponding ten-year federal bonds. For corporate bonds, the default rates and spreads over government bonds should be taken into account. Private debt is a niche market, strongly reliant on individual management decisions.

It's no easier to make general assessment statements for hedge funds as an asset class, as this asset class is a popular one for those seeking yields independent from the market. Each strategy, and each manager, must be analyzed meticulously.

In the past, private equity could be expected to return several percentage points above stocks. Given the number of systematic benefits for this asset class, such levels of performance seem attainable in the future as well.

Among the systematic benefits of private equity are:

- **Corporate Governance,** and with it in particular incentive systems for the management of the target company
- **Depth of information,** i.e. extensive access to corporate data
- **Long-term orientation** as a publicly traded joint stock corporation. Medium to long-term management decisions can be made to increase returns, even if this produces less attractive numbers for the short term. For publicly traded companies, this is frequently a critical point.

It is difficult to make general blanket statements about real estate. Depending on the location, it is a field where the macroeconomic situation can have a massive impact on the value of individual properties—or no impact at all. Common macroeconomic influence factors include demographic trends, economic growth, interest rates, demand, inventory, new construction levels, etc.

Gold is especially difficult to assess. There are supply and demand models, but these are also susceptible to purchase or sales by central banks—events that cannot necessarily be predicted in advance. What can be assessed, for example, is the equivalent value of a stock or stock market expressed in ounces of gold. This at least provides some view of trends, an important step is assessment.

As previously mentioned, interest rates represent another long-term consideration here. When the real interest rate is positive, cash investments will continue to earn interest even after accounting for inflation. As such they offer an attractive alternative to gold, as gold does not produce this positive wealth-generating effect.

4.1.12 Active and Passive Fund Management

One controversial topic is whether it's worthwhile to trust an active manager with the money, or whether a passive index fund represents a more sensible form of investment.

What does active and passive management mean? For many liquid asset classes such as stocks and bonds, there are market indices comprised of a portfolio of stocks and bonds. A fund representing this kind of index is known as an Exchange Traded Fund, or ETF. The index fund only acquires those securities that are actually listed in the relevant index. The weighting for the individual securities is tied extremely closely to the weighting of the corresponding index. A management fee is charged for replicating the index, although this is generally lower than that for an active manager, meaning that index fund returns the value results of the comparative index minus costs. The fund manager does not make active decisions about the composition of the funds, but rather reproduces the index portfolio as precisely as possible. Hence the description as "passive management."

An active fund manager has a greater degree of freedom in composing the portfolio. Individual analytical skills and the option to deviate from index weighting can be harnessed to outperform the index. The difference between the index results and the fund's results is known as the "alpha."

A number of analyses have suggested that many active managers have difficulty outperforming comparative indexes once costs are factored in. From an academic perspective, this reflects the idea that (capital) markets work efficiently. Studies have found that it is not possible to gain an informational advantage through analysis that leads to above-average value growth compared with the market index.

So how can it be that a relatively strong number of investors manage to outperform "the market" over time? The most famous is Warren Buffet, whose exceptional investing choices have made him into one of the world's wealthiest individuals (*Forbes, accessed 1 Aug 2015*).

And if the capital markets are efficient, then the question remains as to how price bubbles appear again and again on those same capital markets. Example: the high-tech stock bubble (1998 to 2000)? How about the real estate price bubble in the US, Ireland and Spain? How can it be that in 1989 real estate prices in Japan rose so sharply that the 110,000 m^2 of ground beneath the Japanese Imperial Palace was worth just as much as all the property of California (421,000 km^2)?

These and other questions raise real doubt about the theoretical concept of "Homo oeconomicus," the "rational agent," and about the theory of efficient markets in which no market participant can possibly derive an informational edge.

Such a theory would certainly not be derived from the behavior and the decisions of individual investors. It is probably more effectively situated in the roots of human behavior itself (herd instincts, greed, fear) as filtered through various legal frameworks and across different investment time horizons. A family oriented toward long-term investments will probably only rarely make a rapid decision to buy or sell based on a company's quarterly results. The outlook is completely different for hedge funds focused on an investment horizon measured in fractions of seconds. The field of behavioral finance may provide interesting insights in this regard.

Investments must be reviewed based on the previously discussed principle of due diligence, with proper weighing of the economic risks and opportunities after costs and taxes. The various national tax policies alone have a significant impact on the attractiveness of the investments and require closer examination.

4.1.13 Selection of a Manager

Before one can answer the question of which manager holds the greatest promise for success, one must first understand which asset classes can benefit from an active manager. This means evaluating the asset classes for which active management can add the most value. This analysis should also extend to those asset classes in which even outstanding managers can only add a relatively minor amount of value.

What asset classes are most conducive to an active manager achieving performance above the market average? (See Fig. 4.7).

It is clear that managerial analysis offers the greatest potential benefit in the illiquid asset classes, private equity, and hedge funds. Real estate was not considered in this review, but likely will rate similarly high. The distribution of the results is relatively higher for illiquid assets than for liquid asset classes, which tends to justify the effort put into analysis.

It should furthermore be noted that illiquid asset classes do not have standardized indices of value in the way the stocks do. These investments are not freely investible; while it is possible to calculate and publish values, they remain strictly theoretical until concrete market pricing is sought. The best option is to seek a comparison with other market participants, known as the 'peer group,' and to limit that comparison to a single market segment.

The question of implementation is therefore limited to the liquid asset classes, and in particular to stocks and bonds. Index funds are highly affordable for the established markets, including the USA, Japan and Europe, although this benefit is mitigated through investments in other regions or sub-asset classes.

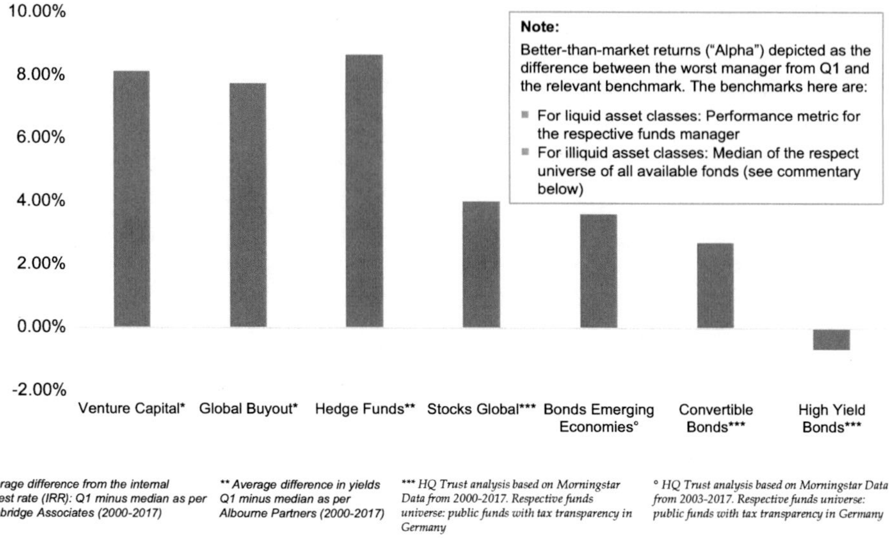

Fig. 4.7 Selection of the manager, average annual higher returns

Active managers can leverage larger volumes to negotiate more attractive and advantageous conditions. Bundling can thus also be used by good active managers to achieve attractive conditions, giving investors the chance to target value growth above the market average—which, by definition, is impossible for passive index investments.

In summary: If the analysis indicates a good and promising manager would be beneficial, then everything speaks to making that investment with the goal of achieving results that outperform the market. Anyone who solely wishes to be involved with the growth of the market would be well served to invest in index funds, i.e. passively.

4.2 Wealth Management Through Asset Accounting and Reporting

Asset accounting forms the basis for a great many different analyses and must thus be understood as a decisive factor in the family office system landscape. All asset-related business transactions are recorded in the asset account. Those records are then used by corporate accounting to formulate profit-and-loss calculations, cash flow projections, ROI and cost figures and a balance sheet. One extremely important component of asset accounting is performance assessment.

Effective accounting provides the informational foundation for three different levels:

- At the **commercial level,** it provides companies obligated to draw up a balance sheet with the various elements of this, including the balance of accounts, profit & loss calculation and the annual statement of accounts.
- At the level of **balance sheet for tax purposes,** it lays out the base commercial data.
- At the **assessment level,** it establishes the net worth on a specific date. This level is an internal affair, not a legally mandated one. Hence each individual or family can decide how to assess investments, such as based on the cost of acquisition or the strict lowest value principle.

In general, accounting systems are oriented toward the generally accepted accounting principles and, for performance assessments, the GIP standards (the Global Investment Performance Standards®). The asset report offers a manageable presentation of the aforementioned analyses and other controlling benchmarks. Reporting has a clear mission: providing the wealthy party with an ongoing overview of the status of their entire fortune. Complex asset portfolios make this more difficult. The challenge is to present the content as transparently as possible, to encourage identification of and countermeasures against risks.

Data consistency is crucial, as otherwise no accurate aggregation of the individual components, including total assets and earning statements, is possible. Individual transactions can be traced via these earning statements and bookings to the corresponding profit and loss accounts. Discussions with the wealth holders can then move quickly between the uppermost aggregation level, i.e. consolidation, down to the individual transaction level and back. If the underlying numbers cannot be presented in a coherent and comprehensible manner, then the entire set of figures will quickly be questioned. The desire for transparency is especially strong among investors when times are difficult.

This report is then used to make strategic decisions on asset steering, and supplements the ongoing performance and risk controlling processes. Furthermore, costs must be explored alongside other aspects, such as the positioning of the wealth in relationship to the investment guidelines. These various aspects make it clear that the requirements posed on the reporting department are shaped by the intended recipient of the report. The owning family as a whole will have other needs here than the family officer, tax accountant or controller.

The generalization that the members of the family will only want the bird's eye view is clearly insufficient. It is however reasonable to presume that their interests have a specific focus: The family ultimately wants to know whether their wealth has grown or not. The asset report should thus include an executive summary that allows the family to review the most important information in just a few pages.

A controller can then hone in on areas such as costs, compliance with investment guidelines and performance review. The quality of the tax assessment and tabulation of various taxes upon completion of the year can be a big aid to a tax accountant, especially if the data is prepared pre-sorted based on income and underlying taxation classes so that it can be funneled directly into the tax return.

The asset accounting and associated asset report are then used for performance review and asset oversight. The assessments can, in simple terms, be broken down into inventory assessments on specific dates or into performance reviews over periods. Inventory assessments serve to answer the following questions, among others:

- How much are the assets worth?
- What is the structure of the assets?
- In which assets is the family invested: stocks, bonds, equity holdings, real estate, etc., and in which currencies? How high are the absolute values and the relative percentage values?
- What are the largest individual items?
- Have the investment guidelines been followed?
- Which capital contributions or withdrawals were made?

The performance review is intended primarily to determine whether the assets were successfully grown during the reporting period. This involves, among other questions:

- Which investments grew?
- Where were losses suffered?
- What capital movement was observed?
- How large was the impact of foreign currencies?
- How did value grow or shrink based on the exchange rate between local and international currencies?

If asset management is being outsourced, then the reporting department should be in a position to prepare all information for each administrator, as well as an amalgamated asset report.

4.2.1 Performance Calculations

Performance calculation involves the mathematical assessment of investments and their value trends. The value trends encompass both realized and unrealized results. Already accrued interest, dividends and other earned gains or losses go into the realized results. Gains or losses that have not yet been collected form the unrealized results. The value trends are calculated for each asset component and then aggregated across all investments and portfolios into an overall value trend report.

There are two types of performance calculation (see Table 4.1): Cash-weight performance, which accounts for capital inflow and outflow and the amount of invested capital, is evaluated at the total assets levels, making it an important metric for the family. Time-weighted performance by contrast forms the proper basis for assessing a manager's performance. The calculation contains the adjusted capital flows that the administrator cannot influence because the timing of the inflow or outflow of resources was dictated by the family.

In the end, if the value growth is equal in both cases there is nevertheless a significant difference in the percental performance. This can be traced back to the capital flow at the end of Period 1. For money-weighted performance, the value trend is determined on the basis of the average fixed capital (1000 + 500 = 1500: 2 = 750) for the overall time period. By contrast, capital flows do not play a role in time-weighted performance, as each capital flow starts a new performance period (1.1 × 1.2 = 1.32).

The performance of the comparative indices is always calculated and presented based on time weighting. At the total asset level, if a comparison against the cash-weighted performance basis is to be made, then the index perfor-

Table 4.1 Sample calculation: year 1: +100 EUR, year 2: +100 EUR

	Money-weighted performance	Time-weighted performance
Period 1		
Start of investment:	1000 EUR	1000 EUR
Profit (+10%):	100 EUR	100 EUR
Total:	1100 EUR	1100 EUR
Withdrawal:	600 EUR	600 EUR
Period 2		
Interim sum:	500 EUR	500 EUR
Profit (+20%):	100 EUR	100 EUR
Final asset:	600 EUR	600 EUR
Difference:	+26.7%	+32%

mance must first be 'translated' into cash-weighted performance. In addition, all flows must be 'invested' within the index at the respective points in times and value amounts.

4.2.2 Controlling and Performance Review

General controlling tasks involve cost controlling, exchange rate controlling, controlling of invoices, controlling of compliance with investment guidelines and the identification of risks, such as concentration risks. It shows that an analysis of allocation decisions is also essential for effective asset controlling. Were the decisions that were made at the various decision-making levels good ones, and how strong were their impacts?

These tiers of strategic and tactical performance and the picking performance must be quantifiable and deliver proper insights for medium-term oversight of the assets. The major instruments for this are contribution and attribution analysis. The contribution analysis indicates where the performance drivers are found, while the attribution analysis indicates why that is the case.

The assessments provide important anchors for performance discussions. When meeting with managers, these results can be used as evidence of which areas were handled with more or less success and influence allocation and mandate assignment decisions. If for example one manager has shown strength in the allocation of assets, while a different manager makes good selections at the specific stock level, then it may be possible to combine these into one mandate.

Strategic asset allocation indicates which asset classes will be pursued over the long term. Decision-making at the tactical allocation level encompasses decisions in terms of weighting of the asset classes. These decisions are oriented toward the short to medium term. Beyond this, tactical decisions can also include regional assessments, such as instructions to weigh US stocks higher or lower than European ones. The lowest decision-making level is picking—i.e. the decision to buy share A or share B.

The performance analysis is oriented on ex ante structures and the actor's level of responsibilities. There are various approaches possible even under the same strategic allocation instructions.

Imagine total assets of 200 mn. EUR, divided between two managers each with 100 mn. EUR and the same strategic instructions (50% stocks, 50% bonds).

Variant 1: no instructions on allocation decision

Manager A: 100 mn. EUR: stocks + bonds

Manager B: 100 mn. EUR: stocks + bonds

The managers make their allocation decisions by determining the weighting of the asset classes, in this case stocks and bonds. This decision should reflect the attractiveness of each asset class and be based on solid, justifiable analysis. Beyond this, the selection (i.e. picking of stocks) is handled by the managers themselves.

Variant 2: Instructions for allocation decision

Manager C: 100 mn. EUR exclusively in stocks

Manager D: 100 mn. EUR exclusively in bonds

The decision on asset class allocation is not in the hands of the managers; they are solely responsible for making picks within their respective asset class. As a result, each manager can only be compared and evaluated based on the specific assigned asset class. In this case, the decision whether 100 mn. EUR per asset class or some other amount is to be invested in the asset classes was decided in advance by the family (resolving the question of which asset class has the best prospects).

The long-term strategic goals are identical in both variants: 50% stocks and 50% bonds. The difference comes at the decision-making level. In variant 1, the family is making the strategic decision and leaving the subordinate rounds of decision (tactics and picking) to the managers.

In variant 2, the strategic and tactical decision have been made in advance by the family, meaning that they must weigh their trust in the skills and aptitudes of the manager and then on how to weight the asset classes. They must first have formed an opinion on the attractiveness of the respective investment classes and must continue following the data so as to take advantage of movement on the market. Given their commission to move within an asset class, managers C and D do not have the option to re-configure between asset classes.

4.2.3 Relative Benchmark

A family office looking to assess wealth managers will encounter the following questions:

- What methods are available for assessing manager performance?
- Which returns have already been achieved?
- Is Manager A's 7% return necessarily better than Manager B's 6%? Which factors must be taken into account?
- Which volatility is acceptable for the value trends?

A tool known as the "Sharpe ratio" is used to evaluate the returns against the backdrop of risk and portfolio fluctuation. It creates a ratio of targeted portfolio yields above the risk-free interest rate to portfolio fluctuation, known as the "reward-to-variability." This is helpful for comparing different results.

A representative comparative index is typically needed to classify performance. Good, suitable indices will represent an actual investable universe. It is not helpful for an index to be determined purely synthetically, as the goal here is to invest the wealth in the real world.

Beyond this, the family or family office must know the details of how the index is split so as to account for the implications associated with that. From the family's standpoint, does the selected comparative index reflect the desired investment universe and its risk environment? When examining the cumulative assets and the cumulative asset environment, a hybrid benchmark from the strategic investment class indices can be formed with relevant weighting.

4.2.4 Absolute Benchmark

In general, the family will specify that their assets must be retained in real terms plus a certain percentage of growth. It must be remembered that these specifications must be set over an extended time horizon, such as several years. In principle, all available asset classes represent a higher amount of fluctuation than the inflation rate.

Absolute benchmarks do not focus on the strategic allocation, but rather on the tactical allocation and on selection. For example, if a return of 4% per annum is specified, then only investments that might potentially offer that level of ROI during the measurement period will be examined.

Relative benchmarks work differently. If, for example, an index contains 50% US government bonds, then few managers would be willing to pass up on the allocation altogether, even if they assess the investment negatively. This deviation factor is known as "tracking error."

4.2.5 Investment Policies and Cost Controlling

The conversion from strategic allocation to the asset classes and sub-asset classes is defined during the final step, in the form of investment policies. The investment policy forms an essential part of any wealth management contract and are legally binding.

Each family decides for itself how detailed the stipulations should be. The issue is typically decided based on the respective responsibilities. Another aspect for consideration is the complexity of the reporting. The number of index requirements rises in proportion to the number of asset classes and sub-asset classes; if this grows too large, it threatens any sense of clarity and comprehensibility.

Many index requirements will end up increasing the intensity of the interdependencies and the complexity of the analysis. The so-called 'cross-product,' i.e. the portion of the performance that cannot be clearly assigned, tends to expand, while the explanatory content shrinks. In debating a proper level of complexity for their performance benchmarks, a family should be honest about whether they possess the know-how to assess the data or whether they would rather simply trust the consultant's analysis.

Cost controlling is an important aspect of cumulative asset controlling. All levels must be recorded and reported. Service provider costs tend to be contractually fixed, so the underlying metrics and calculations themselves should be reviewed. Single family offices also face costs for the office, personnel, IT, travel costs, etc. Fees for wealth management are generally determined on a percentage basis. It is then supplemented with transaction-related costs by banks, such as portfolio fees, transaction fees and other costs. While securities transactions represent a standard service, experience teaches that unexpected elements can arise here as well.

4.2.6 Efficiency in Bookkeeping

Bookkeeping remains, even today, largely bound up with manual time and expense. Property management firms normally have no uniform standard. Similar, depository banks issue their invoices, holdings lists, etc. in a variety of formats. As a result, the grand majority of postings still must be performed manually by a bookkeeper. Data can also be transmitted electronically, but that convenience brings with it a certain degree of programming and upkeep costs. It is typically of real benefit only when the economy of scale applies, i.e. if a variety of accounts and portfolios are administered by one depository bank and the data can be transmitted using a single interface.

Economies of scale can also be applied in the areas of securities master data and reporting, insofar as securities appear multiple times among the assets and the reporting pages are programmed and configured for a number of customers. Where transactions have already posted in an IT system, it makes sense to harness that labor and create a system where the data can be exported to other systems such as a portfolio management system for further re-use.

While standard reporting practices call for all assets to be listed, it is essential that all liabilities be listed as well. On the balance sheet, the asset values can be found in the assets column (see Table 4.2).

Many families bundle their assets via wealth management firms, with the capital accounts contained on the liabilities column. Each family member is a

Table 4.2 Typical balance sheet

Assets	Liabilities
Stocks	Equity
Bonds	
Real estate	
Shareholdings	
Gold	

shareholder in the family business. For underage children, a guardianship court must be involved in any inclusion as a shareholder.

Several equity accounts are typically maintained. The share ratio per shareholder is produced from the total deposits, including liability deposits. Over the course of time, those ratios tend to shift as some family members withdraw more funds than others. Because bookkeeping for equity accounts is complicated, the company contract should explicitly specify deposit and withdrawal windows. Suitable regulation of how to handle overdrafts of accounts is also required, including interest rates on negative balances and the time frames by which the account must be zeroed out. Otherwise there is the potential for some shareholders to benefit during good years from excessive "loans," to the detriment of the other shareholders. The same applies to handling of positive balances.

Profit-taking or changes to the equity account must be reviewed for tax implications. There are two fundamental tax tiers: at the corporate level and at the level of the shareholder. Insofar as the company has a legal form such as a limited partnership that is transparent from a tax perspective, then this first level does not apply (see Table 4.3).

Table 4.3 Decision-making process for asset allocation

1st step	Addressing total assets or partial assets?
2nd step	Determination of risk environment
3rd step	Establishment of yield specifications
4th step	Reconciliation of yield specifications and risk environment
5th step	Determination of the strategic asset allocation based on own goals
6th step	Internal or external management: Accounting for own strengths and weaknesses, composition of clear decision tiers and determination of responsibilities
7th step	If external management is used: Focusing of the manager on an asset class or on allocation
8th step	Composition of investment guidelines and awarding of mandate
9th step	Construction of reporting systems or commissioning of an accountancy
10th step	Neutral performance review

From Germany: "Fundamental strategies have to be defined and voted on."

Interview with Christoph Zapp

This interview touches on questions of founding or joining a family office, challenges during the founding phase and thereafter, strategies for staffing the family office and the importance of family governance.

This interview was conducted by Christoph Weber.

Mr. Zapp, you have first-hand experience in the establishment and operation of a single family office, as well as in consulting on large private real estate portfolios for client families. What moves a family to found their own family office instead of becoming a client in a multi family office?
Christopher Zapp: A sense of control and self-determination are the primary driving forces, as well as a perpetual mistrust on the part of ultra high net worth private investors toward third parties such as banks and wealth managers. When it comes to family-owned businesses, you're typically dealing with people who have been deeply involved in the company and built up their own fortune, or whose fathers did so. Eventually their wealth achieved a critical mass too large for them to handle on their own. At that point, a wealthy individual must decide whether to hand over the money to a third party or to build up internal structures that he or she can influence directly. This latter case is often preferred when dealing with accumulated wealth of over 150 mn. euros. Third parties are then only commissioned in situations where a strong bond of trust already exists, such as when recommended or after a long period of mutual familiarization.

Christoph Zapp *is a shareholder in Zapp AG, a family-run company in the steel industry whose history stretches back over 300 years. He is also a member of the Zapp family's single family office, founded in the late 1990s and a charter member of the Verbandes unabhängiger Family Offices e. V. He is also the managing partner in PAMERA Real Estate Partners GmbH, a multi family office specializing in real estate. His work there has taught him valuable lessons in advising wealthy families in the field of real estate investments and development projects.*

Based on your experience, what is the difference between the services offered by bank-bound and by bank-independent family office structures?
CZ: Bank-bound structures are tied to banks, and so are inherently product-driven in one way or another. What I mean is that such organizations face pressure to present the bank's products (funds, etc.) to the customer. Many bank-bound providers of family office services may protest otherwise, claiming their services are completely independent from the parent firm, but I just don't see that as being the case. The chance to cross sell is just too tempting for the bank not try to emphasize its own services and products to the clients via the family office structure. In many ways this is completely understandable, but the portfolio owner always needs to keep this in the back of his mind. Bank-agnostic family office structures, by contrast, are completely free to compare between different investment products and are more likely to select what they see as the best prospects for their clients. A clear plus for me.

What special challenges do families face during the founding phase of a single family office?
CZ: Many, unfortunately. One of the big issues: highly divergent interests within the family, not least due to the age differences inherent to the various generations. To accommodate for this, it's essential that a fundamental strategy be defined from the start for the family office: continued growth of the wealth (greater risk) vs. pure wealth conservation (hedging and securing). The selection of managers is also a crucial aspect: The internal managers for the family office must be identified first, followed by the various external managers, wealth managers and investment partners for the various asset classes. That search for internal managers can be particularly long and difficult. A long-term commitment is usually needed. In fact, if the chemistry isn't strong between the family and the family officer, the situation is probably destined to fail. Constantly rotating personnel in the family office is detrimental to both the family and the family officer.

What are the biggest mistakes that you can make during the founding phase and how can they be avoided?
CZ: You have to give yourself time in the early phases to think through the problems I just mentioned. A clear structure for the family office must be in place from the start, and the core strategies must be defined and approved. Only then should investments be made. People often make the mistake of getting right into investments, instead of first establishing structures to manage those investments. This typically leads to poor decisions and lost money. There are various negative examples of newly founded family offices that even years later are still trying to recover from those initial errors.

Are there different requirements when recruiting personnel for a single family office as opposed to a multi family office? Are special social skills required for a single family office?
CZ: You're touching on a really tricky aspect, as I already briefly mentioned. In a single family office, the social fit between family officer and the family must be very strong. The goal here is to build ties that will endure for years, even decades. There must be an ability to weather changing moods. The family officer in particular has to be prepared to stand up front in a big room at times, exposed to the temperaments of the principals. With that said, the employees at multi family offices must also be selected carefully. They too need strong social skills and expert knowledge. But it's ultimately simpler and easier to make personnel changes at a multi family office than at a single family office. What does apply to both structures: loyalty and a strong sense of ethics are a must.

What factors influence the personnel strategies for a single family office or a multi family office? What role does the size of the portfolio to be managed play, or the number of family (households) and asset classes to be managed?
CZ: Each of these aspects plays a role in determining how big a staff is required. What I primarily look at, though, is the degree to which outsourcing will be used within a given family office. The original task of the family office is controlling, in the sense of its proper economic definition: definition of investment strategies – execution of investments – ongoing auditing of the investments. Everything else, such as tax and legal consultation and operative management of investments, can be outsourced. So to my mind, it's not inconceivable that a family office with just three employees could manage and control assets totaling several hundreds of millions.

A single family office supports a family in its very specific needs and specific asset allocation. A multi family office, by contrast, is responsible for multiple families whose specific requirements profile may differ greatly in some cases. Do you see conflicts of interest between the client families?
CZ: Yes, this kind of conflict of interest can arise in a multi family office, but these situations can also be effectively managed. The magic word here is "transparency": There must be open discussion on this point within the multi family office and with each client. At PAMERA, my real estate-focused multi family office, we sometimes identify a potential investment object that might fit two or three families equally well. When something like this occurs, we sit down around a table with the relevant families and talk it through. This of course only works if the pool of clients is not comprised of too many families, and if the multi family office doesn't take on too many clients predisposed toward conflict. It falls to the managing director of the multi family office to

act in a sensible manner, focused on the long term interests of her clients. That can be a much bigger obstacle for bank-dependent family office structures.

Let's assume that a family has the type of asset volumes that lend themselves to the economical operation of a single family office. What criteria must be fulfilled before you would recommend founding a single family office, commissioning an independent multi family office or joining a bank-dependent single family office?
CZ: My opinion on this matter is unfortunately quite unyielding: I would always counsel for a single family office, with the possible exception of a small multi family office for families with pre-existing bonds and a desire to work together. For the reasons I've already discussed, I simply cannot recommend a bank-dependent family office. There is another potential option as well, one that combines the benefits of a single family office and a multi family office. It's actually becoming more common. Here how it might work: A single family office manages the overall asset pool, but then works together with specialized multi family offices on specific asset classes, such as in the areas of real estate or private equity.

In your opinion, which services should a single family office always handle on its own? Which ones can or should be outsourced?
CZ: As I mentioned, the controlling of investments is the original task for a single family office and must be handled internally. This includes of course the selection of external managers and general asset reporting for the family. Topics such as tax accounting, legal counsel, insurance management etc. are better handled via professional external partners who can be replaced if their performance is not satisfactory.

What role do you feel family governance plays in the range of services for a family office?
CZ: One important soft factor, albeit one that each family office must decide on its own, is the level of detail it wishes to receive. The bigger the family, the more weight this aspect carries. If a single family office is handling dozens of clients within a family, then family governance structures must be in place, I feel. Those are often tightly related to a legacy business, if one still exists.

Should a family office retain its own experts for this, or commission this from third parties?
CZ: The family governance documents should be defined in cooperation with external professionals versed in best practice approaches. In my view, implementation and control should then be handled internally within the family. An internal audit should be conducted every few years by an external partner to ensure that the family governance guidelines are in fact being correctly implemented.

By your reckoning, what are the minimum requirements for IT structure (hardware and software) for a single family office?

CZ: In general, all that's needed is the standard infrastructure for any normal office. The one place where the requirements get much stricter is in terms of IT security. Some family offices have been "hardening" themselves as targets by avoiding cloud-based IT solutions in particular. Due to various scandals (buzzword: "NSA"), many families are proceeding with great caution, and rightly so.

Which costs should be expected by the operator of a mid-sized single family office and/or multi family office? Is there a direct correlation between the costs and the size of the assets being managed?

CZ: To my mind, the costs are more closely related to the degree of outsourcing involved, not the size of the assets. A mid-sized single family office (10+ employees) or a multi family office will certainly quickly range into the low single digit millions. Single family offices generally work on the 'cost center' principle, while multi family offices should be set up as profit centers, albeit with reduced profit targets. Quality must come before quantity (profits).

5

Reliable Handling of Legal and Tax Issues

Jens Escher

The members of a family office, their assets and any companies that they maintain, directly or indirectly, are subject to a ceaseless stream of different legal and taxation questions. Depending on how the family office is structured, these issues are either handled internally by in-house attorneys and/or tax consultants, or in collaboration with a network of external specialists. Whichever is the case, the family office is responsible for ensuring that legal and tax-related topics are addressed in a timely and reliable manner. The family's full trust relies on this point.

5.1 Internal or External Advisors

If the family office does not employ its own in-house lawyers or tax advisors, then the family office is responsible for identifying, commissioning and coordinating external consultants to handle these legal/tax issues. From a taxation standpoint, in-house activities can limit themselves to the collation of receipts for the family members' annual income tax filings and their safe transfer to the commissioned tax accountant. Whatever the structure, the family office must arrange for tax compliance by all family members (and, where applicable, any organizations they run).

As the implementation of specific projects approaches (such as the acquisition of a share in a company or a land purchase), then the internal activities may be restricted to assessment of the legal/tax-related opinions solicited from external consultants and reporting to the family. It is a major benefit for the

B. Canessa et al., *The Family Office*, https://doi.org/10.1007/978-3-319-99085-9_5

internal tax/law liaison to have a good "gut feeling" for situations in which thorny legal or tax issues could arise, so as to arrange for the involvement of an external consultant. For example, if a family member wishes to marry and is seeking advice on proper framing of a prenuptial agreement, then a suitable consultant can be contacted. Another potentially tricky issue involves plans by a family member to move abroad for an extended period or even permanently, as this can raise tax questions for equity holdings (such as in the family company after an anticipated succession). A tax consultant should be involved as a proactive measure.

The larger the assets under management by the family office and the greater the pool of family members being serviced, the likelier it is that hiring in-house attorneys and tax accountants will be worthwhile. These employees would then be tasked with reviewing specific contracts and/or draft contracts for family members and the organizations they run, as well as setting up or restructuring companies. In-house tax accountants can initiate ongoing tax preparation for family members and the organizations they run or—depending on their particular expertise—deliver comprehensive tax advice.

Even so, there is typically still significant need for a network of external specialists to address specific legal or tax-related topics as they arise. In many cases these professionals are simply commissioned internally to serve as sparring partners. Internal consultants can work for only one family (single family office) or for a strictly limited circle of families, while external consultants can work with multiple families, applying their experience from a wide variety of situations.

External consultants typically bring a much higher degree of specialization than would be practical to hire in-house at the family office. It makes little sense economically to retain legal and tax accountants for specialized situations that only occur very rarely. Yet given the wide range of highly complex legal and tax issues that are likely to arise for a family office, external experts will invariably be needed—especially since many of these topics are constantly evolving (see also Fischer and Syring in Farkas-Richling et al. 2012, p. 529 f.). There is another benefit to bringing in external talent: exposure to the latest developments on the market and to insights gained by external consultants through their work for other clients.

It should not be underestimated that external consultants themselves maintain national and international networks. Given the mobility that can be expected of affluent family members in the modern world and the need to maintain international investment structures, this international component can be of significant importance. Specialists working in-house for the family office are responsible for ensuring comprehensive and effective communication with the external consultants.

In many cases, family offices chose appropriate consultants based on their own experiences or based on the recommendations of other family offices. The selection of consultants and the awarding of commissions is the responsibility of the family office's executive team, with veto power ultimately held by the family itself. The family office can also present its family members with a set of potential candidates and then undertake quality monitoring and performance evaluations after the jobs are commissioned (see also Fischer and Syring in Farkas-Richling et al. 2012, p. 530).

Practical Tip: Organization of Legal and Tax Advising

As a family's portfolio of assets grows in size, so too does the degree of complexity associated with tax and legal matters. This is especially true for families with a broad international footprint. Be sure to talk with your "house" attorney and personal accountant about potential topics that may require external specialists, either as sparring partners or project managers. You may also wish to consider building up your own legal and tax infrastructure within the family office if it will provide for greater efficiency at a reasonable cost point. Do remember, however, that the benefits of having an exclusive legal and tax team must be weighted out against the risk that their knowledge may stagnate once they are no longer being exposed to the different scenarios inherent to serving many different clients.

5.2 Legal and Tax-Related Tasks

Family offices must handle an extremely diverse range of legal and tax-related questions and tasks. These can involve the private affairs of the family members or assets and investments at the broader family level and at the organizations they run.

Table 5.1 (below) shows typical legal and tax tasks for a family office:

Table 5.1 Typical legal/taxation tasks for a family office

Topics	Concrete tasks, example
General contract management, including internal and external contracts	Proper filing, monitoring of contract durations, identification of necessary action steps
Family constitution	Composition of new or adjustment of existing contracts in coordination with the family and accounting for the stipulations of the family constitution
Contract between family members or owned organizations, such as loans	Ensuring contracts are documented in writing, administration
Wills, testaments, prenuptial agreements	Administration, notification about stipulations regarding children in the event of marriage, comparison of future contracts of all kinds for conflicting obligations; identification of necessary changes
Health care proxies, living wills	Administration, identification of need for changes
Other powers of attorney	Administration of general powers of attorney, power of attorney for matters related to commercial register
Income tax	Collation of all documents required for tax filing; internal or external preparation; taxation issues related to capital gains and losses; monitoring of loss carry forward and their claim status; potential targeted use of losses
Monitoring of tax deductibility of costs	Which costs accrue? Can these be deducted?
Departure of family members	Tax support, review of impact on inheritance/matrimonial property law
Inheritances/bequeaths	Support and coordination of bequeaths; preparation or support in preparation of tax filings; creation of overviews of consumption of tax exempt amounts and deduction of bequeathed amounts from statutory shares
Essential structural questions related to asset allocation	In particular: test of which holding vehicle is suitable for which investment, legally and from a tax standpoint
Review of shareholder's agreements	In particular review of contracts of private funds for market conformity, legal and tax-related consequences
Overview of all shareholding structures	Maintaining overview of all shareholdings among family members and all organizational structures within a holding
General management of law and tax issues	Identification of potential legal/tax opportunities/risks; interface to external legal and tax consultants

From the United Kingdom: "First, we need to determine what their motivations are."

Interview with Nicholas Warr

This interview touches on in-house vs. outsourced legal counsel, choice of jurisdiction, insight into interfaces between legal advisors and family offices and the value of soft skills.

This interview was conducted by Steven Sidore.

Your firm provides a program of legal services for ultra high net worth families and individuals. From your standpoint, at what point is it worthwhile for a family office to maintain their legal counsel in house and at what point does it make sense to take advantage of external resources like yours?
Nicholas Warr: I don't think the point relates to a monetary sum. It's more the complexity of the investments coupled with other factors, such as whether there's still a legacy family business involved. It also depends on what the daily legal needs are and how much assistance they need in managing external legal relationships. If you've got a complex trading business, then there may be a number of legal relationships that need managing, and it's helpful and more efficient to have that managed by an internal person.

For example, a large portion of what I do—my day job, so to speak—is the internal constructs of the family office. That involves arranging ownership structures and how they govern the behaviors of individuals, which is normally transmitted via family governance instruments such as a family charter or family constitution.

Nicholas Warr *is a partner in the Private Client department and Head of the International Private Wealth group of Taylor Wessing. He specializes in advising ultra high net worth individuals and families with interests mainly on fiscal and succession planning. His practice is international in nature and he represents individuals, families and family offices in the Middle East, the USA and Europe, as well as the UK. The majority of his clients have personal and business interests in a number of different jurisdictions.*

When you're giving advice to a family office, how do you advise them in terms of where to establish their jurisdiction? Does it matter particularly?
NW: Again this depends on a number of factors. One: is there a legacy family business that is operating? Secondly: if there is already a core of expertise, where is that situated? Thirdly: tax implications of both the office itself and the family members.

It's not as though there's a one-size-fits-all-solution. To the contrary, one must appreciate that the family office is a very, very broad church and it means different things to different people.

How do you channel clients towards the appropriate resource levels?
NW: First, we need to determine what their motivations are and what the aims are for the family office. Is this something that they've thought through and require i.e. do they require a multi-generational structure or merely to meet the needs of that immediate generation? You'd think it would always be the former, but you'd be amazed how often it is the latter.

Once you have established the real requirement, we can then properly look at how to resource it. This could range from hiring a comprehensive team deployed to manage the day to day trading businesses, to an individual/individuals with the skills to apply in-depth quantitative analysis on external investments, right through to a person employed to simply support the family's day-to-day needs.

How do you normally interact with a family office?
Are you typically consulting with the family officer, or presenting directly to the family itself?
NW: This really does vary according to the location and size of the family office and how sophisticated it is. For example, if the family office is very sophisticated and headquartered in London, I would tend to speak with the MD almost every morning. This would serve as an ongoing review of the projects we've got on the go at any one time, which is continually evolving. I would then meet with the principals probably once a month and the whole family once a quarter. That's one end of the spectrum.

At the other end could be a family located in the Middle East, in this situation I would meet the principal more often but only communicate with the family office once per quarter.

And then somewhere in between is a family office that works with us only on a project-by-project basis, as we are one of a number of legal firms who this particular family office uses. They mix and match depending on what their legal requirements are.

So, for example, one day we'll be asked to advise them on a transaction and then hear nothing for months, and then we'll get an instruction on, say, a reputation management project.

During the establishment of a new family office, which areas are most likely to produce problems, from your legal standpoint?

NW: Problems are most likely to arise if the thought process behind the creation of a family office is not done thoroughly enough. By that I mean where someone has met someone else and decided they need a family office, they then set out in a direction to create one and this may not be the right solution to their needs.

When this happens, not enough up-front analysis is done on the cost/benefit analysis. For example, hiring a large team of highly paid and highly skilled investment individuals is not necessarily required if the family just has an operating businesses making widgets. This is a complete mis-deployment of human capital and financial resource.

Do soft skills play a major factor for legal advisors to family offices?

NW: I think as far as the daily interactions are concerned, there's got to be a large amount of EQ as there are interesting dynamics in all families which need to be navigated carefully. It is also about actually identifying what the family really needs, which requires a lot of listening, a lot of refining and testing, because sometimes they don't know what they want.

Bibliography

Farkas-Richling D, Fischer TR, Richter A (Hrsg) (2012) Private banking und family office, 2nd edn. Schäffer-Poeschel, Stuttgart

6

Succession Planning

Alexander Koeberle-Schmid and Jens Escher

High net worth individuals should think about succession planning early, at least five and preferably ten years before the intended handover. This allows time to frame a smooth and effective transition of assets and leadership, accounting for the different goals and interests of the various family members.

Any succession strategy should be formulated to facilitate agreement between the retiring and the ascending generation. The family office can in some cases provide an employee to shepherd this process, or it can engage an external succession specialist. It is important to remember that the entire issue of succession often represents an emotional minefield. An external specialist, unencumbered by personal or financial ties, is often better positioned to navigate difficult constellations.

The negotiated succession strategy should include plans on how leadership and assets will be transferred. Once drafted, it must still be codified into a succession plan to be implemented operationally, financially, legally and in accordance with the tax code—at both the personnel and family levels. The family office can provide support with these tasks, or external auditors, lawyers, accountants and coaches can be commissioned.

6.1 Forward-Looking Succession Planning

Alexander Koeberle-Schmid

Despite the many potential hurdles, a smooth transition between generations is an achievable goal. Certain facts must however be accepted from the start. For one, it is helpful to acknowledge that generational transitions rarely run

B. Canessa et al., *The Family Office*, https://doi.org/10.1007/978-3-319-99085-9_6

in a straight line. This can be expected from almost any complex process with elements of business and organizational politics, family dynamics, financial pressures, legal and tax considerations and personal emotions. Success here relies on bringing each of these factors into harmony. Beyond this, the interests, goals and needs of the people involved must be explored and made transparent to one other. Only once all parties understand what the others are expecting can a process towards a consensual succession strategy truly begin.

Both parties must thus start with a true readiness to relinquish or assume responsibility, respectively. This applies whether the assets to be transferred are liquid or bound in a corporation. The same two central questions arise for both corporate and for family assets managed by a family office: Who will assume leadership of the family office and, if still involved in managing a company, who will take over the management position or at least take over the non-executive board or even chairman position? Who will receive what from the family assets in the family office and who will receive which shares of the corporate assets? Consideration must also be given to what will happen with the private assets that belong solely to the wealthy individual.

These questions are at the heart of the succession strategy. A 3 × 4 model built around three tiers (succession goals/succession model/succession details) can be applied towards a strategy that encompasses issues of leadership, ownership and assets, family and each individual person (see Fig. 6.1, published in a similar form in Koeberle-Schmid and Unger (2019)). This strategy ultimately produces an operative succession plan that addresses in precise terms the questions of "who/what/when."

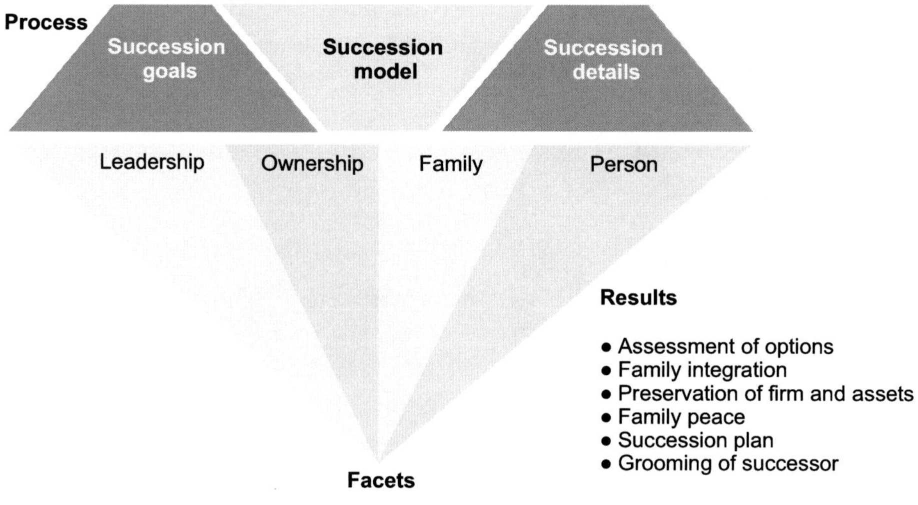

Fig. 6.1 3 × 4 succession strategy

This process offers several benefits. It ensures that the different options for the transfer of ownership of assets, as well as leadership of the single family office and/or the family business, are all discussed. In concrete terms, this includes questions such as: Will the daughter receive the liquid assets in the family office and the son the company? What does this mean for the future ownership and leadership of the family office? Or will liquid assets and corporate ones instead be transferred in equal portions? Will shareholders be entrusted with reviewing the work of the family officer and executive management of the corporation solely via a board of directors or oversight council, and not take an active role in operations as family officer or executive board member? This and many other succession questions are assessed together. Furthermore, all family members are drawn into the process sooner or later—an important prerequisite for preserving family harmony, especially for the generation after the passing of the current legal owner of the assets. The fortune is more likely to remain intact, giving the family greater reach and power as investors.

Before a succession strategy can be formulated, the real state of affairs must first be surveyed: What is the current situation within the family office and any companies in which the family has invested, in terms of strategy, leadership, structure, asset allocation and profitability? In this context, the question should also be posed as to how many persons can be effectively served by the pool of wealth. Large fortunes can naturally bear more owners than small ones.

The family dynamic must also be examined. Are parents, children, grandchildren and nieces/nephews coming together with confidence and mutual trust, or are there still "old scores to settle" from the past? Are there suitable candidates to assume control of the family office and of the companies the family is invested in? And which goals do the individual persons have in terms of the transfer of assets and leadership responsibility in the family office and the firms in which the family is invested?

Once these initial circumstances have been clarified, the next step is to define objectives for the succession process. In the broadest sense, this may simply reflect a desire to transition influence and assets successfully. At the leadership level, the concern centers much more around long-term definition of vision, values and objectives for the family office and its investment strategy as well as asset allocation. To this end, a determination is made as to the degree in which the family is involved in the leadership of the family office and in the firms in which the family is invested. At the ownership level, the family must indicate how they would like to see their wealth structured between joint family and private individual wealth. This is reinforced by defining the family's expectations of the family office. At the family level, all affected parties must gain clarity on their shared vision, values and objectives. Finally, at the personal level, the focus is on formulating individual goals in terms of leadership, the family office, ownership, the family and the individual's own personal development, and sharing those insights with others. This may potentially be formulated through a set of wishes for the transition—at the very least, the party relinquishing responsibility should contemplate and share her wishes for the transition.

As a second step, a suitable succession model for the handover of the family office and the other assets should be formulated (see Fig. 6.2). Who will assume leadership of the family office and who will take over responsibilities in the businesses in which the family is invested? Who will receive how much of the family fortune? Who gets which of the assets? And what will happen with the individual private assets? What role will the advisory council, the family council or the investment council play after the transition? Who will take over non-executive positions in the family office's board, or in the boards of the companies in which the family is invested? All of these are formulated in a precise and coherent succession model.

As soon as it is clear how leadership and ownership of the wealth will be passed on to the next generation and who will serve in the leading and monitoring positions in the family office and the firms in which the family is invested, it is time to move on to the detail stage. Nailing down these details involves discussion and agreement on rights and obligations, organizational questions, information and decision-making hierarchies. It is important that the requirements for the management team and the family office as well as a potential advisory council and board of directors be defined. Details on the transfer of the assets should be formulated together with a last will and testament that covers unexpected emergencies.

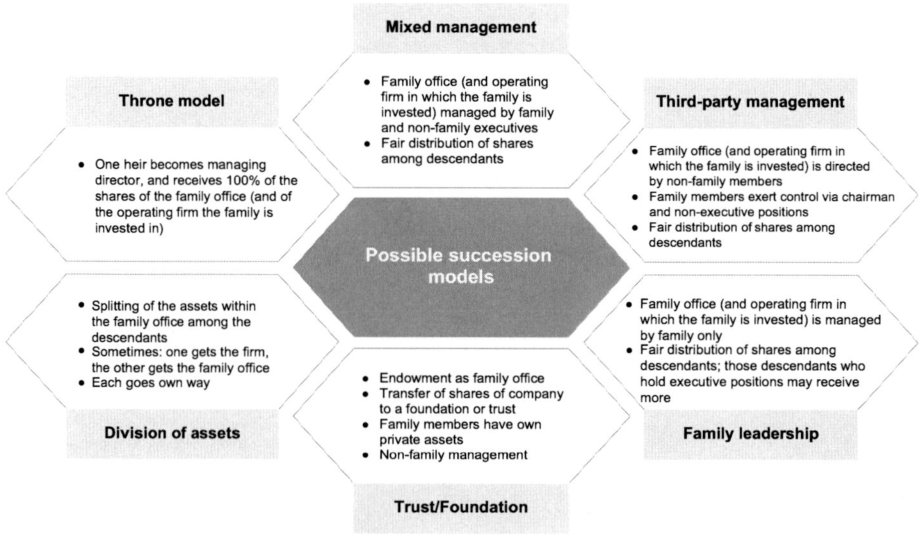

Fig. 6.2 Potential succession models

The family office succession check list (Table 6.1) provides an initial review of key items to clarify when planning successions. This same list can also frequently be used for legacy family businesses. Should the participants discover that they lack answers for any given section, they can then give extra focus to those topics during their discussions.

Table 6.1 Succession checklist

Leadership of family office	**Yes**	**No**
The family office has a mutually acceptable vision and mission, set of objectives and a strategy to achieve those objectives, all based on strong shared values		
The economic situation is very good (strong yields from the family office, assessed based on the risk strategy; high yields from the businesses in which the family is invested, with a stable financing structure; assets invested in line with the owners' risk specifications)		
The organizational structure is clear and delineates clear responsibilities and decision-making processes in the family office and in regards to the firms in which the family is invested		
Management (of the family office and other firms it owns in part or whole) is competent and working towards attaining the goals		
The advisory, supervisory and/or investment council features competent members and provides comprehensive consultation and/or undertakes controlling of ownership of family assets		
There is unity within the family about how the ownership of the assets will be bequeathed		
The legal claims to assets by descendants and partners have been taken into account		
The discussion of the family about future challenges for the family office and the firms it owns in part or whole may be emotional in substance, but are conducted with respect and a sense of purpose, and are not rubber stamped		
The current and future wealth holders are clear about the rights and obligations that come with that role and accept that responsibility		
Handling of profits (retention of profits, dividends/transfer from reserves, profits from sales) is clearly regulated and all shareholders have signed off		
Family	**Yes**	**No**
The family members have a strong relationship with one another		
The family meets regularly to preserve tradition and enjoy each other's company		
All are in agreement that a balance must be established between assets and family interests, and that personal interests are subordinate to this		
The family supports the decision regarding the transition of the assets and leadership		

(continued)

Table 6.1 (continued)

Conflicts within the family have been settled and themes discussed; this is how the family stays together in difficult situations		
Person	**Yes**	**No**
The family member(s) proposed as successor for positions is/are qualified, properly initiated and has/have had a chance to prove her skill		
A contingency plan has been established in the event that the family members working for the family (as successor) do not thrive in the role		
Old age care for the party relinquishing responsibility and his or her partner (and with it their own private assets) are sufficient and independent from the success of the family office		
The family member relinquishing power has and accepts a clear plan for 'letting go'		
Emergency plans (will, power of attorney, etc.) are in place for all involved parties		
Process	**Yes**	**No**
A detailed and binding plan is in place for the transfer of assets and, where applicable, leadership of the family office and positions in the companies the family is invested in. This document lays out the timing, roles and areas of responsibility		
The succession will be/is jointly composed, accounting for the interests of the various stakeholders and the overarching goal of shared preservation of wealth across generations		
All legal aspects related to asset and leadership transition have been clarified and laid out contractually between all participants		
Tax consequences related to the handover of assets have been calculated and prepared for		
The stakeholders, e. g. family members, employees, business partners, have been informed, sufficiently and in an appropriate form, about the switch of leadership and assets and corresponding symbols of the transition have been defined		

Developed by/copyright Alexander Koeberle-Schmid

6.2 Handover of Leadership Responsibility

Alexander Koeberle-Schmid

Practical Example: Questions about Succession

For over 40 years, Rueben Brock has served as owner of an automotive supplier company that he himself inherited as a young man after the sudden death of his father. His physician has now issued him an ultimatum to lessen his load. And even he has noticed: I need to hand off my work—perhaps to my oldest daughter. At the same time, Mr. Brock is debating how things will continue with the leadership of the family office. It is structured as a sub-department within the family holding and to date he has personally overseen its work. Yet if his daughter assumes leadership of the operating company

(*continued*)

(continued)

and his two other children are to be involved in the holding, then it remains to be clarified who will lead the family office going forward. Initially he would like to do this himself, with the idea of professionalizing the family office once he has successfully grown its wealth. For the medium term, he can imagine hiring a family officer from outside the family to build up a team and establish suitable structures. He envisions the board of directors for the family holding comprised of his daughter, the family officer, his son and himself. He also wishes to elect three non-family, non-executive board members that will serve in both a consulting and controlling function. One will be an investment banker, another one a restructuring and M&A expert, and the third one a director at another family-run automotive supplier. They together with Mr. Brock will also form an investment committee to support the family office. In addition to that they will work with a succession expert who will support father and daughter through the leadership succession process as a coach and mediator. He can imagine establishing a separate investment council next to the board of directors at some subsequent point to handle the key questions of the family office. Beyond this, there will also be a three-person advisory council focused solely on issues related to the operating business. This would ensure that family office and operating business are completely separated at a structural level. But for now this is all just plans on paper.

All family members working for the family or more specifically: for the family office or in a firm they are invested in, will eventually be faced with the need to set out rules for succession and/or transfer of leadership. Even when only a single family office is in play, these questions will emerge once the lead family officer, a member of the family, finally begins contemplating stepping down. Things grow much more complicated if management of one of the companies in which the family and the family office need to be addressed at the same time. (The following differentiates fundamentally between the family office and a business in which the family is invested, as many families retain a legacy operating business alongside their family office. In situations where a family office is all that remains, the complexity is reduced to questions of leadership succession for the family office.) This step represents a radical break for all involved. Proper preparation is essential for the transfer of power and the re-orientation of the structures for the assets (family office and possibly the firms the family is invested in). After all, these positions involve a great deal of responsibility. An employee of the family office or, even better, an external succession consultant can provide support through this process.

6.2.1 Defining the Fundamentals of Leadership Transition

By the time the family officer or reigning executive of the family company acknowledges a desire to step down in the foreseeable future, it is already well past time for the circle of owners to discuss a few essential questions: Who is qualified to serve as a successor? Should the successor for the family office and if applicable also for the firms in which the family is invested, come from within the family or outside it? Should the director of the company also have responsibility for the family office, or are boundaries between the organizations needed? Is there a suitable family member who has real interest in a role in the family office and/or one of the companies in which the family is invested? What is an appropriate skills profile for the director of the operating business, and, separately, for the family officer?

For family offices as well as for the firms in which the family is invested, several options for succession typically emerge in the aftermath of this first step:

- The leadership is transferred to one or more family members.
- The family hands over leadership to persons from outside the family.
- A mixed solution is used, with family members and non-family members put in place for both family office and the firms in which the family is invested (for example, the business is helmed by a family member, but the family office by someone from outside the family)

6.2.2 Evaluating a Suitable Successor

When evaluating potential successors from within the family, the normal process of evaluating professional and personal competency can sometimes be inadequate. If the proposed replacement should be a family member, for example, then the family might establish its own custom set of guidelines to identify the right person:

- Only the best qualified candidate will be selected.
- All qualified family members will be considered.
- The oldest child receives the leadership position.
- The oldest son will receive it.
- Women may not hold leadership positions.
- Only one family member per branch can assume a leadership position.

There is a noticeable trend among families toward tapping only those family members for leadership positions who actually possess the necessary competency for the position. It must be acknowledged that a significantly different set of knowledge, skills and experiences are needed to run a family office as opposed to a commercial enterprise. A corporate executive requires more business-management knowledge, while the family officer must possess financial knowledge in assessing suitable investment of assets. These are two completely different skill sets, attitudes and bases of experience. Both roles require strong communications skills, senses of responsibility and ability to resolve conflicts, while the corporate executive also needs a strong conviction and ability to get things done. Both must be capable of motivating others and thinking strategically. And they need to have strong interpersonal skills that allow them to initiate and maintain social relationships within the family. For a young executive, these skills can potentially be acquired through theoretical training such as an MBA program, supplemented with practical business experience, either at the family's company or an external one. For a potential family officer, the training track likely leads through a stint in investment banking or asset management. A continuously evolving leadership development plan is an indispensable tool in grooming a young leader for his or her eventual position in leadership and to accept responsibility for the organization's performance. An impartial succession coach can provide tremendous help in this regard.

6.2.3 Professional Management of Leadership Transition

Once the model for leadership transition has been defined and a suitable successor has been identified, both the party relinquishing and the party receiving power must come to an agreement on how the leadership transition will proceed at a concrete level, and how long the transition phase will last. Are both sides interested in a flexible transition during which responsibility is transferred in stages? Or is a complete handover at a concrete date and time preferred?

Mutual trust and open communication are key prerequisites for a professional transition without conflict between family members. A transfer will best succeed when each side's motives and interests are clear to all involved, especially if the responsibility for the family office is to be transferred from one family member to another of the next generation: the rising leader wants the responsibility, but also the freedom to make decisions independently and prove his worth. The person relinquishing power, especially when it is a family member, is looking to secure the continued prosperity of the family, to grow its wealth and secure dividends, as well as to retain an informed status. A specially commissioned employee of the family office, educated in coaching and best practices for succession, or an independent third party can help frame expectations and build buy-in on both sides. For example, the rising leader can commit to securing the continued prosperity of the family wealth and to invest the family's assets prudently via the family office. In return, the retiring leader can once again confirm that he is ready to relinquish power. The exiting leader needs to trust the rising one and be willing to cede at least a portion of control. In return, the rising leader should keep him informed through a routine series of succession meetings.

Once the transition of power has been negotiated and planned, the relevant stakeholders need to be informed, even if this is "just" a few employees in the family office. Involvement of the employees is an essential step for acceptance of the new boss. It is also important to bring all committees and sub-committees, as well as all family members, on board in advance to ensure that no one feels circumvented.

After that point, the news can be distributed via internal and external channels, depending on the number of stakeholders and whether an operating business and family office are involved or just a family office. This can be handled through closely targeted measures such as personal introductions and transition discussions with key stakeholders or by much broader channels such as the family office newsletter or even a press release. Some retiring power-holders use a celebratory event to announce their leave and name their successor publicly. The festive framework underscores the positive atmosphere surrounding the handover, providing an important symbol for continuity of the prosperity and, where applicable, the company. Other trappings of power such as the prime parking space, head position at the conference table during the weekly family office meetings, the family officer telephone number, or the founder's pocket watch, passed to the rising leader on the day that the former leader steps down, can help drive home the point, especially when other family members are involved.

The retiring member, who is stepping away from a strictly regimented work life with massive responsibility, power and money, should be given time and latitude to prepare for that step. The leadership transfer is a major personal transformation whose impact must be respected. Plans for life "after the family office," a sensible new area of activity and new projects can help senior "let go" and "let it be." While freedom and flexibility install a sense of peace and quiet outside the family office for some retiring figures and their families, other former entrepreneurs and high net worth individuals ultimately feel dissatisfied with a mere life of travel. Productive outlets for these impulses can include humanitarian aid in crisis areas or support and mentoring of students as they work to implement innovative business ideas. Jobs that have a sense of purpose, and potentially which also have an impact on society, are needed to give back a bit of one's own success and wealth.

Naturally these aspects are no guarantee that the transfer of power will run smoothly, even when specially trained employees from the family office or an external consultant are used to support the process. The retiring and the rising generation are always human, with strong personalities that can frequently clash. This makes it all the more important for all participants to adhere to the road map for the transition of power and to identify conflicts before they escalate.

Practical Example: Succession of a Family Officer

Some years ago four siblings sold their company and limited themselves to investing via a single family office run by an experienced family officer (not a member of the family). The four siblings have now reached between 60 and 75 years of age. The assets are to be transferred to their seven children, step by step. One of those descendants has conducted a successful career in asset management, and hence the question is posed whether he might assume leadership of the family office. The four siblings decide to work together with a moderator and two employees from the family office on establishing a profile for the future family officer. In the process, procedural guidelines are developed to regulate the prerequisites for a family member to assume leadership of the family office, including a stipulation that any candidate must have worked successfully in the financial industry for at least ten years. The decision is also made that employees of the family office are only eligible to work until the end of their 65th year of life. The siblings decide to establish a professional investment council. This includes all four siblings, until the completion of their 80th year of life, as well as three experts: an investment banker, a real estate specialist and an auditor versed in accounting and law. The members of the board from outside the family should then decide whether the nephew is suitable for the position of family officer.

6.3 Transferring of Wealth

Jens Escher

The transfer of leadership is not the only significant succession-related question requiring clarification. Mechanisms for transferring the assets themselves must also usually be defined. Even once a decision has been reached on how business and private assets, as well as shares in a family office, are to be gifted or bequeathed, those intentions should be recorded in binding form, either as contracts or testamentary dispositions. The goal is to implement the personal and economic objectives of all participants as effectively as possible despite a gauntlet of potential disrupting factors, including inheritance, family, corporate and tax law. These changes should also of course go hand in hand with the leadership transition (see Fig. 6.2).

6.3.1 Wealth Succession Following a Death

It is fortunate that questions of succession regarding wealth and assets rarely occur solely as a result of death, because the consequences can be massive. Structured leadership transitions, built around a transition phase and a gradual incorporation of the rising generation into its new role, can be thwarted entirely when the entire succession process is unexpectedly triggered by an inheritance event. Admittedly, perfect planning is difficult and there are in fact certain asset items that the senior generation should never transfer prematurely, even as part of an accelerated inheritance case (e. g. the family home). And the precise timing on inheritance events is, by their very nature, often unexpected. Yet where wealthy individuals fail to record their wishes for such an event in advance, probate courts are left to handle the matter. This generally has unwanted side effects, as the estate as a whole is then distributed to the successors based on the principles of intestate succession. Depending on the legal system, this typically involves a community of heirs comprised of descendants and surviving spouses. There are therefore no guarantees that distribution of the corporate assets and the shares in a family office will run according to the wishes of the deceased person (the 'decedent'), or even in the best interests of the company or family office. If there is no will to be executed, then the beneficiaries—after distribution of the inheritance and compliance with any corporate law requirements—are free to do as they please with the wealth they have inherited. This is often contrary to the wishes of the decedent, as it exposes young wealthy individuals to temptations they may not be equipped to handle.

Against this backdrop, succession planning for assets should always be made early and in writing. These plans should be reviewed at regular interviews for potential improvements, including any new legal or tax rules that might necessitate changes.

Common components of estate and succession planning include:

- **Last will and testament**
- **Succession clauses in shareholder's agreements** (harmonized with the will)
- **Prenuptial agreement** (with stipulations compliant with matrimonial property law to govern equalization of accrued gains)
- **Power of attorney** (authorization to represent the individual's affairs in personal and property law matters)
- **Living will** (medical instructions for the attending physicians)

When composing a last will and testament, special consideration must be given that instructions involving disinherited parties are actually enforceable, as the laws regulating statutory shares can in some cases override the desires of the bequeather. Beyond this, the surviving spouse can also be entitled to special compensation related to the equalization of accrued gains, presuming no other prenuptial terms are in place. Such claims may have to be paid by the inheritors in cash, which must factor into liquidation planning alongside the anticipated inheritance tax. For larger fortunes with numerous illiquid assets (real estate, closed-end funds, corporate holdings) in particular, one of the tasks of the family officer is to regularly review the liquidity situation should an inheritance case arise.

Prudent planning can avoid massive strain on the beneficiaries related to forced shares and equalization of accrued gains. For example, beneficiaries can be asked to sign away their right to intestate inheritance. Such agreements can be signed in advance by some or all potential descendants. Along the same lines, prenuptial agreements can be put in place to limit or eliminate any special compensation related to the increase in value of the shared assets. In all cases, the possibility should be explored that the value of the assets in a family office and other companies left behind by the decedent should be excluded from the calculations of potential claims. There may also be the option to limit the size of potential claims to forced shares of the inheritance by transferring funds to the preferred heirs while the bequeather is still alive. The applicable inheritance and family law for the respective jurisdiction will determine which limits apply to the addressed methods of estate planning.

Another important component of a will: defining an executor for the probate process. The executor ensures the execution of the will and manages the disbursement to the descendants. Where allowed by law, the executor can even be given a permanent power of execution to manage the inheritance for a specific period (in Germany, for example, up to 30 years in standard cases). Beyond this, there are a variety of other options for estate planning that allow the testator to ensure the desired legal effects after death (such as the founding of trusts, bequests, distributions, conditions, etc.). In particular, explicit instructions should be recorded for the shares of a family office.

Specialized external consultants should be engaged to assist with the composition of such stipulations and documents. Beyond the aforementioned liquidity planning in the event of an inheritance case, the family office should also handle routine coordination of relevant tasks and document management and may also be tasked with monitoring the need to make revisions. This latter situation can occur for example if interim transfers of individual asset items are to be made while the bequeather is still alive, as well as upon new marriages and divorces, or following births and deaths, the departure and arrival of family members or entrance into new ventures covered by corporate law.

6.3.2 Accelerated Wealth Succession

Beyond any statutory regulations regarding wealth succession in inheritance cases, accelerated wealth succession can play a major role in the estate planning of high net worth individuals, owners of a family office or the shareholders of a family-owned business. After all, this issue is central to effective generational transitioning of leadership and a controlled acclimation of the rising generation to their coming responsibilities. Estate planning can be implemented, practiced and where necessary revised by the transferring party.

For the transferring party, accelerated wealth succession offers the distinct advantage that corporate law structures can be established intentionally and in advance to allow for the desired rolling transfer of assets and to ensure the integrity of the fortune. Intangible assets are often first moved prior to gifting to a newly created family holding firm whose shares are then transferred to the rising generation (along with shares of corporate investments, where applicable). In some cases the transfer is conducted successively. The same mechanism can be used for shares in a family office.

In corporate law, which applies if the family office is a separate legal entitiy or if the assets are held through companies in a holding structure, there is usually the option of securing key participation rights for the donor, such as a special right to act or vote within the management council, a veto right for shareholder votes or enhanced voting rights. Alternatively, control rights or a board of directors tied to the shareholder's agreement can be implemented, with the donor retaining a significant role in it. The rules of the shareholder's agreement can also potentially be used to limit the beneficiaries' ability to activate their shares or profits, such as through restricted transferability clauses and limitation to withdrawals or reserve transfers. The circle of potential shareholders can also be limited in some cases through stipulations in the shareholder's agreement (such as to the donor and his biological descendants), to prevent an unwanted ascension by third parties outside the family related to an inheritance case.

Beyond the retention of controlling rights, the financial security of the donor can also be a relevant issue, especially if shares of a company are to be transferred that still serve as a primary source of income. A transfer involving 'reservation of usufruct' or trust agreements including a life interest for the settlor (in common law jurisdictions) can be suitable methods to ensure that the donor still receives yields from the transferred asset blocks. In such a scenario any growth in the transferred assets would then fall to the beneficiary, which is advantageous from an inheritance tax standpoint. Entrepreneurs in particular should act early to accumulate a store of private wealth separate from the family office and the companies the family is invested in, so as to secure means for retirement and a bit of independence from the business and investment success or failure of their successor. There are also a variety of other contractual models available.

From a taxation perspective, accelerated inheritance has a fundamental benefit that the timing of the transfer of assets can be planned—a factor not available in the event of death. Given the frequent changes that are made to tax law, this can be a significant factor. For example, the most advantageous windows for certain transactions from a taxation perspective can be sought, such as when the anticipated transfer date falls at a time that either triggers or doesn't trigger certain taxation criteria, whichever is more beneficial. The impacts of income and gift taxes related to the transfer can be examined from all sides in advance of the desired date, including the obtainment of an official ruling from the local tax authorities if desired. Because the transferred wealth and its value on the day of transfer are in many countries subject to gift taxation, the selected transfer date can have an impact on the structure of the gift tax that is triggered.

An inheritance process that is begun early and conducted in multiple steps may offer multiple opportunities to pass portions of the gift completely free of inheritance or gift taxes. Profits from the transferred assets are the responsibility of the beneficiaries, which can reduce the giver's income tax load (progressive impact based on the distribution of income among several persons) and can prevent any such income from falling under inheritance tax as assets of the bequeathing generation.

As part of the accelerated inheritance, the family office is responsible for coordinating the process, collaborating with external consultants and ensuring that all necessary information on the subject is available. During the implementation of the succession project, the family office is generally responsible for monitoring changes to the legal, taxation or economic framework around the intended transfer (such as the need to change a will or a marriage or inheritance contract). Yet future events are not the only important ones. Circumstances from the past, such as the signing of a shareholders agreement or a recent restructuring, can also have a significant influence on the design of the accelerated inheritance. In this last situation in particular, a family officer familiar with the family's situation and with comprehensive knowledge of existing contracts and processes from recent years represents as an ideal liaison to the external consultants hired for a specific succession project.

6.4 Mediation: Helpful for Succession, and More

Alexander Koeberle-Schmid

In theory, families that have a family office and possibly in addition are invested in a company should be mentally and emotionally prepared for the fact that they will eventually need to manage transitions. After all, one nearly universal goal for building affluence and influence is the desire to pass the family assets on to children, nephews and grandchildren. In practice, though, leaders are often unwilling or unable to relinquish responsibility. This may be because the succession isn't voluntary, but rather dictated by medical circumstances. Or because the retiring party believes that the rising generation isn't (yet) ready to carry the weight and responsibility. Or perhaps the current generation simply still enjoys the thrill of managing the family's wealth.

These conditions are ripe for big family fights, and sometimes they lead to irrevocable splintering and splits. The negative consequences, especially for families with a large pool of wealth in a family office, can be massive and lasting. After all, the assets in and of themselves cannot build emotional relationships. Fights over wealth in particular can easily cause permanent damage to family relationships. Diametrically opposed opinions on topics such as investments, disbursements, dividend payments, services within the family office, employment, succession, board of directors, advisory council positions or new investment council staffing can lead to deep conflicts in business-owning families.

In many cases, the parties then escalate the conflict spiral. One common progression: After a phase of ineffectual argumentation and persuasion, each side tries to raise the pressure through alliances with other shareholders, unapproved and unilateral actions or the use of employees as pawns. Lawyers are then engaged, forcing otherwise uninvolved family members to choose sides and further driving a wedge into the family's sense of identity. The conflict festers, taking on a chronic feel and mutating into emotional disorder. The urge to listen to different positions and understand mutual interests and motivations dwindles. The incentive to search together for an objective solution is lost. Feelings of betrayal and hurt, of rage and disgust are allowed to dominate. Insults, allegations and baseless accusations hinder any chance of resolving the situation internally.

Conflicts are, however, part of life. Preventing them completely is a utopian goal. Handling them constructively—that's where science becomes art. To prevent or de-escalate a destructive battle, many family offices have found it helpful to involve an impartial third party. A professional mediator trained in the conflict field of "succession in families" is a good candidate for this role.

The mediator can help the family navigate safely through the emotional minefield of expectation, interests and needs. Her goal is to help both parties better understand each other better, to acknowledge emotions and to classify actions accordingly. Beyond this, she supports both generations in the development of individual solutions. In many cases, this gives rise to entirely new ideas and results that the two competing parties hadn't considered at all.

Types of Conflict

Being in a conflict situation often means that the parties do not see the possibility of coming to a common solution, a consensus. One effective way to move past this hurdle is a mediation process to help each side better understand the needs, interests, and motives of the other parties. However, equally important is to cut through the conflict situation by achieving transparency about the different conflicts. The following six conflicts are common in families owning a family office (Table 6.2).

Table 6.2 Types of conflict and possible solutions in family offices

Types of conflict	Examples	Possible solutions
Value conflict Values are usually not negotiable and are at the foundation of personal identity. Values are a core principle and standard. They are defended if challenged. They normally arise when family members did not grow up with the same set of values transferred from their parents and when there is no family legacy put in place. They are especially frequent when there is less attachment of the family towards the wealth and when the attitude towards the family wealth is more like an investor.	• Different attitudes towards risks and thus asset distribution • Renewing the portfolio and the strategy of the family office vs. preserving the family legacy and not divesting because there is a resistance towards change	• Shedding light on the conflict and on the different motives and reasons for the opposing argumentations • Definition of common family values, discussion about the history of the family business and the family wealth • Definition of values for working together • Establishing a family office education program and the attitude of a responsible owner • Discussion about risk appetite and about attitudes towards change

(*continued*)

Table 6.2 (continued)

Types of conflict	Examples	Possible solutions
Data conflict Transparency about decisions and wealth is crucial when trust defines the relationship among family members. It is problematic if there is a lack of communication, misinformation, unaligned interpretation of data or procedures and contradicting views that come through different sources of information, i.e. different data about the same issue. Even when the same data is available, misunderstandings and improper interpretation of data can lead to data conflicts.	• Inaccurate information about the total wealth, its distribution • Changing numbers in reporting each month due to mistakes in the reporting system • Family members and family office not transparent about decisions	• Elaborate reporting and controlling system in place, that is easy to understand, IT based and preferably available via a secure internet connection • Open discussions about investment strategy and asset allocation • Regular reporting on decisions • Regular meetings of family members with the family office
Structural conflict Ownership structures and management structures are organized that make it difficult to come to clear decisions. Different share distribution among the different assets can increase the variety of interests and goals. Structural conflicts also arise due to a lack of authority to resolve problems, competition for limited resources and divergent priorities.	• Ownership shares of family assets differ between the family members, causing different priorities • Management of the family office is not aligned with management of the firms the family is invested in • The governance is not clearly structured with missing definition of responsibilities of the different bodies	• Detailed decision, information, and responsibility distribution • Investment pooled in a family holding (one ownership position only) • Good governance aligned with the asset distribution • Having non-family, non-executive members in the board or other councils
Task conflict Task conflicts are about goals and strategies. These conflicts are quite normal because family members can have different points of views about their goals for the family office and which services the family office should deliver to the family members. They can become problematic if they are discussed at an emotional level rather than an objective one.	• Disagreement about the goals for the family office • Disagreement about which services are offered by the family office • Disagreement about the strategy of the family office and of the firms the family is invested in	• Clearly defined goals for the family office • Defined investment strategy that is revised regularly • Mutually developed family strategy and definition of measures to ensure cohesion among family members

(*continued*)

Table 6.2 (continued)

Types of conflict	Examples	Possible solutions
Process conflict Process conflicts are about how to reach a goal. To use a metaphor: the task conflict is about the final destination. Process conflict is about whether to take a taxi, bus, train or plane to reach the destination. It is also quite normal that family members have different opinions about how to reach a goal. If you set a goal of 5 percent annual ROI, a variety of different portfolios can achieve this. Process conflicts become problematic when family members have for instance different risk appetites, different expectations regarding dividends, different cash flow needs, and different views about which member of the next generation should become the next family officer.	• Family members having different levels of requesting services from the family office • Confusion among the members of the bodies of the family office (management, board, advisory council, investment council) about responsibilities, leading to questioning of difficult discussions and parallel decision making	• Clear policies regarding leadership succession • Clear policies regarding all money issues (dividend distribution, return on investment distribution, etc.) • Accepted distribution of rights and obligation of family owners, board members, family officers etc. in place • Policies about decision making in the family office and among the family members • Policies regarding decreasing and increasing the shares in the family office, the invested capital • List of services that can be requested from the family office and at which price
Relationship conflict This critical type of conflict is personal in nature and normally occurs when the aforementioned conflicts are left resolved and emotions fester. Stereotyping, personal animosities, poor communication, using others as tools for one's own interest and goals, reacting highly emotionally—all this fuel relationship conflicts. It can arise very easily within families because family members have known each other for a long period and communication is very often direct and personal.	• Emotional debate among the siblings about the next family officer from the family—without any perspective of making a decision • A lack of communication prevents a necessary discussion on shifting assets to prevent financial losses	• Mediation process to get the conflicting situations discussed • Trying to establish mutual respect and love through extensive discussions about motives and aspirations • Acting in accordance to the commonly defined strategies, rules, procedures, and policies

Mediation Process

Successful mediation absolutely requires that all participants agree to the involvement of a mediator—and work in good faith with her. Once these conditions have been met, the mediation can run through the following four steps.

The first step is to define positions: This phase involves listening to the viewpoints of the retiring and the rising generation, separately from one another. Each formulates concretely what he expects from the other side. The mediator initially just listens. In order for representatives of both sides to open up to her, she needs to earn trust. This includes behaving in a strictly impartial manner and at no point revealing her own opinion. As a neutral listener, she compiles a list of the requirements from each side and tries to structure the points of conflict. The retiring party may, in a time where ownership and leadership is handed over to the next generation for example, declare that he wishes for continued voting rights, wishes to remain informed, demands dividends in a certain amount and wishes to retain 10 percent of the assets in the family office until his death. The rising generation by contrast may declare that they require more freedom of action, more latitude to make decisions and a wish to receive a portion of the assets now.

The second step is to reveal interests, motives, feelings and needs: The mediator must determine why the parties are behaving as they are. What's behind it? This requires clever questioning that awakens self-reflection in both sides. She may for example doggedly pursue the question of why which position is important to the participants. As a result, the retiring party may admit that he is concerned about losing influence and wealth—and to not being happy with the new-found freedom. Beyond this, he may want more security and sees risks in the potential that the rising party may pursue a riskier strategy with the family office's assets. The rising party in turn may simply finally want the chance to prove his worth, be independent, shape the family office and the investment to his vision, and earn more estimation from the retiring party. It is the mediator's task to foster understanding by both sides for each other, typically by presenting each side's wishes and expectations in their own words. Both sides will learn to understand each other better in this way and will be better equipped to interpret the other's motivations and behavior. In many cases, behavior by others that is perceived as negative can lead to conflict, with each party believing they understand the motivation of the other. Yet the motivation is often different than anticipated.

The third step is to agree upon criteria for a solution: With an eye towards the interests, objectives and motivations, the parties now begin working together on potential solutions. In many cases this is actually fun, as the two parties reconciled during the second step after coming to understand each other's viewpoints. The various options are now jointly assessed, with the goal of forming a consensus. This includes, for example, working together to frame the succession process so that everyone knows which tasks and responsibilities the one side will be assuming, and when the other party holds the reins for a decision.

The fourth and final step is to sign binding contracts: The mutually agreed terms should be codified by both generations in a contract. This includes a generational contract with articles of association and a bestowal deed, the testament and employment contracts.

Open communication is of prime importance during mediation. Both sides should express their expectations and concerns openly at all times. Trust is very important for the transition to run without conflict. And this can occur only when mutual interests, motives, objectives and needs are made clear.

Practical Tip: How a Family Officer Can Help in the Succession Process

The following recommendations can help family officers to prevent conflicts from arising in the family for which they work. Especially in the time when ownership and management of the family assets is being handed over to the next generation, the family officer can recommend the following aspects to the family:

- **Create a healthy communication environment:** Encourage open dialogue and freedom to express feelings and thoughts. Establish a code of conduct within the family to minimize conflict. Encourage family members to pose questions before making assumptions, practice active listening, and avoid personalizing the issue.
- **Formulate a leadership development plan:** The rising generation should already have proven their leadership and profit responsibility before accepting the reins. For this to happen, work with the younger generation to develop a plan that defines in stages what, when, how and why something is to be done. This is especially important if the members of the rising generation are to be trained outside the family office. And engage a coach who can support "Junior" through the transition process.
- **Prepare for afterwards:** The retiring party should compose his thoughts on what is being gained by the transition. Support him and brainstorm along with him about how to use the new free time: hobbies, family or volunteer work.
- **Define communications rules:** Try to avoid competition and rivalry among the family members. Work toward the goal of both the retiring and rising generation discussing their fears and expectations. Derive rules and objectives from this with the participants. Clarify who will receive which information, who will decide on new investments, who is involved with major asset reallocations and—so as to speak with one voice—who will answer questions from employees, banks and other shareholders.

(*continued*)

(continued)

- **Set occasions to celebrate:** the family should be informed about a set point in time for the handover of the keys and the assets. Anchor the family's appreciation of the change by commemorating the handover with a symbolic act: a golden watch, a Christmastime speech, or an anniversary.
- **Involve a mediator:** Whether or not there is a conflict, contemplate whether a mediator, either active or in the background, might help better structure the succession plans and ensure that all interests are properly represented. Cutting corners here can mean massively higher costs later on if conflict arises—and even threaten the continued existence of the family and its assets.

Practical Tip: How a Family Officer Can Help Solving Conflicts

Sometimes family members find themselves in conflict but are unwilling to involve a mediator. The following steps might help them resolve their conflicts on their own:

1. **Improve the environment:** Create an atmosphere of openness, constructive criticism and problem solving.
2. **Set the stage:** Emphasize that it is important to work together to reach a mutually satisfactory solution and make the first step towards this.
3. **Evaluate the situation:** Describe the conflict situation from your own perspective as clearly, objectively, and specifically as you can to the other person. Say what you think, see, feel, hear.
4. **Remove distractions and bystanders:** Do not use other people to influence the other person or to reach your goals.
5. **Gain perspective:** Ask questions to understand the other person's ideas, thoughts, values, perspectives. Repeat what the other person has said to promote mutual understanding.
6. **Outline the points:** List all your points and also list the other persons' points.
7. **Try to structure the conflicts:** Use the six types of conflicts to structure your situation. Establish an order of the different points together.
8. **Gain mutual agreement on the conflict:** Identify the topics where you already have a mutual agreement and note the issues where you have a disagreement.
9. **State your perspective:** Clearly articulate your points per conflict/conflict type (clearly formulate your position). Also formulate why the points are important to you. Be sure to ask the other person about their position and identify why the different aspects are important.
10. **Formulate solution criterion:** After you and the other party have understood why the different issues are important to each other, ask: what needs to be assured when finding a good mutual solution?

(continued)

(continued)

11. **Identify potential solutions:** With the solution criterion in mind, use the chart of different types of conflicts to begin brainstorming various mutually satisfying solutions.
12. **Evaluate the solutions:** Work together to evaluate the different factors that make the solutions mutually satisfying.
13. **Choose the solutions:** Select the solutions that meet all the parties' needs. Consider that your solution also satisfies the other person at the same time (in relation also to the solution criterion). Remember: the goal is not to achieve unilateral victory for one side or the other. It is about finding a mutually satisfying solution.
14. **Develop an action plan:** Decide on specific actions that you and the other party wish to undertake to put the solution into reality.
15. **Let it be:** When you have come to a solution, do not reheat a solved conflict.

From Germany: "We've stayed together as a family for generations."

Interview with Christian-Titus Klaiber

This interview explores the choices that face high net worth families after a cash event, the challenges of family governance and getting buy-in from later generations for the family office and the emotional value of charitable foundations.

The interview was conducted by Alexander Koeberle-Schmid.

Mr. Klaiber, you are a member of a well-known industrial family here in Germany, the Leitz family. Over 15 years ago, the fourth generation made the decision to sell Leitz, the family's legacy company. What's there in its place today?
Christian-Titus Klaiber: Well, we don't have factories any more. We sold all our shares in the company to the Esselte Group. So nowadays there's a family office on the one side and the Louis Leitz Stiftung on the other.

What changed for you all after the sale?
CTK: The business was well over a hundred years old by the time we sold it. My great-great-grandfather Louis Leitz first founded his workshop to produce metal parts for organizational tools back on 1 July 1871. In 1896 he invented the Leitz folder, which you'll still find today. In this case, 'running the operating business' means: We always produced office supplies and sold them worldwide. 15 years ago, in the aftermath of the sale, all we were left with was cash. Which posed the question: Were we going to remain together and undertake something jointly, or was everyone just going to take their own share of the capital and go? We decided to remain together as a family.

Christian-Titus Klaiber *is the deputy chairman of the Leitz Family Office shareholders' committee. He and his relatives in the shareholders' committee work to promote long-term cohesiveness in the family and control that its assets continue to grow over time.*

In fact, we were unanimous on the point. The family gets along very well with each other and recognized that in the aftermath of the sale it made much more sense financially for us to stay a cohesive unit. For starters, we have an entirely different magnitude of influence when we invest our money as a group. And it also protects shareholders working in other fields, the ones who weren't economists, auditors or bankers. If you'd simply transferred the money to their accounts, they would've been left to ask themselves: So now what am I going to do with all this?

Did all of the family members sign on after the sale of the company, i.e. did all the proceeds from the sale go into the family office?
CTK: I think there were six shareholders who left the family association. For a variety of personal reasons they wished to invest their money on their own. They didn't want to be bound by communal decisions. And they were furthermore of the opinion that they had sufficient knowledge to invest their money on their own. There's no doubt that upon sale there will be an initial wave of withdrawals. But I'd say that the rest of the family applied over 90% percent of the sales price to the family office.

How many shareholders in the family office are there today?
CTK: We currently have 45 shareholders. Each family member receives a small share when he or she reaches 18 years of age, and so automatically becomes a shareholder. The idea is that you grow into the family and into the responsibility that goes along with this kind of wealth, and have time to better understand the issues.

What is your family office responsible for managing?
CTK: Our family office serves as the final instance of approval for asset investment. The asset portfolio as such is outsourced to professional wealth managers. We formulate the strategy, so to say, but not the operative elements. We don't undertake tactical asset investment. The family office is thus a final approving body for any asset investment and makes strategic decisions on such investments. It also coordinates our asset controlling and asset reporting. An external service provider has actually been contracted to handle this work, but the family office collates it all for us. The family office handles tax planning and tax returns for all stakeholders. In the past, all insurance policies were also handled centrally within our family office. That's no longer quite as prevalent any more. The family office plans the general shareholder meetings, which are held twice a year. It also coordinates all of the activities and events that we conduct to reinforce our family identity, such as the "Day of the Fifth Generation," joint skiing excursions among the fifth generation and continuing education events. So, we're talking about really concrete family governance measures. This

is where the families, and the members of the family, gather and meet, and where the fifth generation also comes together. What we don't have is a central organization for all of the security questions on the part of the shareholders.

Who pays for the services of the family office?
CTK: It's all paid centrally from one big pot. There's no cost center-style breakdown. Everyone has agreed to this. In our family, there's a principle of mutual give and take. As long as it works for everyone, the whole system is stable. There are years where one person utilizes the family office more strongly and other years when someone else does.

What is the leadership structure for your family office?
CTK: The stakeholders choose a shareholders' council from their own ranks, which in turn selects a chairperson and a deputy chairperson. My uncle is the chairman and I'm his deputy. We have a family office advisor. That gentleman is an auditor and tax accountant.

So you're a member of the shareholders' council for your family office. What are its responsibilities?
CTK: The shareholders' council represents the interests of the shareholders. It's akin to an advisory council or supervisory board in a company. For example, it sets the investment strategy, meaning it defines the bandwidths within which investments should be made in the various investment classes. The shareholders' council makes the strategic decisions that are then conveyed to the asset managers.

What are the responsibilities of the shareholders' council in terms of family governance measures?
CTK: For example, we'll be holding our "Day of the Fifth Generation" next year in Bad Homburg. Members of my generation who haven't been as deeply involved in the details of the family office are invited to join us for a day in Bad Homburg and gain some insight into what exactly we do here in the family office, what the various asset classes are, who the people are behind all that work, and so on.

What were the origins of this "Day of the Fifth Generation?"
CTK: It was actually my idea, and we took it up in the shareholders' council. First, I talked with the central contact person for the fifth generation and the person who organizes continuing education events within the shareholders' council and we decided: "It's a good idea, let's do it." The family office is handling the operative implementation.

What does a session of the shareholders' committee look like?
CTK: In concrete terms, we discuss all topics openly. Following classic parliamentary rules, everyone is welcome to offer his or her opinion and the

discussion remains open until a solution is found. We've got quite a wide range of characters in the committee, with different professional backgrounds. At the end of the day, we've always managed to come to a mutually agreeable solution—even if discussions have dragged on quite late at times.

Where do you meet for the sessions—since you no longer have the corporate headquarters.
CTK: We have an office in Stuttgart, where our family office is based. That's the central meeting point for our family. After the sale, the Louis Leitz headquarters in Stuttgart-Feuerbach was no longer available for meeting. We initially met at fancy hotels, but it didn't really work for us. Even since we've had our family office, we have always met there. The round table in our conference room is a tangible symbol of its role as a place for all sides to come together. Everyone gathers around this table, makes communal decisions and works to find solutions.

The topic of succession is a relevant one for you as well—in the establishment of shareholders and in the control of the family office. How are you nurturing your successors?
CTK: A generational passing of the torch is coming for us soon. The fourth generation is now between 50 and 75 years old, while the fifth generation is between 30 and 45. For right now, the fourth generation retains the ultimate decision-making authority. That responsibility is increasingly being passed to the fifth generation, however. I'm the deputy chairman of the shareholders' committee right now and am assuming a growing share of the responsibility—including from my uncle.

In summary: What do you see from your perspective as the success factors for family offices?
CTK: You need loyal and discreet employees. After all, they're dealing directly with the members of the family. For example, the central contact person for all shareholders has been working for us for over 40 years (initially at Leitz, now for us in the family office). My grandfather first hired her. Beyond this, you need external expertise in wealth management, law and taxation. Because simply being a nice guy isn't enough. Clear decision-making paths are also essential. And all sides must be clear on which topics are handled on our own within the family office and which tasks we will pass on to external consultants. For that to work, skill profiles need to be defined for people working in the family office. That applies to family members in the committees as well.

Putting the family office aside for a moment, you are also engaged in the Louis Leitz Foundation. What moved you to create your own foundation?
CTK: We were always entrepreneurial in nature. As Swabians and as owners of a family-run company, the well-being of our employees and their families

has always been very important to us. In some cases we've had generations of different families—grandparents, children and grandchildren—all come to work for us. We were a very important employer at the local level. When we sold our company, the fifth generation in particular felt that there were issues that needed addressing: are we going to be satisfied with this monetary wealth, or is there also value in taking a portion of that inheritance, this economic success, and giving back to society? We also wanted to establish a framework that would promote ideal togetherness. And so the foundation was created. It is focused on education, training and employment. That reflects our tradition.

How is the family involved in the foundation's work?
CTK: Over 90% of all shareholders are also benefactors. All on a voluntary basis. We have a foundation board, with a chairperson and deputy. Both are members of the family. The members of the foundation board, also members of the family, oversee various projects as sponsors. These projects are then presented twice a year after our shareholders' meeting. The responsible parties report on how the money was used. And that motivates the shareholders as well.

What projects are you supporting?
CTK: The "Seehaus" in Leonberg, as an example. It works to re-integrate youths with a criminal past into society. My mother is involved with the SELF project in Kassel. It's a program for children without parents, or whose parents have abandoned them. We help them get started in a career. In concrete terms, my mother sponsors three youths and provides them with assistance. What stands out about our foundation work is that the members of the foundation are personally involved with the projects they sponsor. We want to be present in the projects as a family, something we see as a success factor.

Which other success factors do you see for good foundation work?
CTK: The shareholders and members of the foundation need transparency on where the money is going. There need to be lean structures to keep administrative costs down. A foundation always needs to be aware that it's not just managing itself, it's also responsible for ensuring that the money is reaching the people who need it. Beyond that, a mix of generations is important. If the foundation is solely run by the 'golden generation' and is unable to pull in the younger generation, then at some point the board turns 90 and finds it hard to continue its work. So we must question our own methods and processes. Things that were modern 20 years ago can be perceived by young trustees, themselves little more than 20 years old, as being no longer modern at all.

Looking back over the past 15 years, what would you change going forward?
CTK: 15 years after selling our company, we're still together as a family. In many places large segments have already been transferred from the fourth to the fifth generation, or the process is underway. We all get along very well within the family. To that extent I'd say: The family office has been a success and is likely to continue being so. With that said, we need to be diligent in ensuring that the family office stays lean. And we need to work on a smooth, shared transition between the generations in the years to come. The groundwork has been laid for that. We have well-educated and interested fifth-generation family members. That means continuing the shared spirit and remaining thankful about being a member of the Leitz family. And we always need to continue working on that.

So you feel that your efforts have been a success?
CTK: In terms of the economic success: staying together and investing jointly through a family office has definitely paid off. In terms of the societal impact of our foundational work: the projects have genuinely had a positive impact on our society, because the project sponsors from the family are personally involved. And perhaps most importantly: The family has stayed together across generations.

Bibliography

Koeberle-Schmid A, Unger M (2019) Nachfolge im Familienunternehmen. Beck Verlag, München

7

Organizing the Family: Family Governance

Alexander Koeberle-Schmid

Pride in being part of a family with a history of owning a business. A sense of honor in investing family wealth in other companies, thus securing jobs for communities. Joy in participating in a positive, conflict-free family environment. Acknowledging shared values and passing them on to the children. Honoring and maintaining traditions and rituals. Helping one another and staying together for the long run, even when the businesses the family is invested in encounter tough times or the stock markets have a bad run. These are the common traits of emotionally stable families that own or owned a family business and are now part of a family office.

Family governance can help promote this kind of stability. It is built atop a foundation of concrete measures that encourage the entire family to form positive associations and effective interpersonal relationships with each other and with their shared organizations. These include family reunion days or weekends, joint tours of the companies the family is invested in, rules for interpersonal interactions and conflict resolution, young future shareholder days, continuing education offerings for wealthy families and mentoring or coaching for the next generation.

Effective family governance does more than just promote healthier emotional relationships among family members. It fosters loyalty and self-identification in ways that mere investing of wealth and running a company cannot. This starts with rules on how the family may influence the family office and the legacy business, a principle that almost paradoxically strengthens the bond between family and family office. Important components of successful family governance include policy rules, decision paths and notification chains, but that is not all. Committees must be formed and roles must be

B. Canessa et al., *The Family Office*, https://doi.org/10.1007/978-3-319-99085-9_7

negotiated, up to and including advisory councils, supervisory councils, family managers, family councils, investment councils or quorum requirements at shareholders meetings.

Practical Example: Cohesiveness and Identification with the Family Office

Family members who feel good about the unity of their family often make statements such as: We are capable of addressing even sensitive topics openly. We come to a consensus, even if we have divergent opinions. In our family we have the feeling that we belong together and are there for one another. I receive a lot from my family without the sense that something is being expected in return.

Family members who feel a strong bond with the family office say: Preserving family traditions is important to us as a family, regardless of whether our assets are exclusively invested via our family office. I am aware and interested in what is happening to our wealth in the family office and the impact of our investments on society and the employees of the companies in which we are investing. I feel myself to be a part of the family office. The family office and our charitable foundation are an important part of me. I am involved in the family office, put my energy into it, prepare thoroughly for meetings, watch the stock markets and intensively analyze our planned corporate investments. I feel close to the employees of the family office.

Family Governance across Generations

How broad do the family governance measures need to be? Their scope and depth should ultimately reflect the size and composition of the family, its relationship to the family office and the size and diversity of the managed wealth. Unlike a legacy business, the family office in and of itself is unlikely to have much emotional pull for the family. If the family office is the only common institution for the family, then family governance measures are an effective way to promote a stronger internal identification with the family office. On the flip side, a lack of information or involvement with decisions can lead to disinterest and even rejection by the next generation.

The cycles inherent to any owning family should thus be understood as having an impact on family governance. An illustrative example:

- In the **first generation**, there is a company; ownership and leadership typically lie in the same hand. Poor decisions cause twice the damage, especially when someone is alone at the peak of a company. At a time when business is good, the entrepreneur considers putting a portion of the profits into a family office for management. The expertise of a banker and an investment specialist are needed for this to work.

(continued)

(continued)

- The **second generation** pursues a two-pronged approach to company leadership: A pair of siblings run the company together. Another brother, who is a lawyer and tax accountant, manages the family office. This constellation requires a different leadership structure: a board of directors is established at the company to serve as a sparring partner and to break ties when opinions are split. Questions of succession arise: Should the son follow the father, or is one of the nephews the better choice? It must also be clarified how the cousins will get to know each other and form a relationship with the family office. After all, the third generation will not be growing up together, which brings both advantages and disadvantages: Individuals can be more professional and less emotional with one another, but the relationship toward the assets becomes more akin to that of a shareholder in a publicly held firm.
- The **third generation** tends to encompass more shareholders, meaning the main issues are notification and voting rights: who gets to develop and vote on corporate and investment strategies? Who is allowed access to the balance sheets and P&L calculations, how much of the profits will remain in the company, how much will be managed by the family office, and how will returns from cash investments be handled? Or should the legacy business be sold and the entire pool of wealth be managed by the family office? These crucial issues involving power and money are prime candidates to cause conflict—even if fights over money and influence can permanently damage a company or family office or even set it on a path to ruination.

Overview of Family Governance Measures

Starting with the second and third generations, where the shareholders begin pursuing different walks of life and the "family glue" slowly begins to dissolve, instruments become necessary to promote cohesion. A family council or family manager can offer concrete help here. He/it is responsible for organizing joint family reunion weekends and training programs for young shareholders, such as seminars on better understanding of balance sheets and the fundamentals of strategy. Stable relationships require fair, transparent and rigorous rules, especially in questions of succession and public appearances. The goal is to promote responsible owners, dedicated to the long-term success of the family wealth and at minimum the preservation of wealth and cohesiveness of the family; people who think in generations.

When they do, they ultimately structure their own wealth in the company or in the family office to last for generations. This requires vision, clearly defined values and goals, a forward-looking family strategy and a sustainable family office investment strategy. This includes leadership structures for the family and the family office that are capable of adapting to changing situations. Those structures are then documented in a family constitution.

7.1 Family Constitution and Family Charter for Family Office

There are certain questions a family officer should pose to the owning family: How can conflicts be avoided between regular shareholders and family leaders? What should happen if the children absolutely refuse to go along with the desires of their father? Or when multiple grandchildren are struggling with each other for control and oversight of the family office? Differences of opinion occur in any family—but if left unresolved, they can quickly put an entire investment portfolio at risk, even one with a rich portfolio of liquid assets in a family office.

During the first generation, ownership and leadership responsibility typically reside in one person. Over time, the number of members in an owning family tends to increase, sometimes exponentially. In situations where the family office is the "only" vehicle for asset investment and the emotional anchor of a shared company is no longer present, the "family glue" can slowly dissipate. Other instruments are needed to promote closeness and cohesiveness within the family. Among the most effective tools are rules defining succession, remuneration, notification rights and dividends, as well as family reunion days and continuing education days for younger family members.

The Importance of the Family Constitution

No company can afford to engage in a "war on two fronts" for very long. Companies are fighting every day for market share; family offices also face

Practical Example: Explosive Topics

Owning families are likely to encounter a number of thorny issues, such as different distribution of shares between multiple siblings. The following topics can represent true minefields:

- From a group of eight cousins, three have left the family-owned company. The others are now in a heated discussion about how to prevent further conflict-related departures among the shareholders.
- A father accuses his son of no longer providing him with all of the information from the family office that he needs. As a result of this, the father withdraws the majority of profits from the family office and invests them in his own real estate holdings. And his daughter, who works in the controlling department, complains that her salary is too low.

(*continued*)

(continued)

- After his uncle cuts him off during an executive meeting, the nephew is barely able to contain his rage. On top of this, his aunt is refusing to agree to foregoing a round of dividends, a move that is needed to undertake a promising expansion into the USA. A niece is complaining that she can't use the family office to invest her husband's assets. And another cousin wants to implement an investment fund for family ventures but is unable to secure a majority vote for this.

When conflicts like these are not sufficiently addressed and answered, they can eventually rupture the peace and with it the continued existence of both family office and the family itself.

daily pressure to earn adequate returns on their invested capital. Rivalries within the owner family are detrimental to this effort.

In their book "Governance in Family Enterprises," Alexander Koeberle-Schmid, Denise Kenyon-Rouvinez and Ernesto Poza describe all important aspects of family business governance and how to implement a family constitution. In their view, early implementation of a family constitution or charter can help manage the expectations of family members. These are not extended arms of existing corporate and investment strategy, which must be continuously adjusted for the current economic conditions. They are instead shared statements regarding the universal questions at play in every family: power, money, love, personal fulfilment.

Studies have found that while increasing, the number of families that have their own family charter ultimately still remains stubbornly low. The benefits of a family constitution are often not appreciated. It lays out in writing a set of fair, transparent and rigorous rules for the family office and the family itself that are then accepted by all shareholders. It cultivates stability, secures a solid base of communication and ensures that decisions are transparent. It also establishes a framework for conflicting interests to be addressed and resolved.

Joint composition of a family charter promotes togetherness in the family and works to avoid conflicts. In many cases, members of an owner family find themselves finally addressing the unpleasant or conflict-laden topics that they had, for better or worse, previously swept under the rug. They must now work together to compose a strategy for the family in terms of the family office and its assets, accounting for the entirely different viewpoints of all involved.

A family constitution has a stabilizing effect for the family, both internally and externally, as it does more than just set down policies. It also establishes a benchmark for how all members of the family should comport themselves. Beyond this, it installs professional decision-making structures, defines responsibilities and forms a basis for unity within the family. The owners and their dependents gain a deeper understanding of the needs of the family office and the companies and asset forms they are invested in.

Critical topics should be discussed during peaceable times: Who among us has control, and when will I enter the executive ranks of the family office? Who will inherit what? What happens if my cousin and I disagree on something?

The best way to avoid discord on such questions is to address them openly. As the number of family members grows, this can be a difficult process, especially if the individuals involved don't know each other well. An institutional exchange can be an effective bridge. A family constitution might for example call for family reunion days to get to know one another and discuss—and resolve—potential points of conflict. The idea that families should create rules for handling of their wealth is nothing new. Noble houses of bygone times always had such rules as well. What's new is that the rules are no longer dictated from above by one person, but instead are worked out in consensus.

The family charter is based upon an acknowledgement by the family that their collective wealth is best preserved for the long term through shared ownership. Sustained growth of that wealth demands vision, clearly defined goals and guidelines for the family office as to which risks the executive team may enter into and which asset classes are to be avoided.

Presuming the wealth does continue growing, it is also sensible for the executive team of the family office or the company to provide an advisory or investment council. This too can be established in the family charter. An investment council serves as a sparring partner and provides advice on key investment decisions (or may have a crucial veto power); it can also help break deadlocks and—in the interests of the shareholders—prevent poor decisions. The investment council must be comprised of competent representatives—which does not inherently mean the senior boss. A family council or family manager also promotes togetherness and a flow of information from the family office to the family. Either is responsible for the shared family reunion days and can work to ensure that the ascension of family members into the family office is transparent and handled according to the negotiated policies.

The charter also gives information about employment, remuneration, dividends and the rights and obligations of each individual family member. These topics have direct influence on the personal happiness of each owner: How satisfied is a family member in the position that he holds in the family office? What level of involvement must each shareholder have with the family office? What dividend levels are necessary at an individual level to live from?

'Being happy' here means belonging to a strong community to which one can contribute and within which one can grow. For this reason, the family charter offers opportunities for each individual to join bodies like the advisory council, become a member of the investment council, or an active owner, family manager, organizer of the family reunion weekends or the controller for the family office.

Practical Tip: Understanding the Family Constitution

Tailor the content of a family charter to your specific family: It can be framed as short and concise or long and comprehensive, whatever is needed. It allows the family to come to agreement on the factors that ensure preservation of the family wealth. The terms are formulated through workshops, interviews and written drafts. Family leaders and family members should be included in this process to reassure the different constituencies that their interests are being represented. The actual composition of the family constitution is best handled with the support of a family office specialist.

Clarify the process for composing a family constitution: A family constitution is a document signed by the owners that encompasses all strategies, structures and rules that provide guidance to the comportment of the regular shareholders and family leaders. It documents the vision and values that determine the leadership of the family office. It defines the goals of the family office, as well as for the family itself, and establishes the investment and corporate strategy. It defines decision-making processes and documents the fundamental underlying principles. It defines the roles of the family within the family office and boosts the engagement on the part of the family members. With that said, it does not resolve any conflicts. It merely provides an instrument for constructive problem resolution.

The checklist in Table 7.1 will help you review whether the most important topics for a family constitution have been defined for the families, the family office and their wealth.

Table 7.1 Family constitution checklist

	Yes	No
Vision		
The vision, values and objectives for the family office are clearly defined		
The vision, values and objectives for the family are clearly defined		
The owners have defined in writing their expectations for and their commitment to the family office		
Family Strategy		
Clear rules have been put in place about which obligations family leaders have toward the family office		
All owners have committed in writing who they wish to inherit their joint and individual assets in the family office, as well as their individual private assets (such as through deeds of gift, wills or inheritance deeds)		
The appointment of the managing director for the family office is conducted through a fair and defined decision-making process		
Clear rules are in place for family members regarding the qualifications, skills and experience they must possess to work in the family office		
Successors to the leadership ranks of the family office from the next generation of the family have a suitable individual leadership development plan		
The departure of the retiring party from leadership of the family office has been planned in detail and documented		
Rules for removing the executive managers of the family office in the event of poor performance and non-attainment of goals are defined and will be triggered if such a situation actually arises		
Clear rules are defined for employment by family members for non-executive levels in the family office		
The awarding of contracts to family members by the family office is clearly regulated (conditions, decision-making processes)		
The assets are organized so that clear decision-making paths and responsibilities are in place		
The assets are clearly structured so as to reduce the complexity of ownership by the family		
Asset and investment strategies are defined		
Clear rules are defined regarding the services that members of the family can draw from the family office (such as personal security, car, mobile phone, insurance, etc.)		
Clear rules are in place as to how information flows to the family about the state of the family office and the development of the investments, as well as extraordinary events		
Supplemental communications media (such as newsletter, intranet) are established		
Family office governance		
Written policies are in place as to who can become owner of the asset in the family office		

(*continued*)

Table 7.1 (continued)

	Yes	No
Rights and obligations of the owners of the family office are codified in writing		
The procedures for buying, selling, gifting and bequeathing shares in the family office are comprehensively regulated		
Dividend/withdrawal options are comprehensively regulated		
The responsibility of the advisory council/oversight board (appointment and removal of executives, consulting and monitoring) are defined and implemented		
The process for appointing the advisory and oversight council members and the members of the investment council is clearly regulated and also accounts for minority owners		
It is clearly established that non-family members are appointed to the advisory/oversight council and investment council		
A qualifications profile for members of the advisory/oversight council and investment council has been clearly defined and is reviewed on a regular basis		
There are clearly established rules on how executive meetings are conducted in the family office to ensure that it runs effectively (number, information, decision-making process, agenda)		
A clearly defined professional and personal qualifications profile is in place for executive positions in the family office		
Compensation for the executives of the family office is clearly defined (including pegging to long-term growth and value appreciation targets)		
A sufficient number of meetings is held to harmonize and make decisions within the executive team of the family office, and participants in those meetings agree to proceed constructively		
The responsibilities for executives of the family office are clearly defined and do not overlap, with their corresponding decision-making processes clearly defined		
Comprehensive Directors and Officers insurance is in place for all members of the advisor and oversight council and all members of the investment council		
Risk, compliance and controlling systems are in place; these organs report to the advisory council/oversight council and the investment council		
Family Governance		
A family council and/or a family manager is put into place to address the central issues for the family		
The family chooses joint activities (such as family reunion days or weekends, young future owner days) and ensures that these are actually conducted		
Processes for the next generation to acquire its share of the wealth are defined (such as through a junior advisory council or get-togethers and continuing education)		
Clearly defined resolution mechanisms are in place should conflicts arise		
The owner family has professional structures in place to conduct its charitable engagement		
A family fund or family bank supports family members with special conditions for the implementation of their own entrepreneurial projects		

Developed by/copyright Alexander Koeberle-Schmid

7.2 Family Activities to Reinforce Cohesion

Belonging to a strong family contributes directly to one's sense of happiness. There is a certain joy unlike any other in meeting up with cousins at birthdays, holidays, religious ceremonies and weddings. Each successful celebration within the family circle helps reduce any feelings that one is only participating in such events out of a sense of obligation.

In growing families, the distance between the individual members inevitably increases. Individual paths are pursued and separate families are founded. Attitudes, lifestyles, generations, degrees of relation and living spaces vary. Families with a family office do have certain advantages over 'normal' families. Namely: the large-scale shared project that is the successful operation of a family office. Most owning families desire fervently that affluence be passed on to the next generation. No matter how large a given individual's share of the overall fortune might be or his or her attitude toward the family: Association brings with it rights and obligations—such as the right to information and dividends or the obligation to conclude prenuptial agreements.

Strengthening the "Family Glue"

Over the generations, as the number of claimants to the wealth grow, their shared emotional connections tend to diminish. Family members regard each other more and more frequently as co-investors. Steps are needed to counteract this by promoting internal cohesion and burnishing identification with the family and the family office. One option are joint activities, organized either strictly as leisure events or within the context of the family fortune.

Family activities to strengthen the "glue of the family" can be as diverse as the family itself. Here are a few examples:

- **Family gatherings**: The extended circle of owners includes spouses, life companions and children who are not shareholders. This community is often very large, and in many cases is best served through an annual family gathering. The family gathering has no rights or obligations in a strict sense, but it is often used as an occasion to provide family members with important information about the family office. They are informed about strategies and new developments of the investment of the family office, and discussion is encouraged.
- **Events accompanying the family office shareholder meeting**: Supplemental events can serve to bring together the shareholders outside the framework of the meeting itself and open up a valuable informal forum to pose questions

(*continued*)

(continued)

to the family office executive team. In many cases a specific amount of time is reserved for open questions. The program of events also typically includes a shared dinner or "morning pint" on the next day, with all family members invited. A separate set of activities is offered for all those not invited to the shareholders meeting or Q&A session because they are not official owners of the family office. For larger shareholder groups, regional meetings can be held during the year, including reports by the family office executives on past and future developments.

- **Family reunions and family weekends**: The goal here is to encourage shared fun, become better acquainted and help the different members engage in conversations across generations. One fixed weekend a year is picked, potentially for its importance to the founder of the company, and all family members are expected to be present. The range of options is virtually limitless: concert trips, rafting tours, sailing excursions, ropes courses, joint cocktail mixing classes, rugby matches—virtually anything that is a fun, shared experience that can't simply be bought and which leaves fond memories. For this same reason, a sport like golf, which breaks people into small groups, may be less appropriate. These weekends can then be tied to trips to the businesses the family is invested in and the family office, such as for a presentation of new strategies, analysis of asset development and amendments to the family constitution.

Planning and Organization of Family Activities

The family office, under the leadership of the family manager or family council, often handles the planning and organization of the family activities. The family manager plans out the key elements of the individual events, coordinates with other family members and then transfers operative execution to the family office.

A family intranet aids internal communication between family members, and in the process promotes the cohesiveness of the family. It also makes it easier to organize joint activities and continuing education measures. The family office can issue invitations to events via the family intranet and send reports and photos. Information about recent corporate or portfolio trends can be posted, as can decisions by the advisory council and recommendations of the investment committee. Discussion forums can be established for questions to be posed to the family office. Whether it is newsletters, birthday greetings, a family tree or photos from the first steps of a new family member—any occasion to encourage dialog among the family members and between family and family office and establish the basis for mutual trust and esteem is welcome.

7.3 Involving Succeeding Generations: Continuing Education within the Family

Are owners, parents and children informed about the doings of the family office? Do they have questions such as: What and how much do we own? What were Grandfather's goals and values back then—and what about now? How can I rise to become an executive in the family office? Can I work in some other part of the family office? What experience must I have? Who is responsible for professional monitoring of the family office? Where do we stand overall in terms of financials, assets, yields and risks? Which yield benchmarks are used to assess the performance of our family office? Who is allowed to attend shareholder meetings? What happens if I have a difference of opinion with a cousin? Which family gatherings must I attend? And what's the procedure should one of the executives die unexpectedly?

Continuing educational measures are an effective tool as families grow. They allow each family member to further his or her own development, to live up to his or her responsibility to be an informed member of a wealthy family and to ask critical questions about decisions made by the family officer and the consequences of such decisions.

The path to becoming a responsible member of a wealthy family often traverses the following components:

- Wealthy individuals behave responsibly by teaching their children **the benefits and obligations of affluence and how to behave objectively, intelligently and responsibly when arguing with others.** Imagine for example a change of strategy that would necessitate suspending dividends for several years. The best chance for achieving acceptance for this measure is to ensure that all affected parties understand the reasons behind it. A medium term drop in stock values is easier to weather if the asset allocation and individual investments are better understood. A responsibility-minded member of a wealthy family has faith in the future of the family and the family office. Entrepreneurship and investment knowledge are important to him or her. Mutual respect as well as self-realization are important topics. He or she is constantly developing, but not in ways that threaten the family or its fortune. Because he or she is happy to be a member of the family.
- **He can competently assess consultants and managers.** He can distinguish between those consultants that act in their own interest and in those who act in the interest of the owners and the family. He has a good understanding of the motives of the other. And he encourages others to openly voice their opinion to get honest feedback.

(*continued*)

(continued)

- **He is good at establishing connections with other family members** and willingly helps other family members develop. He also has a good sense of which topics could potentially flare up into conflict and addresses them before they can ignite.
- **She is prepared to invest in the future of the family office.** She incorporates spouses and life partners actively into this effort. She attempts to make solid decisions to the benefit of the long-term wealth growth. She behaves consistently and holds herself accountable. And she obeys the rules laid out in the family constitution.

Those capable of embodying these ideals are truly exemplary and responsible wealthy individuals. Continuing education measures for the members of the family should help engender the following characteristics in the successor generation in particular:

- promoting entrepreneurial and investment thought
- development of responsible, dedicated, duty-minded and knowledgeable high net worth individuals
- informing and involving the next generation
- protecting the family's assets
- developing the next generation of committee members

Continuing education helps the family members be clear about their goals and their future roles. Career options can be discussed and tested. Beyond this, skills and competencies that can't be learned at school or university can be acquired. This promotes greater self-confidence and esteem when dealing with other family members, their interests and objectives.

Practical Example: Families Keep Learning Together

Once per year, the "Next Gen" descendants of a family can come together for an investment tour to prepare for their future role as owners of their family office. The cousins have already visited three firms in which they hold a minority investment, viewing the production line and talking to the executives of the companies. Next year they'll head to France and the year after that they will travel with their families to the USA to view other firms they are invested in, to get to know the American management team, talk with other American owner families and to visit a conference on family offices.

(*continued*)

(continued)

A family academy run by another family that owns a publicly held company and a family office offers a well-crafted continuing education program for its roughly 70 shareholders under the age of 30, all from the fifth and sixth generation. Twice per year the next generation runs through a sample set of questions of the type that can arise in the family business or the family office, all under the watchful eye of family office specialists and managers from the business or the family office. There are also other courses offered at regular intervals by an experienced auditor. Participants learn how to read documents such as balance sheets, P&L calculations and the annual report. There are also stipends available each year for family business programs at renowned universities in Switzerland and the USA. A junior advisory council is formed with selected young owners, preparing them for their monitoring duties in the advisory board.

A family-owned financial investment firm, founded in 1876, is today home to 1900 employees in four countries. It was bought out in 2010. In the aftermath of that event, the family had to re-establish its bonds. Because of the way the family branches were organized, the young family members hardly knew each other, and in fact knew little about the business itself. The family office, founded in 2015, was also completely foreign to them. To remedy this, the entire class of descendants aged 15 to 35 were invited to tour the various subsidiaries and learn about the history of the firm, conflict management, rhetoric, balance sheets, asset investment, controlling, finance, governance and team building.

A different family sold its legacy business 14 years ago and now manages its assets via its single family office. It designed a comprehensive continuing education program that all family members are expected to complete. The next round of the program involves the presentation of a dashboard that will provide the shareholders, who currently live in various locations around the globe, with access to up-to-date data on their investment portfolio at any time. The primary focus is on conveying a proper understanding of the figures.

Topics for Continuing Education

Continuing education varies in nature and style from family to family. It may be that for a small family all that is needed are regular sessions to bring all members up to date, with individual members then free to seek out advanced training as needed from external coaches. For larger families, it can be an extra boost to the "family glue" to institutionalize the continuing education of its next generation owners. Regardless of the size of the family, the following steps should be taken when establishing a continuing education program for the family, all supported by the family office:

- Raising the competency level of the family members in accordance with their age and querying each individual's continuing educational objectives
- Developing a core competency profile for family members in the various age classes
- Establishing different audiences within the family
- Defining education goals for specific audiences and then discussing these with the family members
- Developing education programs for specific age groups
- Conducting education courses and assessing feedback on an ongoing basis
- Adjustments to individual education course based on feedback and changing framework conditions (content, method, materials)
- Reviewing education goals and adjusting the continuing education program

The continuing education program is targeted at the owners, partners of all owners and their children, i.e. the next generation, which is typically not employed in the family office or in one of the firms the family is invested in. The greater the degree to which they are integrated, the greater their satisfaction and trust in the leadership of the family office. Figure 7.1 shows which concrete information can be conveyed.

Wealth-related knowledge	**Ownership knowledge**
• Stock exchange • Wealth analysis, structuring, management and controlling • Balance sheet and controlling – evaluation of financial, asset, profit and risk situations • General legal, taxation, inheritance law • Business management and strategy basics	• Succession • Family business governance • Conflict dynamics • Multi-generation development paths for families • Assessment of managers and consultants
Knowledge of own family	**Personal knowledge**
• The history of the family, the company and family office, including key events • Current strategy, technological, financial and investment challenges • Future market developments • Annual statements with additional balance sheet background • Asset situation, with explanatory reports	• Career paths (personal aptitudes and interests) • Health (physical activity, nutrition, mental strength) • Education

Fig. 7.1 Potential continuing education options for families

A good example of this includes continuing education programs for young future shareholders. These typically cover descendants ranging from 15 to 30 years of age who would benefit from instruction on life as responsible wealthy individuals. The youths and young adults should be trained on how to research information on their own and to interpret and assess corporate and asset-related information: What are methods for understanding the accounting data from companies in general and the reporting from the family office? What special elements are at play in family offices? What are the different asset classes and how is a risk-optimized portfolio constructed? A stock exchange simulation is conceivable. And naturally this younger generation will be interested in hearing the history and traditions of the family. They learn about their rights and obligations and how they can apply their own personal strengths to boost the family and the family office. Rhetoric, role-playing workshops and conflict management are other potential topics.

The succeeding generation will also surely have interest in performing a practical internship in the family office or at one of the companies the family is invested in. This can occur either while in secondary school or university. The juniors familiarize themselves with the bankers, service providers, family officers, the investment strategy and how various specific asset picks are assessed. The potential inheritors also see first-hand the level of dedication on the part of the employees in their work to preserve and grow the family's wealth.

The family officer can serve either as a coordinator or an organizer for these family continuing education events. An education committee, the family council or the family manager provide advice and ensure acceptance by the family. The family office helps with the scheduling, planning, organization and execution of the education events, the mailing of invitations and regular notification of the individual family members.

Practical Tip: Manage Continuing Education for the Family More Professionally via the Family Office

- Involve the family members and imbue them with co-responsibility for the strategic orientation of the continuing education program.
- Establish a continuing education committee and integrate it into the governance.
- Orient the continuing educational program toward the goals of the family and the family office.
- Tweak the continuing education program on an ongoing basis
- Recruit specialists as speakers for the individual educational measures.

7.4 Achieving Personal Goals Through Coaching

The family office can serve as an advisor and a mentor, or potentially also as a coach for the members of the family. Coaching is always understood as a partnership through which a family member draws support in achieving personal and professional goals. Coaching is also relevant to holding a role in the family office, as well as within the family and as a wealthy individual.

Coaching involves an active learning and modification of attitudes and behaviors. Family members who enter into a program of coaching can learn how to improve their own performance and quality of life. In the sessions, the family member seeking support (coachee) determines the topics of exploration. The coach listens intently and observes the coachee's behavior, and then poses well-considered questions. Through this process, the coachee gains a comprehensive understanding of himself and his role in the complex world of the family and the family office. The coachee is in a position to become active and to make the changes necessary to achieve his goals. This might be a satisfactory position in the family office, or engagement as an active, devoted owner, or finding a way to follow his or her individual calling, such as by becoming a doctor, artist or manager of another company.

Coaching can also be helpful in a variety of other situations, such as positioning the family to aid the family officer when decisions need to be made, in improving leadership skills or in bettering interactions among siblings. It can help wealthy individuals become clear in their goals and strategies in terms of the family office. But not only that—the potential avenues of support through coaching are manifold, as it always involves how a coachee can reach his personal goals more quickly through the help of a coach.

Practical Tip: Coaching for Successors

A set of best-practice coaching questions has been developed for family members interested in rising to a posting in the family office. Before individual answers can be formulated, however, one overarching question must first be answered: Do you really wish to join the family office as an employee or even executive or not?

Identity: Being Yourself

- Vision and Values: How do you envision your life (dreams, goals, wishes)? How do you intend to reach your goals (mission)? What values drive you? What attitudes are preventing you from reaching your goal?

(continued)

(continued)

- Interests: What are your personal interests? How can you implement these in the family office?
- Competencies: What type of things do you find easy? Where can you apply your competencies (within the family office) in an especially effective way?
- Knowledge and experience: What knowledge do you need to enter properly into the family office? What knowledge and experiences do you still wish to acquire?
- With reference to the family office: What do the family's wealth and the family office mean for you (especially in terms of working in the family office): Obligation, opportunity or calling? How do you view others in the family office? How do you handle the fear of failure (including existential angst)?

Leadership: For You and Others

- Leadership: What does leadership mean to you? What messages would you want to send to your co-workers? How would you wish to position yourself in the family office? Where does your motivation come from, and how you focus it in difficult situations?
- Leadership style: What is your leadership style, how does it differ from that of your predecessor and how do you bring your own style to bear? How would you imagine delegating work contracts, jobs and responsibility? How would you go about making good decisions?
- Public speaking, difficult situations: How convincing are you when talking before a group? How can you escape when backed into a corner? How do you handle failure (in the family office)?
- Pressure, stress and health: How do you handle stress and pressure without sacrificing your health?
- First 100 days: What would you want to do in the first 100 days of your work as a family member working in the family office? What would you want to do in the first 100 days of your work as a managing director or CEO?
- Rituals and symbols: Which rituals and symbols are important for you to be accepted as the next family officer? How should the transfer be communicated?
- Negotiation of hiring: What is the best way to negotiate your contract and remuneration with your father, with the shareholders?
- Free time, small family, work/life balance: How will you establish a healthy balance between your nuclear family, your free time, your work, the larger family of owners, your family office, and the relevant stakeholders? How will you ensure that you are truly present for your partner/spouse, children and parents?

Interaction: Positioning Yourself in the Power Structure

- Dynamic between family office and family: Which internal forces and expectations in the family office and the family do you face, and how to you channel these appropriately? What do your siblings do, and how does that fit their goals and visions?

(*continued*)

(continued)

- Power and networks: Who holds the informal power? Who supports them? Who undermines them? How do you intend to position yourself in the power structure? How can you build up networks, and how can these persons be of help for you? How would you handle a potential 'sandwich' situation if you're already a shareholder and work on the level just below the uppermost tier of the family office?
- Collaboration: How might you handle the change in stature that will result in the move into an executive decision, when your former colleagues suddenly must acknowledge you as Mr. Brewer, not just Frank? How would you improve the cooperation within the executive management team?
- Conflict and conflict management: How do you handle conflicts with your managers, your colleagues, with employees, with family members and with your predecessor? How can you improve your ability to manage conflict and promote your desired solutions?
- Relationship with predecessor: What expectations do you have from the retiring party? Which concessions are you willing to make for them? How will you establish a collaboration of trust with them? What do you hope to gain from your predecessor, and what not? How do you handle competition between you and your predecessor? How can your predecessor make you a success? How would you inform your predecessor that you only need his counsel when requested?
- Criticism, praise and recognition: How do you understand criticism, recognition, estimation and self-realization for yourself and for your predecessor? How do you demand recognition and estimation?
- Training as a successor: How can you grow interest for the family office in your children?

Strategy and Implementation: Driving Yourself and the Family Office Forward

- Career development: Where are you currently in your life? What would be a suitable career move for you now? How do you design your development plan for your activity in the family office?
- Create something new, blaze a trail: Follow in the footsteps of your predecessor or go your own way and deviate from the model—what's your preference? How can you bring your family office into modern times? What resources and what support do you need to be successful in your work in the family office?

Practical Tip: Coaching for the Person Ceding Power

A different set of questions are used for the family owner or family member ceding power in the family office. The following topics and questions have been drawn from the extensive experience in coaching persons preparing to cede power in companies and family offices to the next generation. The effort of formulating responses to these questions can help the transition run more smoothly:

"Me": Being Instead of Having

- Identity: What would you have done with yourself if you'd decided to exit the family office at some earlier point? Who will you be after handing over leadership? What will still make you special?
- Values and self-worth: Which values are important to you? Are the things you've achieved sufficient too?
- Sensibility: What should the people who matter to you say about you in the period after you've left the family office?
- Reflection on lessons: What lessons would you like to further explore? Which of their topics captivate you, and what do they mean for you?
- Living environment: Where and how do you wish to live (together) in the future?
- Loss: How do you practice the "ability to let it go?" How can you say an effective goodbye to your current work? Why is there doubt that you ultimately won't/can't hand over power?
- Past: What topics do you feel you need to gain clarity on for yourself?

Behavior: Doing Sensible Things and Intentionally Staying Hands-Off with Others

- Dreams: Do you still have unachieved dreams? If yes, what are they?
- Goals: Which goals do you have for yourself in the coming years? How can you make your life simpler (do less) yet deeper (more intense)?
- Concerns: Which fears do you have about working less or no longer work in the family office? How are you coping with them?
- Qualities: What qualities have you shown over the course of your work in the family office? How will you bring these qualities with you so that they are still part of your life going forward?
- Work outside the family office: How can you enjoy "nice things" without feeling the pressure to work and earn money? What jobs do you want to do, including of an entrepreneurial nature? To which organizations do you want to apply your expertise and know-how? Which passions and interests do you want to pursue (together), which leisure activities do you want to explore (together) after the completion of your family office work?
- Integration into the family office: What influence do you hope to still have after the transfer of power in the family office? Which information do you hope to receive regularly from the family office? When do you want to have a say in decisions? Which role(s) do you want to adopt in the family office, and for how long?

(*continued*)

(continued)

- Health care: How can you ensure that your body and mind are healthy and fit?
- Financial security: What liquidity and financial nest egg do you require? How are you shielding yourself against financial loss?
- Timing: What timing is appropriate for the different parts of the transition process?

Interaction: Societal "Warming" and Being Proud

- Caring society: How do you want to help other people (including financially)? Which voluntary work appeals to you still?
- Family activities: Which tasks would you like to handle for the immediate and extended family? Which family obligations would you like to fulfill?
- Partner/spouse: What do you mean to each other? What would you like to experience with your partner? How would you like to support one another?
- Interplay with successor: Is your successor ready to accept power, and will he? How will you handle the fact that your child will soon rank above you in the family office? How can you pass on your knowledge without strings? How do you offer esteem, and how would you expect to be shown respect?

From the USA: "The family and family office needed to have a broader voice if it was going to be sustainable."

Interview with Larry Donckers

This interview touches on the pluses and minuses of strong leadership from a legacy business, the challenges of getting buy-in on family (self)-governance, and strategies for involving later generations.

This interview was conducted by Peter Preller.

Were you involved with the family office from the beginning?
Larry Donckers: Yes. The family's operating company, a stevedoring business, was founded in 1949. The family decided to sell a minority interest to an infrastructure fund in 2007 so that the business finally had shareholders with resources and so that the family had resources with which to diversify and further advance its long term estate and gift planning. That sale and its proceeds was the genesis to create the family office.

At that time, my primary role with the family was at the operating company in various financial functions. They gave me the opportunity to start the family office with the family leadership, or stay with the operating company. I obviously choose to start the family office with the family principals in 2007, and it's been a learning experience from the get-go.

Larry Donckers *is Vice President and General Manager of Progeny 3, Inc., a single-family office established in 2007, following the sale of a minority interest in the Smith-Hemingway family's operating businesses. He assisted the family in establishing Progeny 3, Inc., and is responsible for the office operations on a day-to-day basis and is a member of the family's Investment Committee.*

Within the family office community, he is a member of the Family Office Exchange's Executive Council, the Wigmore Association, and represents Progeny 3 as a director and founding member of the Private Investor Coalition, a national advocacy group comprised of single family offices based in Washington D.C. He has been a member of the board of directors of the local chapter of the Financial Executives Institute and remains a member of the Washington Society of CPA's and the AICPA.

Was it a difficult process to shepherd the family along?

LD: I think one of the advantages I had is that the family had been managing the operating company business for three generations, so they understood the concepts of governance, leadership and what they hoped to achieve with the family office because of the experiences they gained in an operating company business.

I personally think of a family office as being a small business in many respects. You really have to plan in advance of the governance and consider the structures you want to have in place and need to establish. How involved will the family principals be? Do you want to develop in-house resources or outsource services?

There's a myriad of questions you need to give thought to and then have very deliberate thinking in terms of what you want that office to become and the types of services you expect to offer—who you're serving, how many generations, how many households, how you deliver the services. All those types of considerations and many more come into play. What I've learned is that it is an evolutionary process to an extent. Initially you plan for core services but over time, ancillary services and managing client relationships become equally important.

Were family governance regulations or a family charter discussed from the first moment or was it more of an evolution?

LD: It really was an evolutionary process with the president and CEO of the family office, a family member from the third generation providing the direction. He provided the vision for the family office and was also responsible for managing the family's operating business as its CEO.

I worked together with him to implement the structure he had in mind along with other family leaders, which was very helpful in terms of what he saw as the vision for the family office and the governance the family wanted to establish. Early on, he understood what resources we wanted to have in-house. As an example, he realized the benefits of building an experienced and professional core group and eventually having an internal CIO investment team so that the family could better manage and control investment decisions.

It also worked in our favor that we were very deliberate and thoughtful about deploying the cash from the sale. We were very patient. You may recall that 2007 and 2008 were very challenging times for investments. It was fortuitous that we were slow to invest the family's capital.

Was the slow pace intentional?

LD: Yes, in a way. We wanted to understand all the various types of investments that were pitched to us, even though he was well-versed given his background both as an attorney and a CPA, plus, he was experienced and savvy in terms of managing a global company. Nonetheless, it was a good decision to pace ourselves.

On the governance side, we've made good progress, but we didn't have a family charter or a constitution at this time. The family initially developed a mission statement. And that was one of the first family office achievements that involved many other family members.

What discussion was held with the family members about involvement? The options range from totally involved to not involved at all. And what about the next generation?

LD: We knew it was important to get the family involved in the process, so in terms of governance, the mission statement was developed fairly early on. They also developed what I would call a set of "white papers" on a variety of topics. For example, family-related documents that captured the expectations of family members—participation, communication, how to become good stewards of their wealth—many elements that are pieces of a family charter or a family constitution, but less formal at this stage by design, to provide a narrative and context to describe the family's values.

So, much of our progress has been an evolutionary process. This past year, just after our tenth anniversary of the family office, the family established a family council. It's a pool of representatives that includes spouses, the next generation—many key elements that are so important and vital to the sustainability of the family office.

This broader participation of family members didn't happen right away. Decision-making for the family within the operating company was long led by my boss (G3), who remains as the chairman of the operating company, together with his uncle (G2). They currently serve as trustees of the family trusts that represents majority ownership of the operating company, and provided the liquidity created from the partial sale. With the success of the family's business and the confidence gained from family members to manage the company, it's no surprise that they were leading the charge and direction of the family office. So that's been an evolutionary process in terms of elements of the governance and family transition outside of managing the company.

The person driving the growth of a huge business can often have a dominant personality. Transitioning leadership to the rest of the family can sometimes be a problem. What is your experience in this area?

LD: Transition can certainly be a challenge. In our case, we have a family member who took over management of the business at a very young age from his uncle and grew it internationally. They have 250 locations throughout the world, so he really expanded the business and gained an enormous amount of experience in those circles and representing the family, which had ultimate confidence in him.

But at some point you have to transition. And they've done a very good job of planning as they have a succession plan in place for the trustees. And then there's the family council, a concept I've been supporting for several years. It's terrific to see it established because that will give them a broader base for family participation and developing relationships among the next generation, which is spread out, both in age and geographic location.

As the family continues to grow, relationships will change and it will become more difficult and challenging to build the same types of relationships among cousins than among the previous generation.

Is the family council one person or several persons?
LD: The family has set up a governance structure around the council. In the lead up to its formation, several outside advisors spoke about governance structures, levels of authority and decision making, and other family offices also shared their experiences. At the end of the day, the family decided that the council shall consist of seven members and be cross-generational. Currently, there's members from G3 and G4 that comprise the council….

So the council consists of family members?
LD: Yes, including spouses.

How do you educate the next, and later generations about why the SFO is a useful thing, from an economical point of view—sharing costs and teaming on investments and also non-financial aspects?
LD: That is clearly one of the challenges of communicating with the next generation and creating deeper relationships. As a family office, we currently have those types of relationships with the third generation. They were involved when the family office was created, that's where the wealth lies, and in many ways, we've grown and evolved together.

This next generation is busy with their lives … starting families, going to college, or seeking and starting their first job. To be quite honest, we've got a lot of work to do in that area, in how we express and communicate our value proposition. We need to create and take advantage of opportunities to connect with the next generation. As an example, in 2016 we had a family gathering with all generations and everyone met over a weekend. It was one of the first times that we had an opportunity to share family office experiences, investment portfolio information, services provided and topics like that at a very high level with the next gens. It was an opportunity to make it interesting.

And that went off very well. It was also a first step that ultimately led to the development of the family council. I think with the council, there's a lot of opportunity to deepen those relationships. But it's going to take work, a collaborative effort on the part of the family and the family office.

Was it tough to convince the family of the need for a family council? After all, it involves time and effort.

LD: Yes, absolutely. There has been very strong leadership in the family over several generations. From the current CEO of the family office who started the family office with the vision and very strong patriarchal leadership along with his uncle, there was an unrecognized need to broaden participation. And I think part of the challenge was conveying how important it was … they always spoke with one voice in managing the operating company for generations, even though there were two family trusts set up, one for each family branch.

And here, the challenge was that the family really needed to think about having a broader voice if the family office was going to be sustainable over multiple generations.

So, while it was a process that took some time for family leadership to buy in to the concept of a family council, and then develop distinct lines of authority between family matters and those of the family's operating business, the benefits that a family council could provide have been wholly supported. And that was critical, I think, to getting approval.

I'm very proud of the family members who stepped up to launch the family council. I participated as an ad-hoc member to support a family steering committee that spent close to a year developing the framework and criteria of their family council initiative and presented it to the second and third generations to get their buy-in prior to launch. It took considerable guidance from advisors, discussion and internal meetings to find answers and obtain a consensus to questions like: "What is a family?" "What are the documents that we want to have to govern this council?" … all the different situations that might come up and for those that haven't been identified.

It's been a long, but rewarding process. The family held their first family council meeting in December. We're all very green to this and new to the process, but I think it's going to have tremendous benefits in the years and generations to come.

What challenges have already emerged?

LD: For any family council to function, you need participation. And once you get started, you need to make sure that the members don't lose interest. You've got to keep that momentum going. Perhaps the CEO realized that the family wasn't ready in the beginning when the family office was first created. It does take time for the family to adjust to the idea … that's another aspect that is equally important.

Now the challenge is to keep it moving forward. So that's where we are now, making sure we keep the momentum. And it's a lot of work.

Does the structure of the family office support this effort?
LD: Yes, it absolutely does. We're very much an investment-centric office. It all starts with client relationships and the structure of the family's investment vehicles. There are two primary family trusts, one for each family branch and those create the glue for us in terms of the beneficiaries and our investment policies.

There is also a third entity, an LLC, that consists of a number of clients, as individual family members of the LLC. These individual family members could take distributions from the LLC and reinvest with another advisor. Consequently, we're at risk with those member accounts. This recognition relates directly to my earlier comments regarding communication of our value proposition and deepening client relationships.

What pressure does that put on you as the family officer to educate?
LD: We have to take proactive measures. We have to do things to put ourselves in front of that generation and demonstrate how the family office creates value, and to deepen those relationships. As an example, we publish an annual report each year. The report has evolved along with the office itself, and at this stage, I would say it's equal to many public companies' annual reports. The content reflects a collaboration among family leadership and office management. It's a glossy, professionally bound report. And this past year we created two supplements to accompany the core report.

The first section is a family report. There are lots of photos, a higher level of reporting that's intended for a broader family audience. Its content reflects on family gatherings throughout the year, how they participated, how philanthropy is progressing.

The second section is the core report. That's more about the family office performance itself, in terms of our departmental reports, milestones, strategic office goals—although we all have individual goals as well. In this section we report on our progress toward the office's strategic goals versus individual ones.

And the third section is the appendix, which consists of details about our individual employee goals and financial details on the operating company and the family office operating results.

These three supplements comprise our annual report to the family—perhaps 200 pages in the aggregate—each section is in-depth and has become something that we publish regularly and many use as a resource throughout the year. That's just one example to demonstrate value, but one we are proud of and one that requires a significant number of hours from many employees and family members alike.

How do you manage the different risk adversity of the family members? The fifth generation's shares will be smaller than for the third's. How do you manage the fact that some persons could be more risk averse than others within your allocation or the investments you do?

LD: In terms of different investment risks and tolerances: that is something that we've needed to address. Due to the terms in the family trusts, they are considered pot trusts, not individual shares, and thus we had neither the ability nor the need to do that. And only in the last couple of years through the third entity (LLC) that I mentioned previously, where individual member shares exist, did we recently develop individual investment silos to relate to their individual risk tolerances and liquidity needs. And so that's what we've been able to accomplish—provide different and individual asset allocations and investment risk options within that entity. This will be a model that we expect to carry forward to provide additional solutions for our family clients.

Bibliography

Koeberle-Schmid A, Kenyon-Rouvinez D, Poza E (2014) Governance in family enterprises. Palgrave Macmillan, Basingstoke, Hampshire

8

Effective Structuring of Philanthropic Engagement

Alexander Koeberle-Schmid

There are many different ways for affluent families to engage in charity. Some opt to donate to social or regional projects; others prefer establishing a family-run foundation or non-profit company. Differentiation should however be made between the family's private philanthropic engagement and a corporation's commitment to Corporate Social Responsibility (CSR), for families where there is still a legacy company alongside the family office. CSR is frequently a matter of external communication. Philanthropic engagement, by contrast, is typically conducted privately by individuals or a family, making it more appropriate as a function of the family office. In some cases it is even spun off completely from the family office and established as its own legal entity, such as a charitable foundation.

Charitable engagement by families can come from a variety of motivations: sometimes it derives from a desire on the part of the successful to support the disadvantaged. There are many benefits to establishing a charitable foundation: the entire family can be integrated into the foundation's work, which promotes a greater sense of family identity and cohesion. The foundation can also provide an early opportunity to introduce the next generation to the concept of entrepreneurial responsibility. Descendants can gain a practical outlet for their work, with direct positive feedback in an environment where they experience the value of contribution. It can also give younger family members their first real experience in handling money, helping introduce the importance of managing wealth.

Philanthropic engagement works best when there is a shared common goal. Perhaps the original company founder favored a particular cause, such as

B. Canessa et al., *The Family Office*, https://doi.org/10.1007/978-3-319-99085-9_8

improving access to water in an African country. The next generation can adopt this mission as their own, even after the sale of the company and the application of the sale proceeds to the family office. Or the decision may be made to move on to a different communal goal. What matters is that all family members get behind one major goal and avoid dissipating their energies among too many different projects.

Practical Example: Different Paths to Philanthropic Engagement

Shortly after his 60th birthday, a second-generation entrepreneur received an offer from an American investor. It was an opportunity he simply couldn't let pass by, as he wasn't certain whether one of his four children would follow him into the family business. After the sale, he founded a family office to manage the family's wealth. From time to time the entrepreneur and his wife would engage actively in charitable causes from his region.

When his youngest daughter moved out, it was time to bring a more rigorous structure to their informal philanthropic schedule. A foundation seemed the right choice as a hub to reinforce the binds between the disparate family members, while also promoting the company founder's ideals. Today, that foundation is managed by the four children and supports troubled youths and refugees in underprivileged regions with issues such as vocational training. The goal is to help build the perspectives the disadvantaged need to take control of their own lives. Through their work in the foundation, the four children learned how to work together on a project, including meetings on a regular basis despite the geographical distance between them. A small internal competition even arose as they sought to show which project could produce the best results. For their father, this social engagement is no less important than wealth management or even the family office itself. The children have learned what it means to handle wealth and the impact it can achieve.

The charitable foundation of another affluent business-owning family was founded in 1995. The structures are clearly regulated, with tasks and responsibilities transparently established. The family dictates the financial framework and established a vision for what kind of projects should be taken on. There is a six-person board of trustees, comprised primarily from family members. The chairman is an expert in foundations who works for multiple charitable organizations. He serves as the liaison between the family and the board of directors. The board of trustees conveys the family's vision into a philanthropic strategy that can then be planned, implemented and reviewed by the foundation's board of directors. A catalog of criteria is used to select and promote projects. This is an important prerequisite for ensuring transparency in decisions by either the board of directors or board of trustees. It is supplemented by requirements profiles for the responsible parties within the committees. There must be clarity within the family about the various roles, as this forms the basis for constructive collaboration dedicated to the common good. It also helps avoid the perception that family members who for whatever reason do not rise to a role in the company's management are merely shunted off to posts in the foundation.

Concepts and Strategies for Philanthropic Engagement

It is important that the family office or a philanthropic consultant works together with the family to tailor a concept for the family's philanthropic engagement. This process can take place in stages, depending on the starting situation and ultimate goals. What ultimately matters is that a sustainable process be selected—which projects are truly likely to improve the lives of others, which beneficiaries are intended, etc. For this reason, the motivation of the family should be considered in terms of why and how they wish to become philanthropically active.

Wealthy individuals should consider the following questions as they compose their concept and strategy for the family's philanthropic engagement:

- **Analysis:** Why is there a desire to become active in charity? What are the traditions and values upon which those visions are based? Which contributions have been made in the past? How happy were the family members with the results? What problems emerged and where are improvements needed?
- **Vision and Mission:** What is the vision of successful philanthropic engagement? Given this, which concrete aid topics stand out? Which interests and desires among family members need to be taken into account?
- **Market Analysis:** What projects exist for the selected aid topics? Which players are already active in the selected aid topic? Do the aid topics under consideration need further adjustment?
- **Strategy:** Which aid goals are being defined? Whom do the family members wish to help? Which pools of aid have been defined, and what sums have been assigned to them? Where (geographically) do the family members wish to be active? Based on which guidelines? How should the public be informed of the foundation's work?
- **Structure:** How should the philanthropic work be organized? Which form of assistance will be provided: Donations, grants, external donations, bonds, investment capital? Which aid instruments are suitable: Association, own foundation, not-for-profit company, social investment fund? Which committees are necessary and what should their responsibilities be? Which succession rules should apply?

(continued)

(continued)

- **Planning and Controlling:** Which aid should be provided when, including how and at what volume? What corporate expertise and contacts will be provided by family members, and how much time are they willing to provide? How will success be measured for the promoted projects? Which KPIs will be established? Which measures will be taken if the defined goals are not achieved?
- **Involvement of the Family:** Which roles will result from the philanthropic engagement? Who from the family wishes to be involved? Who will assume which tasks?

Once the strategy is formulated, it is then re-formulated into concrete action steps. The family must play a real role in this. Beyond this, the projects should be monitored and regularly subjected to audits. The following practical tip can help make philanthropic engagement an effective boon for all.

Practical Tip: Effective Philanthropic Engagement

- **Good Governance:** Philanthropic engagement should be managed just as professionally as a company. For this to work, suitable committees, processes, information, decision paths, assignments and responsibilities are needed. Use targets and benchmarks to measure performance.
- **Proactive involvement:** Become involved yourself, and select the right persons, people you'd like to work with. Real personal commitment by the family is needed here. Involve the next generation. Don't just delegate your philanthropic activities to the family office.
- **Effective project management:** Mind that each individual aid project is managed professionally. This includes clear goals, detailed planning and coordination with partners. Ensure that the project is conducted properly and that the success is reviewed. This is the only way to ensure that your projects have a lasting impact.
- **Potential exit strategies:** Each aid project should be reviewed after three to five years. You may find that a project is capable of running without your support, allowing you to withdraw. Or perhaps the need is greater than ever. This is the time to consider expanding the assistance.
- **Regular exchange:** Talk with other families on a regular basis about their projects. Determine whether there is space for a joint aid project, as this can open the door to larger, more impactful projects.

From Lebanon: "Responsible investment is a priority for us and I think it will be more and more the case for younger generations in family offices."

Interview with Nour Abou Adal & Maissa Abou Adal

This interview examines the unique dynamic between family generations within the family office, the importance of philanthropy and the rise of impact investing.

This interview was conducted by Alexander Koeberle-Schmid.

Your legacy family business is based in Lebanon. Can you describe the thought process that went into founding the family office?

Maissa: We have a different approach compared to other families. Back in 2010, we started by focusing first on the core operating business. We kicked off a 10-year transformation process, as this was our priority and the core of our social responsibility vis-à-vis our employees, our partners and our consumers in the region.

Maissa Abou Adal Ghanem *grew up between Lebanon, France and Canada. After graduating from Concordia University in Canada in 1998, she became a sales manager at Sears by age 21. She later joined L'Oréal in Montreal, eventually becoming product manager for the Lancôme brand, before moving to Paris to serve as a trainer for Europe, Middle East and North Africa at Kenzo Parfums (part of the LVMH Group). Her first experience with family businesses came in 2003, when she joined Al Fahim Enterprises (Paris Gallery Group) as a business development manager. In April 2009 she moved back to Lebanon and joined the family business, HOLDAL (Abou Adal Group). She is now a member of the BoD and is in charge of the family philanthropy. Maissa also co-authored a book entitled 'Recettes de Vie' whose profits are 100% dedicated to charities in Lebanon.*

Nour Abou Adal *is a 3rd generation member of HOLDAL, a Lebanese-born family business operating in the fields of FMCG, Pharmaceuticals and Luxury Goods in the Middle East. After earning a degree in Finance and Marketing from McGill University, she first worked in sustainable development as the Marketing Coordinator for the Siwa Sustainable Development Initiative in Egypt's western desert, then in Dubai for Procter & Gamble, handling their Skin Care portfolio across 8 markets in the GCC. Her experiences fueled her passion for people and culture, which in turn pushed her to join the family business in 2012 to focus on change management and organizational culture. She is a member of the investment committee and sees a rich future in challenging the old way of separating business and private sectors from philanthropy.*

Why that focus?

Maissa: We were in an environment of major turmoil. Lebanon, Syria and all these countries in the region have been going through a rough time. So the first priority for us was business transformation and governance, which we kicked off in 2010. We were looking to lay the foundation for a comprehensive and sustainable transformation, to ensure that the company would be ready and fit to adapt to this volatile uncertain and complex world.

The family office is more recent. That process started in 2015 when the family came together not only around the core business but really around the Abou Adal family assets and legacy.

In 2015 we really started thinking: "So: for our generation, for the next generation—what kind of impact do we want to have? What strategy would be best to protect and develop our wealth? What are the means we can use to preserve, develop and transfer the family wealth and legacy between the generations, at least until our children take over?"

Nour: To build on what Maissa said, we don't think of the family office in terms of an 'office'. Up until 2015, it was a one man show handled by our father for over 40 years. Since working on our family governance, we decided to put some structure and processes around it to manage risks, uncertainty and ensure a proper succession.

What was the process for founding a family office?

Maissa: We had to start first with the corporate governance.

Our family business is 70 years old. We're the third generation. The majority of the time was first spent on the family business, reaffirming our commitment to our employees and towards our community.

From there, we moved on to the family governance, which in turn meant exploring each of the spaces, asking questions and structuring things.

What we learned was this: do not overcomplicate the process. There are a lot of people and a lot of consultants that will try to intimidate you as a business, as a family. Keep it simple. Discipline is important. Commitment is important. But keep it simple. Because when you overcomplicate the process, you can miss the boat.

What motivated the family to push forward together on this?

Maissa: The motivation was the same core values that bring us together. Right now we are G3 (Generation 3) moving towards G4. So we have been focusing on our core values and their impact and really trying to show humility in passing on a legacy that we can be proud of to our children.

Nour: We also want to leave an impact on the community we work with and which has put its trust in us. The other motivation was to separate the family interests from the core business interests. That's very important, because the business transformation showed us that while obviously the values are always the same, the family's interests can look a little bit different when seen from a helicopter point of view.

How does philanthropy play into this?

Maissa: Right now the family is involved in both the business and the family office. I'm leading the effort on philanthropy, and that's currently running through the business, where there is a proper CSR/SDG strategy and process. In the future, it will be separate, and our family foundation will see the light of day in 2019.

Philanthropy is already second nature to us. The things that need active attention are family governance on one hand and implementing everything that has been decided on the other. And then testing it and recalibrating it continuously, which is very important too.

Nour: And this where we feel the family office serves its function and draws on the cohesiveness of the family. Our idea of the family involves the spouses and the kids that are not shareholders today, including educating G4 to be responsible shareholders, responsible investors, responsible partners, etc.

So what does the philanthropy look like?

Maissa: Well, we've been active in philanthropy forever, now we're just putting a little bit more process and structure around it. If you look in our annual report that the business publishes every year, there are 3 core pillars to our values, core to what our internal and external community needs. The first one focuses on basic needs, because you are in a region and in a country where we've suffered a lot, especially in the last years, beyond the ongoing war.

We've suffered a lot from poverty that has been increasing in relation to the refugee crisis. So for us basic needs are extremely important i.e. warmth, shelter, food, water. These are givens for Europeans, but for our region there are a lot of people who are really impacted by that.

The second one is around empowering our community through education. Education for children generally, but with a big focus on girls, because today you are in a country and a region where people tend to favor boys, especially in very underprivileged communities. Girls tend to just drop out of schools. And a girl who can continue through primary and secondary school will have a better chance of raising her own daughter who will actually succeed and add value to her community.

So education is another very important pillar for us. But we're talking here about educating underprivileged children.

And the third one is the environment. As a company we have been recycling since 2009, despite the recent garbage crisis we've been going through in Lebanon. We've always been very careful about respecting our environment.

So these are the 3 pillars. And every year we report back on achievements vs. goals. For example, I just presented the 2018 CSR plan last week. The plan offers a very clear 12-month road map based on these 3 pillars.

Starting next year we will also be creating an internal funding program for our employees because we realized that they too are in need. It's going to be focusing on ensuring that promising children can get a proper education, because the public schooling in Lebanon is very weak and it's getting weaker every day with the refugee crisis. So everybody wants their kids in private schools. And their costs keep on increasing. As a parent, you want to ensure that you're taking care of your kids' health and education.

This is part of an external arm which will be working with the operating business to ensure that every single colleague who has kids with very high potential will be able to send them to a decent school, including the financial support to pursue that.

Nour: And this goes back to what we said before about the efforts from the philanthropic point of view. Our work is running through the business right now, but soon you will have two different entities. Within the family office our philosophy or focus is increasingly around impact investing. In fact responsible investment is a priority for us and I think it will be more and more the case for younger generations in family offices.

Of course it's easier said than done. You look at your assets and all of a sudden you think: so many of our assets don't really qualify as impact investing. This not to say we deal in unethical businesses. Far from it. Our values and integrity are at the core of every business and personal decision.

However, drawing the line on what is ethical and what is not is becoming increasingly blurry. The sectors of technology and AI alone raise a ton of questions on that front. How do we truly measure the impact of something still in its infancy?

The essence of what I'm trying to say however is that while family philanthropy is an important part of what we do and who we are, impact investing allows us to integrate philanthropy at the very core of our investments and businesses as opposed to something we do on the side. For instance we recently invested in renewable energy projects in remote areas throughout Asia that are off the main electricity grid. Such investments offer promising returns while at the same time catering to minorities with little access to electricity and also reducing impact on the environment.

Do these investments make good business sense?

Nour: As Maissa says, we work a lot with the competition, especially when it comes to creating a positive impact. One of the things about building proper structures and processes is that it really helps you understand: Where and how are we allocating resources? Who should I take on as a partner to better achieve my goals? A more collaborative approach is essential when forming philanthropic structures. It's not about the formalities, obligations, or that "what looks good." It's pretty much your purpose.

I think our partners are positively surprised most of the time. I guess some of them are still not used to how we assess investment opportunities, because we do consider more than just financial returns. Instead we think: "It might be a nice sounding project, but it's hardly creating value for the world." And that matters to us.

9

Concierge Services by the Family Office

Christoph Weber

The central responsibility of a family office is stewarding a large private fortune—preserving and growing the overall net worth. This is a matter for facts, data and figures. The focus is on operating and financial issues, such as cash flows, streamlining of costs and limiting the risks and costs associated with asset investing.

A professionally structured family office can benefit the family immensely. On the financial side, its effectiveness is measured using a phalanx of metrics. Did it achieve its targeted economic goals? How does its performance grade against the selected indicators? But there is another set of benefits, perhaps even greater in added value: improving the quality of life for its shareholders.

Relaxation and satisfaction are the benchmarks here—notoriously difficult characteristics to quantify. But the underlying foundation is quite clear. What shareholders really want is the confidence that a dedicated, loyal and ultra-professional management team is at their side, assisting with the management of the family's fortune. Only then can the family leader lean back and confidently delegate the operative functions, just as an active entrepreneur does.

The longer the duration of the alliance between the wealthy individual and his family office, the stronger the base of trust that is established with management. The wealthy individual is inclined to release a greater share of the oversight over asset management to the family office, and feels confident in doing so.

In many cases, this willingness to delegate spills over into the sphere of private life and daily needs. Here too the sense of "relief" plays a major role. The wealthy individual recognizes the benefits of liberating himself and his family from unpleasant or time-intensive tasks. This leaves the individual with more time to focus on the operating business, or even on hobbies and leisure activities.

B. Canessa et al., *The Family Office*, https://doi.org/10.1007/978-3-319-99085-9_9

When families transfer private sphere activities to the family office, it is rarely a question of status symbols, vestigial aristocratic behavior models or even membership in the glamourous world of the super-rich, however much the press would wish to depict it as such. It is instead a matter of trust and loyalty, and the chance for the family to win itself additional breathing space.

These services by the family office, where not directly related to asset management, are typically called "Convenience" or "Concierge" services. In many cases, the boundaries between the fields of asset management and support in private-sphere affairs are blurry. The list in Fig. 9.1 provides a partial overview of the tasks that the family office can and often does handle on the family's behalf, with the goal of providing relief in various areas of life.

The option of delegating specific tasks from the family's private life to the family office may be seen as a relief from the family's point of view. Yet commissioning the family office to handle these tasks does not always produce

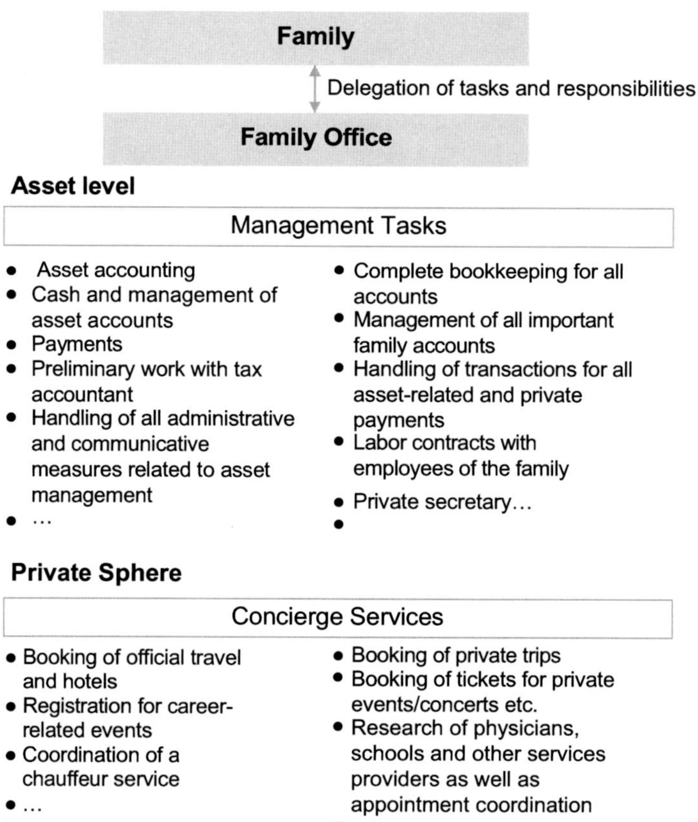

Fig. 9.1 Potential tasks for the family office in various spheres of the family's life

optimal results. For one, the family office employees are not always qualified to provide all services in the most complete and efficient manner (a bookkeeper may in fact not be a terrific travel planner).

Beyond this, the salary of a family officer is often too high to waste on concierge services. For this reason it can be wiser to have an employee from the back office handle these tasks. This choice can also reduce the time that the Family Officer spends on domestic service tasks—which is more time that he can then spend managing the wealth.

Practical Tip: Efficient Usage of Family Office Resources

When considering whether specific "concierge services" should be offered by the family office, be sure to consider whether an external assistant or service firm might not be a more affordable and even higher quality option. The family office can be commissioned to search for qualified providers and to review their work.

10

Organizational Framework for the Family Office

Jens Escher

A family office is normally more than just a "virtual structure," as its executives and staff are not employed directly by the shareholders. If at some point a decision is reached that the family office no longer has a permanent place in the family company, then it is typically spun off into a private company, with its shares held by family members. At a single family office, the owners are members of one family; in a multi family office, they are members of multiple families (see also Chap. 3). From a legal standpoint, the newly spun-off family office is an independent institution. It acts as a partner to the family members by providing services. In situations where it receives portions of the family wealth for the purpose of "wealth pooling," it is also a holding company for those assets (shares of other companies or liquid assets).

10.1 Selection of a Suitable Jurisdiction

Because legal and tax frameworks can vary greatly from jurisdiction to jurisdiction, the ideal legal form for any given family office will always be derived from its specific situation. In fact, for families that are spread out internationally, legal and tax considerations will form a major criterion on one of the most basic points: the country in which the family office should be founded. The family's individual needs and circumstances are paramount, meaning this decision must truly be made based on a case-by-case basis. Beyond economic, legal and tax factors, the following other criteria should be taken under consideration:

B. Canessa et al., *The Family Office*, https://doi.org/10.1007/978-3-319-99085-9_10

- Where are the family members and the essential fixed assets located globally? What changes can be foreseen?
- Which legal forms are possible in the respective jurisdiction (type of company, recognition of foundations and trusts)?
- What is the nature of the tax system?
- Are there regulatory requirements for family offices?
- Is the rule of law sufficiently secure in terms of the legislative, executive and judicial branches?
- What legal standards for communication are in effect?
- Is there a sufficient pool of professional advisors available locally?
- Which visa entry requirements apply to family members?

10.2 Selection of a Suitable Legal Form

The question of the optimal legal form for the family office must always be answered on a case-specific basis. Regardless of which concrete legal forms for companies are available in the individual jurisdictions, most founders end up deciding between some version of a partnership or a corporation. There are frequently also hybrid legal forms available that offer the characteristics of a corporation and a partnership (for example the GmbH & Co. KG in Germany and the LLC in the US). Depending on which specific corporate laws apply, the different types of legal incorporation vary primarily in the following points:

- Management
- Governance
- Limitation of liability
- Public registry entry
- Flexibility of the structure
- Tax treatment

If the family office is also to serve as a holding vehicle for family assets, which can potentially be scattered across the globe, then a holding structure matching the preferred business form must also be identified. Numerous factors can influence this choice, from tax treatment (based for example on the concrete composition of the company's assets) to aspects of liability and risk management. In some individual cases, especially where a very large portfolio of assets is distributed internationally, this can also lead to a partial decentralization of management, with independent management structures established at each subsidiary. Even so, excessive structural complexity should be avoided where possible, as it brings with it unnecessary cost and is more difficult to manage. As such it negates one of the prime reasons for setting up a family office in the first place: boosting efficiency and streamlining costs.

In some individual cases, it may be more advisable to place shares of the family office company in a (family) foundation or trust instead of in the hands of the individual family members. The move to prevent shares from being held personally eliminates any potential questions of succession. At the same time, the family office is also inherently de-coupled from the family from an organizational standpoint. In many such cases, the assets to be managed are also then transferred to the foundation or trust.

Practical Tip: Finding the Right Legal Form

Work together with your advisors to assess your family's specific situation and determine the best legal form for your family office. To prepare for this process, think through the various aspects discussed above and assign your own personal rankings. This information, combined with taxation considerations, should help indicate which company type will best help you realize your goals. In some cases a combination of different companies may be necessary. For example, the family office is established as a partnership to hold all shares on one or more limited liability corporations, which in turn serve as the intermediate holding company for the assets under management by the family office.

10.3 Taxation Aspects

There are a variety of tax-related aspects to be taken into consideration when establishing a family office. If the family office is shifted to a separate legal entity such as a corporation or a partnership, then the family office's income will be taxed based on the selected legal form. From a tax perspective, it also matters whether the family office company solely offers services to family members or whether it also has an asset pooling function. In all cases, the most tax-efficient variant should be selected.

10.3.1 Impact of the Legal Form on Taxation

If the family office is established as a corporation, then it is routinely subjected to direct taxation, insofar as its activities produce taxable earnings. For the family members who are shareholders, this does not normally produce any direct impact tax consequences, presuming the company does not issue profits to the shareholders as dividends and shares of the company (typically within the family) are not sold at a capital gain. In most jurisdictions, a corporation shields its shareholders to some extent from income tax exposure.

A partnership by contrast is typically transparent in terms of income tax. Its profits and losses are attributed to the shareholders in proportion to their respective capital investments or using a deviating profit distribution chart. That flow is then calculated as their own taxable income.

If the family office company limits itself to services for family members and does not manage a pool of self-owned assets, then the impact on taxable income is probably limited, as family offices do not usually provide their services to family members in a normal commercial sense, i.e. based on expectations of earning high profit margins. Given these conditions, no significant tax load can be expected either at the level of the family office corporation or at the shareholder level for a family office run as a partnership. Under some circumstances, these constellations suggest that a legal form that is transparent for tax reasons (such as a partnership) should be selected to allow the shareholders to apply losses by the company directly toward their tax bills. After all, this type of cost is often deductible for shareholders.

The legal form is of particular importance for taxation purposes if the family office company functions as an "asset pool" for the family, or at least as a holding for investments in other companies or firms. This is based in part on the fundamental differentiation made in many legal systems regarding income tax transparency vs. non-transparency for different company types. Beyond this, the tax regulations for individual earned income can change based on the selected legal form. In a corporation, for example, profits from the sale of shares to another corporation, or the dividends that it receives from such, frequently benefit from a so-called 'participation exemption.' Taxation often is not applied until some later distribution of earnings is made to the family members. For this reason, a tax-advantageous retention of earnings and reinvestment are attainable.

The legal form and the structuring for the client's specific situation thus have a significant impact on the ongoing taxation load.

10.3.2 Fee-Based Work for the Family?

Single family offices and classic multi family offices that offer their services solely to members of the owning family are frequently not oriented toward maximizing profits. At the same time, services are generally provided to family members on a fee basis that at minimum covers costs.

From a taxation standpoint, it must be ensured that these services are provided at a customary fee level (in the industry's jargon: the family office charges should be 'at arm's length'). Otherwise, depending on the jurisdiction and legal form of the company, the tax authorities can choose not to recognize the legal relationship between the family office and the family members, which in turn can lead to higher taxes. This should be taken into account from the earliest planning phase of the family office.

Fees paid to the family office are potentially deductible for family members as business expenses or income-related expenses, insofar as there is a defensible connection toward the realization of income on the part of the relevant family member. Where required, the family office should issue itemized invoices for the management of a family member's personal wealth. This process, used in situations such as services related to the management of a personally held rental object, allows for the fees to potentially be deducted from rental income as income-related expenses on the part of the family member. By contrast, if the family member is charged a fee by the family office for services related to the personal sphere (such as convenience services related to flight or hotel bookings or for processing of payments for invoices related to private expenses), such costs are typically not considered tax deductible.

10.3.3 Value Added Tax

Insofar as the family office provides services to family members, those services may be subject to value added tax. This increases the amount to be paid by the family member. Insofar as the family office purchases goods or services subject to VAT tax that are used as part of its own services, that VAT tax may itself be deducted from its VAT debt by the family office (as input VAT, subject to the respective VAT system).

Practical Tip: Value Added Tax

Some additional considerations apply for jurisdictions that levy Value Added Tax. If a family office uses few external consulting services, its invoiced costs to the family will primarily involve the cost transfer for personnel and rental costs. These charges are unlikely to qualify for input tax deduction by the family, meaning the family will be unable to reclaim the Value Added Tax. As such, the family office's services are more expensive in absolute terms than if the family bore the costs directly. (Germany, for example, has a 19% Value Added Tax.) If, however, the family office also serves as an asset pool, then a portion of the family office's total costs relates to the management of self-owned assets and does not have to be passed along to the family with Value Added Tax.

10.4 Regulatory Requirements

Depending on the structure and organization of the family office, special regulatory and licensing requirements may be triggered. In some cases, the family office may even be subject to direct oversight by a government agency. This is especially true in situations where the family office manages the assets of a wider circle of family members, provides consulting on investment decisions or offers comparable services. Regulatory requirements are especially common when assets are pooled from different persons for joint investment purposes. It should be noted, however, that many jurisdictions offer more generous rules for family offices that render services solely to the core family. Beyond regulatory requirements related to the provision of financial services, applicable anti-money laundering rules can apply as well as licensing requirements for any tax or legal consulting services.

At the international level, it is important to note that family offices have in recent years increasingly been a focus of attention in relation to regulation or licensing obligations for the provision of investment advice and asset management. At the same time, family offices are frequently exempted from some regulatory requirements, with the justification that the services are not available to a broad public, but rather only to a strictly limited circle of family and friends. Whether and which such regulatory requirements exist must be reviewed on a case-by-case basis for the respective jurisdiction.

Practical Tip: Clarification of Licensing Obligations with the Relevant Regulatory Agency

When framing the conceptual design of a family office, a specialized consultant should be commissioned early on to determine whether regulatory requirements apply and if so, what steps are needed for licensing. If uncertainty remains, a query should be sent to the relevant regulatory agency for an official determination on what licensing obligations are necessary. This extra up-front effort is an effective way to prevent delays later in the process.

10.5 Structure Suitable for the Situation

How the specific family office should be structured depends strongly on the specific individual circumstances. The legal and tax aspects should reflect a synthesis of the future owner's specific situation and the goals to be pursued by the family office. In this regard, a structure suitable for the individual needs must be developed, without adding unnecessary complexity.

Practical Tip: Configure Your Structure Based on Your Anticipated Needs

The following questions can be helpful orientation aids in designing the structure of your family office:

- Where are the family members and the core of the wealth localized geographically and which changes can be expected in the foreseeable future?
- Which concrete tasks will the family office be entrusted to handle?
- Which tasks should be handled using internal resources and which by external service providers?
- Will the family office company be used as a holding or asset pool for the family?
- Who will be eligible to use the family office's services?
- How will services provided by the family office be charged? Who is responsible if costs overrun income?
- Which conditions must the owner or shareholders of the family office fulfill?
- Who should have control of the family office and which majority rules apply for decisions at the ownership level?
- Which persons will be employed at the family office level and what will their responsibilities be?
- How will the owners of the family office perform an effective oversight review of its executive management?
- What is the decision-making structure?

In terms of the question whether the family office should act as a mere service provider for the family or also as a holding vehicle for all or part of a family's assets, a variety of factors can contribute to the answer. One benefit of the latter kind of design is that a "lean" corporate structure can be established, with a uniform governance framework that avoids multiple parallel companies. Costs for wealth and investment management by the family office can (typically from a taxation standpoint) be deducted from income derived from wealth management, insofar as the company is managing its own corporate assets (Figs. 10.1 and 10.2).

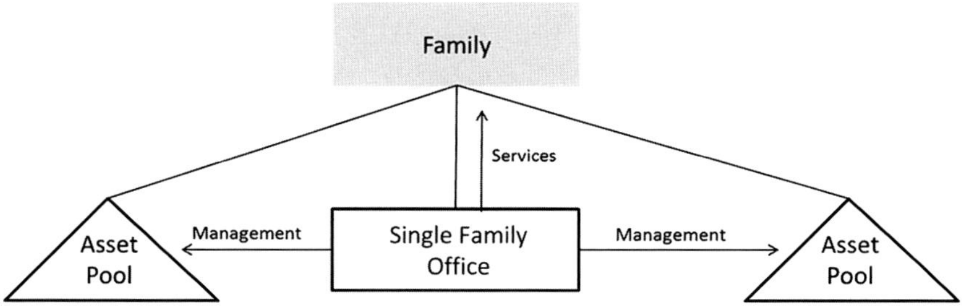

Fig. 10.1 Single family office—service provider model

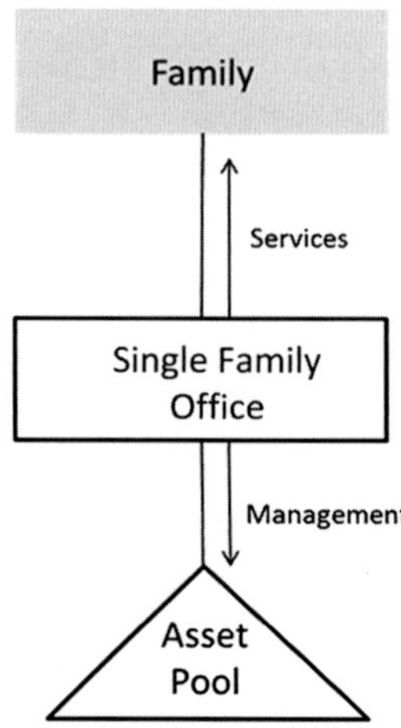

Fig. 10.2 Single family office—holding model

If the family office is entrusted with investing pooled wealth, it may be eligible for certain investment classes (especially in terms of alternative investments) that are not available to family members as individual private investors. On the other hand, consideration must be given that the legal form selected for the family office may, from a taxation standpoint, not be the perfect choice for holding certain investment classes. Beyond this, different liability risks can in some circumstances end up bundled within the same structure.

Even when the family office is designed as a holding for specific asset items or investments, in practice structured "parallel vehicles" are often constructed on a more situational basis to allow family members to acquire and hold other asset investments. If the individual family members do not wish to participate in specific investments or—based on their own preferences for asset allocation—have a different ratio specified for their "primary share," then the formation of additional asset pools alongside the family office is often unavoidable. The same applies in situations in which only certain family members hold shares of the family office, while the group of family members to be serviced goes beyond that more limited circle (Fig. 10.3).

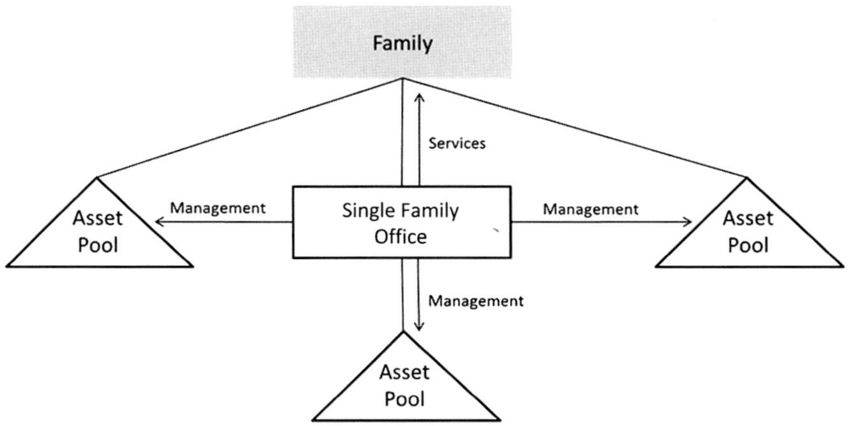

Fig. 10.3 Single family office—holding with side pools model

In particular for a larger circle of family members as shareholders, it may make sense to establish an advisory council at the family office level. It is formed with representatives of the family (in a closed multi family office with representatives of the different owner families) and external specialists (see Chap. 12). The advisory council can assume responsibility for consultation with and monitoring of the executive team, the issuance of by-laws (including investment guidelines) and agreeing to specific individual measures.

Taken together, these considerations should provide an indicator towards an appropriate legal structure for the family office, its necessary internal rules and standards and the process for setting it up. Among the documents that will flow from this decision:

- a corporate agreement (to clarify the relation among owners)
- clarification of regulatory framework for the planned activity and any licensing obligations
- employment contracts for the persons employed by the family office
- rules and regulations for the directors of the family office (including a catalog of transactions that require owner approval), with supplementary investment guidelines for asset allocation as needed; a comprehensive set of compliance rules and standards, as needed (see Sect. 12.3)
- contracts with external service providers
- where applicable: agreements on the transfer of assets from family members to the family office company or a parallel asset pool
- where applicable: supplementary rules governing the relationship between the family office and the family members and the terms and conditions of use

From the United Kingdom: "If you correctly understand the client and manage according to the portfolio plan, you should get the performance you need."

Interview with James Fleming

In this interview Mr. Fleming talks about how a single family office transforms into a multi family one, the importance of understanding a client's psychology, and keys to achieving top performance.

This interview was conducted by Peter Preller.

Sandaire regards itself as the first pioneering UK-based MFO. What's the history there?

James Fleming: Sandaire was founded in the mid 1990s by the Scott family, who for the better part of 100 years were involved in the insurance and banking industries. They eventually sold that insurance business, and, like a lot of families, were faced with the challenge of having monetized their main asset. What to do next?

Now this was a family with a legacy of running a family business, so initially they set up a structure for themselves. As that developed, they at some point felt that structure could be appropriate for one or two other families to use, both to gain the economies of scale as well as to share ideas and to bring a few families together.

James Fleming *brings with him over 30 years of private banking experience. He joins Sandaire from Arbuthnot Latham, where he more recently held the position of Vice Chairman, having previously been Chief Executive from 2012 to 2016 during which time he led the business through a sustained period of growth.*

James started his career at Hambros Bank and moved from the role of Managing Director of SG Hambros (UK) in 2002 to the private bank Coutts & Co where he headed the International Division.

Was the idea to form something akin to an investment club or was it the idea to build a profitable new business?

JF: I wouldn't say at any stage it was as informal as an investment club, no. I think once the idea took root to develop a multi family office, and therefore a business offering family office services, by definition as a business, there was a need to make a profit, because quite simply, as we all know, none of us are in business to make a loss. And neither is it a charitable enterprise either. So there's not a sort of philanthropic element to the structure as such.

The MFO at this point has been alive and well for just over 20 years, managing capital for the underlying 35 families. With each family, there is a need to understand, obviously, the structure of that family, the needs, the circumstances, the requirements, the time horizons, and also the sense of the family dynamics, the structure, how many generations, etc. So a complete thorough knowledge, but also due diligence on the family concerns in order to be able to create an investment plan that matches those factors, those dynamics in each particular family.

How does this differ from a traditional investment office, such as offered by banks?

JF: So I think the first point of differentiation from a traditional investment business is that we are dealing with substantial family wealth in each and every situation. Furthermore, within each family there are multiple persons, multiple personnel, multiple members of the family. So there is a need to create structures, maybe foundations or trust structures, that are creative with a view toward the long term.

Are the members of the Scott family active in the MFO, or is the family just a client and owner?

JF: That's a good question, because if you take the case of Alex Scott personally, so Alex was founder, chairman and chief executive at the outset, some three to four years ago, he stepped back from being Chief Executive and remained as founder and chairman and now today Alex is founder. We have an independent chairman and we have myself as chief executive.

So what I'm describing there is not just a positional change, but an evolution of the business. The aim being today and for the next five years, let's say, to develop a momentum in the business that is almost independent of the core family but very inclusive of the core family.

What skills allowed the founder to make the switch from operating business to family office?

JF: Alex spent the early part of his career within the insurance company and the family's bank, and so gained a good foundation and grounding in financial services with a particular expertise, which was insurance. When he then transitioned into the family office world, and therefore that of investments, clearly there was a need for him to gain a greater understanding of how the investment world works and runs itself.

But that's where you then bring individuals into the business who can bring that technical expertise. The core skill that Alex had throughout this process was that of leadership. And translating that leadership from being in charge of the insurance company to being in charge of the multi family office.

Is there an established body of rules to govern things like whether and how the next generation can entire into the business?

JF: I don't believe there's a written down script that says at a certain age members of the family will join the business. I don't believe that is the case. I think the family owns Sandaire through structures, and Sandaire is now a stand-alone family office. It just happens to be that the core family, the core clients, are the Scott family.

But I think whilst Alex and other senior members of the family may encourage younger members to come towards the MFO, I think that would be on a as-in-when-required basis for the company and as opportunities present themselves.

During the process and getting to know your clients, how do you try to establish their risk thresholds?

JF: I think generally you do see client behaviors and attitudes change as markets evolve and change. By that I mean that when the market is rising, you might typically find clients are very ebullient towards the market and want to take great levels of risk, thinking that the market only ever goes up.

There are risks to that sort of simplistic client perspective that markets always go up. They may initially want to take x degree of risk because it will pay off in the end. And then when they wake up and find that it's dropped 10%, they start to panic and then it's "Why did you put me in this and how did we get here?"

Can you address those concerns at that late stage, or if you're having that conversation is it already too late?

The lessons that the industry has learned over the years, the investment industry, is to have VERY detailed conversations with clients at the outset and to ask quite simplistically: "What are their need circumstances and requirements?" And also to push for a far more detailed understanding of what is their attitude toward risk.

So things such as behavioral finance had gained ever-increasing importance in recent years in the discussion. Questions such as "If you woke up this morning and were down 20%, how would you feel? Do you have the appetite to see through market difficulties market volatility? etc."

And getting an understanding of the client's attitudes through their answers to these questions is a very, very important process. But also, I think, going through history and pointing through various market cycles what levels of returns can be achieved.

And while back testing is only a guide to what happened in the past, it's no guide to what might happen in the future, as much information as you can impart to the client at the outset in this process of formulating an investment plan is very important and will pay you back when markets hit difficult times.

Some family officers say performance is overstated as a criterion. How do you see this topic?

JF: I think it would be foolish to say that performance is not important. It's very true to say that it's one component of an overall service, but it is an important component. If you were my client and you came to see me each quarter, and we never achieved any growth and never achieved the benchmark, etc.—how long do you think you would stay, however nice a cup of coffee I might give you?

If you're here and losing your money, you're not going to stay. So performance is a key component. But I think as important as delivering that performance is understanding the client in the first instance. So, in the management of risk, for example, it would be a very foolish family office that invested in high risk instruments when the client has clearly set out that they have a long-term preservation goal in mind.

So understanding the client and creating a portfolio plan and structure for them in the first place is very, very important. And then managing according to that plan is the second most important thing. And if you do those two things correctly, you should get the performance you need.

11

Client Structure and Communication

Boris Canessa

As with any company, family offices require certain clearly defined structures, rules and framework conditions. These serve as the guidelines for corporate behavior and lay the groundwork for the professional and efficient provision of services that benefits the family office's clients.

Practical Tip: Questions on Client Structure, Notification and Communication

The following list provides helpful questions to be answered and then integrated in writing into the documents, contracts and by-laws for your family office:

- **Client structure:** Who is eligible to use the family office's services? How should "family" (= client) be defined in the context of the family office? Based on which criteria should the clients be segmented?
- **Notification and communication:** What factors must be taken into consideration when communicating with clients of the family office? What technical tools should be used? Which information will be conveyed?
- **Meetings:** What are the respective functions of the various meetings? Who is invited to attend?
- **Decision-making:** Who within the family office is authorized to make decisions, and based on what information?

11.1 Defining the Clientele

One fundamental question: who may be a "client" of the family office? Families seeking to join an existing multi family office will inherently have less influence on this aspect. They should nevertheless clarify the situation by

B. Canessa et al., *The Family Office*, https://doi.org/10.1007/978-3-319-99085-9_11

engaging in dialog with any multi family office they are considering. The answers they receive can provide an important preview of whether the family and its culture are a good fit for the existing customer structure or whether they are more likely to feel like "outsiders," both now and in the future.

If the family office is integrated into the family's legacy business and is solely tasked with management of current corporate assets and shareholders' accounts, then the decision on membership is essentially already settled: with company and family office intertwined, all company shareholders are also clients of the family office. The bigger question in such constellations is whether shareholders are allowed to solicit advice from the family office on holdings not contained in the shareholders' accounts (and if yes: who may and who may not).

Clients of a Single Family Office

When modelling a single family office that is not to be an integral component of the family business, the family office's clients are the ultra high net worth individual and his or her descendants.

Spouses present a thornier issue and are handled in different ways by different single family offices. Many families wish to keep the influence of spouses on the inherited family assets as minimal as possible, especially if the family office is responsible for both the company's investments and current assets in/from the company as well as the accounts of the family members. Yet when spouses are excluded from their family's family office and cannot take advantage of the family office's services, they are less likely to encourage their children to continue its use. Marriages built on mutual trust usually involve discussing issues with a spouse, to seek council and solicit acceptance on decisions. When the spouse is excluded from family office-related deliberations, it is difficult for such topics to be effectively discussed afterward. Beyond this, the decision to exclude spouses does not actually remove the real underlying risk. Whether they are in the family office or not, spouses can cause major structural damage to anyone legally related to them if they make a poor decision or major asset investment blunder. For these and other reasons, we recommend including spouses as clients in the family office.

And what about distant relatives? What about non-biological children who entered the family with a member's spouse? What about widowed spouses, adopted children and divorced spouses? In short: Where does "family" begin and where does "family" end? In many cases, the answers to these questions are simply adopted from older rules regarding "association with the company" and the right to attend family meetings in the context of company business.

There is much to speak for this approach. Yet the family office can also serve as a bridge for positive communication within the family precisely by setting rules for "membership" that are more open than in other areas. The integration of additional family members into discussions and considerations promotes a greater sense of identity and need not necessarily question established structures between the company and family at all. While it is of course impossible to define or plan for every contingency, it often makes sense to establish a thoughtful consensus on who should be eligible as a client in the family office—before allowing the issue to devolve to the emotional level. Wealthy individuals might well ask their own children or adult grandchildren where they would draw the line. After all, family offices are typically founded primarily with the interests of descendants in mind.

There are objective benefits for not making the potential clientele of the family office too narrow. Single family offices are often criticized, justifiably, for being overly insular: Because of their inherent limits to client diversity, they can suffer from a lack of creativity in their concepts and actions. Conflict is famously often the best path to achieving above-average results, and constructive discussions with very different viewpoints and wrestling to determine the right path certainly qualify. This is especially true if the client base is small and shaped by similar ideas and experiences due to their shared daily situations. Sure, it is easier to make decisions when only one option is presented. But are such decisions really the best ones, or likely to break new ground? Allowing the potential clientele for the single family office to be defined more broadly admittedly adds complexity to the process of communication between clients and with the family office. And, of course, those opting to join an existing multi family office will have no influence on the composition of the client base anyways. But these considerations should be explored in as much depth as possible before the decision is made to sign on with a specific provider.

Practical Tip: Compare the Client Structure of Multi Family Offices

When reviewing the catalog of services offered by various multi family offices, be sure to ask the operators for information about their client structure. For discretion reasons only a limited range of information will be available, but it should in all cases include the average net worth of the clients, their professional backgrounds and the representative consulting focuses.

You will not be optimally served by a provider whose existing and desired clients possess a significantly smaller or larger net worth than yourself, or whose assets were not earned through entrepreneurial activities (such as artists or pro athletes) or who require completely different services from their family office than you do.

11.2 Information and Communication with the Clients

Some successful single family offices work on a model whereby the accumulated wealth of all clients (family members) is bundled and then outsiders are commissioned to manage it. This opens the door to a broader range of asset investment vehicles and asset classes (stocks and bonds, real estate, direct investments, private equity, infrastructure investments).

The private conversation between the family office and each individual member is then typically less intensive and focuses more on harmonization of topics of personal interest, such as support in composition of a will, creation of living wills, support for personal lifestyle planning (such as private budget, private tax return, personal lifestyle management or coaching). The same holds true for those family offices that are part of a family business and whose employees are primarily in contact with those family members who hold leadership positions in the family company; here too the assets are generally centrally administered for all family members.

For family offices that advise family members independently and individually and where membership is voluntary, client trust is imperative. Yet such trust is only earned when the family office truly understands the client's ideas, desires and peculiarities and tailors its advice to reflect this. The family office must also know its clients' risk tolerances as well as their preferences for specific investment strategies (and on the flip side their aversion to investment types, perhaps due to earlier losses or bad decisions).

The family office is entrusted with structuring the assets to support each family's desired lifestyle. As part of this, the family office must come to know the rough expense basis for its respective members, including for example hobbies and vacations, domestic help and children. And naturally it must also understand the taxation situation (especially the tax exposures) and side income streams of its individual customers. Because family offices are designed to serve multiple generations, its clients will likely also want advice on questions related to last wills and testaments, the transfer of assets, prenuptial agreements, powers of attorney and living wills. The same applies for multi family offices as well.

This information is usually highly sensitive in nature. Clients will only be willing to divulge it to the family office if they are certain that it will be handled in absolute confidence, and in particular will not be shared with external third parties or other clients. Extra care must be taken to allay these suspicions when family members serve as executives or employees at their own family office, or if the family office is part of the legacy operating company, or if the executive members and employees of the company also manage the family office.

Minutes and Reports

Discussions should be held several times a year (or monthly, if needed) with employees of the family office. Minutes of meetings sent to the clients (family members) recount which decisions were made and which instructions the family member issued to the family office. These written minutes are crucial to preventing misunderstandings. The minutes are especially important for investment decisions, as they ensure that the genesis of any decision can be traced back at some later standpoint. Practically speaking, the minutes also serve as an instance for the shareholders to reconsider or change instructions and decisions if need be. If, for example, a client made a decision in an emotional context, such as following "concerning" news by the media or friends, that threat may appear less critical with the benefit of some extra time for reflection.

Communication with the clients, i.e. family members, is routinely conducted using standardized reports. At predefined intervals (monthly/quarterly) an "asset report" is issued to notify each member about the development of his or her assets (the various portfolios, real estate and investments) and which expenses have accrued (private expenses, wealth management costs, taxes). Together with the meeting minutes and the strategies established therein (target asset allocation, investment decisions) the asset report forms a solid and reviewable basis for assessing performance and for making well grounded, factual and consensus-based decisions for the future. The asset report and meeting minutes are fundamental elements of the discussions between client and family office.

11.3 Consulting Discussions and Meetings

Confidential discussions in small groups between the individual members and the single family office are of central importance. Discussions conducted in a larger circle can also serve an important purpose as well. In this case, spouses and/or children—members of the immediate family—are invited to take part in these discussions. This is a strong step toward establishing joint understanding of the various aspects and objectives of the asset situation, asset investment and strategy. It is thus an important cornerstone of consensus building and dialog within nuclear families. In return, the family office also gains better insight into the dynamics of that nuclear family: its shared values, its points of difference, its concerns and its hopes. This information is then used to determine suitable consultants capable of meeting the specific needs of the individual family members as well as the nuclear family as a whole. Multi family offices are also well advised to organize these discussion circles on a regular basis with the individual families.

Larger meetings can also be conducted with all clients of the single family office. These larger gatherings, which can be also sensible for multi family offices in some instances, can involve the presentation of reports by the asset managers or new products. New investments and the strategic orientation of the family office can be discussed, as well as its personnel structure and the range of services.

Presentation to a larger circle of participants is significantly more efficient than individual discussions. Beyond this, discussions featuring all clients can provide valuable insights for the individual members. Question and answer sessions open the door to greater insights on the part of all clients, especially when certain important aspects are raised that might not otherwise have occurred to the other participants. The exchange establishes a shared core of understanding among the clients, such as regarding expectations for a new product, as well as trust and association among the clients and between client and family office. The larger meetings are also a good venue to discuss the strategic orientation of the family offices or to raise awareness of the family office's personnel structure and the range of services it offers. While no-vote decisions by the patriarch and executive team involve less "effort," jointly formed decisions are more stable and sustainable.

Some successful single family offices bundle their client's accumulated assets into asset pools that are managed by the family office. They thus more closely resemble closed holding companies and allow only for general decisions that cover all asset classes and are equal for all customers. Regular meetings with all customers ensure that they are informed about the jointly administered assets, that they are familiar with existing and future strategies for the individual asset pools and to allow for discussion about reconfiguration between the individual pools or the establishment of new pools. These meetings are similar to general meetings in the family-owned business.

Families bring with them not just business and economic themes, but also personal discussions and shared celebrations. For this reason the family office should organize dinner or other events for all clients. The value of these events should not be underestimated, as trust ultimately relies on positive emotions and these are easier to create if the term "family office" isn't tied solely to the wearisome addressing of problems, but rather also with merry get-togethers.

11.4 Making and Documenting Decisions

In a family office that manages bundled pools of assets collected from all clients, or which solely handles the current corporate assets or assets in the shareholders accounts, decision making must be made centrally. The decision maker in this case is either the relevant department of the company or an external/internal organizational unit created specifically for this purpose. While this centralized process ensures a high degree of efficiency and in many cases a high degree of professionalism, it also neglects certain aspects of the personal needs, hopes and concerns of the individual members.

Yet even if decisions (and especially investment decisions) are not made centrally, the decision-making processes should be made as uniform as possible. "Made uniform" doesn't inherently mean that clients are guided or forced into the same decisions, but rather that the decisions by the clients and the consulting by the family office is made based on a uniform, professional process whose steps can, if necessary, be reconstructed afterward. Investment decisions by the client should be supported in this regard through a clearly defined due diligence process. In addition, extremely high quality asset managers are selected at regular intervals and using objective criteria for various asset classes and are presented to all interested clients. The managers will be subjected to a regular, deep and fundamental performance review based on the investments that they have made. This ensures routine auditing of the performance of the family office. The recurrent audits help members gain trust in the wealth managers, who are aware that they will be subject to regular reviews. On the other hand, if things run well, all members may well arrange for their assets to be managed by these persons.

Because however highly individual decisions should remain in place for the clients of a single family office, rules must be put in place from the start about the scope of the due diligence process for individuals. After all, extensive costs that lead to "just" a few thousand euros of investment can degrade the effectiveness of any family office and lead to critical questions among other family office customers about the sense of such expenses. Clear rules are needed here to avoid conflict: which investment volumes are necessary to activate which specific levels of expense by the family office.

12

Committees, Guidelines and Professional Management Systems

Boris Canessa

A family office's structures should be dictated by its legal form and the tax and regulatory rules it faces. This starts with the client structure, but also extends to the framing of two key committees: the investment council and the advisory council. Core guidelines and professional management systems must be formulated as well.

Practical Tip: Professional Management of the Family Office

It is important to ensure that your family office is managed professionally. The following questions can help clarify whether your family office meets this standard:

- **Investment Council:** What benefits does this kind of committee provide? What are its responsibilities, and how should its members be selected?
- **Risk Management:** Are risks expected solely from "the capital markets"—which components should be present for an effective risk management system? How can organizational risks be minimized?
- **Compliance:** How can a formal set of rules be implemented to avoid liability risks?
- Which areas/activities/aspects should be covered by compliance rules?
- **Fees:** Which fees model should be used for the family office?
- **Ownership:** Who owns the family office (company, family, management)? Where does this have an impact?
- **Advisory council:** What benefits does an advisory council provide? What responsibilities should it have? How should its members be selected?

B. Canessa et al., *The Family Office*, https://doi.org/10.1007/978-3-319-99085-9_12

12.1 Investment Council to Consult on Financial Issues

There exists a bewildering array of asset classes: European stocks, Asian stocks, small cap, private equity Europe, venture capital, large buy-out funds, German real estate, USA real estate, commodities, domestic and foreign infrastructure investments, just to name a few. It's unrealistic to expect a family office, either the single or multi family variety, to field a world-class expert, let alone a team of specialists, for each of them.

Investment councils can mitigate this problem by recruiting external specialists in fields where the family office lacks expertise. As Richard C. Wilson, who runs the Family Office Club, notes: "The role of an Investment Committee is to help make strategic investment decisions, evaluate select fund managers, discuss portfolio construction and risk management approaches and implementation, and to ensure the long-term preservation of capital and implementation of given investment policy they have been given" (Wilson 2014, p. 47).

Investment councils can be formed either for special asset classes, such as private equity or direct investment, or for cross-disciplinary support and advice on asset classes in which the client has already or plans to invest relevant resources. The team can expand its working reach by enlisting qualified members, such as the director of the Economics departments at a large insurance company or bank or of a large and diversified mutual fund. In situations where significant components of a client's wealth are invested within one specific asset class, the investment council should always include experts with exceptional knowledge of that field.

Investment councils typically meet two to three times annually to review existing investments and consult on potential new ones. For family offices that also serve as an investment office managing portfolios and funds on their own, the investment council can also meet more often (monthly). The family office's executive team attends investment council sessions. Clients may also choose to attend; this can be a sensible way to promote better personal awareness about the risks and opportunities associated with the investments, and to observe first-hand the professionalism of the process.

The investment council should have clear tasks and areas of responsibility, where possible set down in writing. An agenda should be prepared and distributed sufficiently far in advance, with detailed research materials on the various agenda items. The meetings are not intended to rubber stamp proposals, but rather to open up a constructive, direct and above all else critical dialog. Opportunities and risks associated with the investments, as well as the legal and tax implications, correlations to existing investments and other investment-related aspects, should be weighed. The task of the investment council is ultimately to provide an insightful, professional and critical sounding board for proposals by the family office's executives—in essence to serve as a sparring partner for the family office team in an effort to uncover errors or problems.

Some clients wish to tap their "business-savvy friends of the family" or "our old trusted tax accountant" or "the former CFO of the company" to serve in the investment council. Such selections are inherently questionable, as these candidates often lack the necessary expertise in the relevant specialist fields. Beyond this, any choice by the client to follow up professional advice from the family office with the request for a second opinion "from old chums" can cloud the consulting structures.

When empaneling the family investment council, it is crucial that the client be steered away from investing in products that are managed or sold by the companies associated with the members of the investment council. This ensures freedom from conflicts of interest, as well as neutrality and professionalism in the decision-making process. Membership in the investment council should never be abused as a channel to flog one's own product.

Practical Tip: Buy or Build?

Imagine that a family office is offered a "magic guarantee." By "magic guarantee," we mean that the family office could clone its own version of Warren Buffet. The cost: four years of investment in a specific team of employees. Would that effort be worth it? Believe it or not, the answer might well be: "No." Because why should you invest in something for four years when you can have it directly now? *Berkshire Hathaway* is a publicly traded firm that can simply be bought—so why spend so much money just to copy it?

So always remember to ask: Is it worthwhile to create something on your own, or is it cheaper and easier to simply buy it outright?

12.2 Risk Management Through the Family Office

One of the key assignments for the investment council is drawing the family office's attention to potential risks. This applies in particular to market risks, risks related to the selected legal construction, tax, regulatory and even political risks.

There is often a pan-generational desire among the clients to "preserve wealth." In practical terms, this means avoiding major risks that could permanently threaten the pool of wealth or otherwise have a massive impact on the client's operating income—such as expected yields that fail to materialize or unexpectedly high expenses or supplementary compensation demands tied to investments. The family office is entrusted with conducting an ongoing review of the correlations between the different risks inherent to the client's assets. This includes determining whether the selected diversification strategy represents a truly effective hedge against loss. These and other risks will have been analyzed at the time the investments were first selected, but require routine monitoring thereafter as well. Families with an operating company will perceive the loss of the company as the largest potential risk. Older and larger families that have sold their legacy business or which for other reasons draw the majority of their financing from income related to their current assets will perceive the loss of that wealth or transfer to "immature" descendants as a major risk. Beyond this, internal family strife (due to a lack of family governance) is also almost always perceived as a risk. Sara S. Hamilton, founder of the Family Office Exchange, says of this:

> Risk, as a concept, varies enormously between families. Even the definition of risk is unique to each family member and shaped by each family's history. For some owners the ultimate risk is the loss of family reputation, while for others it may be the loss of capital or the loss of financial security. … Taking time to reach a common understanding of where the family is vulnerable, and what risks need to be addressed, is important for every family and each family leader. (Daniell and Hamilton 2010, p. 165)

Even the most diligent ongoing monitoring cannot eliminate every risk, but it can make risks tangible and transparent—through discussions with the client and through the asset report. These channels should be used to inform the client in clear and comprehensible ways about the three to five largest risks and their potential impact on his assets, such as volatility, the largest price drop in the last five or ten years, risks related to disproportional leverage or liability, risks related to non-tenancy in real estate or foreign currency financing.

Once informed, the client can make conscious, data-driven choices between opportunities, weighing and reviewing the associated risks and whether—and to what degree—his assets and/or the income needed to maintain his lifestyle might be substantially threatened through one or more correlated risks. The discussion of risks also serves as a chance for the family office to better familiarize themselves with the client's risk tolerance—a pillar of successful consultation. The ongoing review of risk fields also promotes rapid, (more) rational and situationally appropriate reactions in the event that the discussed risks do occur. Alex Scott, the founder of the Sandaire multi family office, and Charles

Peackcok, a Sandaire investment analyst, note on this point: "… risk sits at the heart of investment and should be a key feature in the investment reports" (Archer and Hauser 2015, p. 93).

12.2.1 Insurance Management

Insurance management is an important component of risk management. As a first step, the family office should catalog the various—typically private—asset items held by its members (privately used real estate, artwork, jewelry, antique cars, etc.) as well as liability risks (liability insurance, Directors and Officers [D&O] liability Insurance) and health and/or disability risks.

The family office can review for its members whether all essential asset items and risks are suitably insured (and/or whether they are over insured or even insured multiple times). If this process is being conducted for multiple clients, it is often possible for the family office to negotiate institutional pricing for its clients, winning broader benefits at lower costs.

An independent insurance agent can be commissioned to manage, assess and purchase suitable policies to cover against insurance risks. This can, under some circumstances, represent a crucial task for a multi family office. Personal and family risks are often neglected during this process, either intentionally or unintentionally. Yet the unexpected death of a shareholder without a will or testament can bring massive risks, especially if his heirs are underage (leaving a guardianship court responsible for all decisions). For clients with significant operating income from one activity, especially when that income is used primarily to cover ongoing expenses, any significant disruption of that stream can threaten their standard of living.

Calculations of income, expenditures and assets value trends over the course of time, including their expected future yields, form an important basis in crafting a sustainable strategy for each client to manage risks now and as they age.

There are dangers to leaving the family's corporate assets and the current assets managed by the single family office legally tied together in a joint liability model. If the operating company encounters major problems and is unable to issue dividends for a certain period (or even declares bankruptcy) then the joint liability for the various specific assets can often have catastrophic consequences for the family members. A family office that is integrated fully into the family company actually represents a similar risk, as it threatens the existence (and freedom from conflicts of interest) of the family office at a time when the family members need its advice most.

12.2.2 Internal and Organizational Risks for the Family Office

For the family office, risk management also includes assessments of internal and organizational risks for the family office and measures to eliminate them to the greatest degree possible. This is especially important if the family is solely a client within a commercial multi family office, meaning the family office itself belongs to the management or a third party. Risks are often tied up to brain drain or extended illness on the part of family office employees, or can arise from a loss of information (physical intrusion or hacking attack on the family office's IT infrastructure).

Risks related to bad advice by the family office should also be considered. After a certain point, clients often grow to trust their family office blindly. Family office employees willing to abuse that trust could put the wealth itself at risk. For example, employees might potentially use their powers of attorney to embezzle client funds. Another more indirect, but no less insidious, ethical breach: employees accepting money or other benefits (such as vacations or timepieces) from external service providers (wealth managers, bank employees) in exchange for undeservedly high rankings for and recommendations of those providers.

Risks can also emerge for the family office and the wealth it manages when responsibilities are not clearly regulated. Failure to do so opens the door for important aspects of a family office's work to slip negligently under the oversight radar. Compliance guidelines are an effective way to minimize these internal and external risks.

Practical Tip: Key Aspects of Risk Management

Always remember that there's no such thing as impossible. No matter how settled and established a "fact" may be, no matter how uncritically it is accepted in the press, you must always count on it eventually tumbling down: "The Swiss franc will never be unpegged from the Euro" (and yet it was!), "Oil will never drop below the $70 benchmark" (check the prices!), "Real estate never goes down" (a huge pool of bankrupted investors in the USA, Spain, Portugal, Greece and many other countries might beg to differ). Never put the majority of your wealth in one basket. Shape your portfolio so that the loss of one asset class cannot ruin you. Take measures to ensure that the loss of an investment is limited (and never uncapped)—financial futures, loans in foreign currencies and private partnerships should be strictly avoided. A limited liability corporate structure should always be created before entering into large, risky investments (such as real estate, financial futures, or loans in foreign currencies). Art, real estate, jewelry, physical gold, leveraged real estate purchases and similar asset classes should always be reviewed for appropriate insurance coverage. If your income or your work at the firm are of central importance, then you should insure your ability to work and your general health.

12.3 Establishment of Compliance Guidelines

The German Corporate Governance Codex (DCGK) offers a helpful definition of compliance: it is the responsibility on the part of the executive board to enforce adherence to legal regulations and internal corporate policies. The legislative preamble to Germany's Second Act for the Promotion of Financial Markets provides further clarity on the subject: The creation and development of compliance organizations for those providing securities-related services is an important step in defusing the fundamental potential for conflict between the interests of the company and of the client. In their publication "The New MaRisk Compliance Function," noted compliance experts Timo Boldt, Karsten Büll and Michael Voss explain: "The term Compliance regularly appears together with phrases such as Corporate Governance, Directives, Liability Management, Anti-Corruption, Privacy Protection and Protection of Confidence" (Boldt et al. 2013, p. 9).

Compliance guidelines thus represent an important set of internal rules and standards for promoting the long-term functionality of the single family office. In his book "The Family Office Book," Richard C. Wilson defines one of the core tasks of governance as establishing an "internal watchdog" to ensure that the family office does not undertake any course of action that is not to the benefit of the client. It furthermore needs a review of all activity to ensure that it serves the client's interest. Single family offices often prefer to avoid the entire issue of "Compliance" because it typically involves bureaucracy and legal stipulations that it may perceive as "senseless." For multi family offices, the costs of implementing relevant control mechanisms can also represent a significant financial strain. Yet a serious "organizational accident" can also quickly undermine the existential basis of a client-owned family office. "If you feel somewhat lost by the mention of governance, just think of it as management policies and rules for working together as a family—along with your family office team. These rules govern and enforce the operations discussed…" (Wilson 2014, p. 47).

Peggy Scharf, writing in "Compliance in Credit and Financial Service Institutions," points to the importance of a company-specific definition of compliance that is not overly broad: "Otherwise personnel and resources are tied up unnecessarily, and superfluous controls lead to bureaucracy; yet the definition cannot be set too narrowly either, as then the danger arises that risks will be missed and damages will arise that would have been prevented had suitable controls been in place" (Scharf 2014, p. 71).

Compliance rules should be framed to ensure that the following areas and responsibilities are perpetually handled professionally and in compliance with applicable law:

- The compliance rules should ensure that family office employees **comply with the law and behave in an ethically proper manner.** Employee behavior should also be in harmony with the responsibilities of the family office and the visions and core values of the family. It should contain measures that prevent the exploitation of non-public information by family office employees and secure **the confidentiality of stored files.** The compliance rules and standards should be a part of the employee's contract, or at minimum mentioned therein, and all employees should have to regularly attend training sessions to ensure that they are fresh in mind.
- The rules and standards must also cover core activities related to **IT compliance:** Creation of security requirements, consulting, training, controlling and reporting on the state of IT security, coordination and support for internal and external audits (see also Boldt et al. 2013, p. 143).
- Special rules and control mechanisms are urgently recommended if the family office is given authority to handle **payment transactions.** In this case the compliance rules must include effective control mechanisms to prevent unauthorized/illegal cash or asset transfers by employees of the family office otherwise authorized to conduct transactions, either to benefit themselves or third parties.
- The compliance rules should define **decision-making processes** (especially those involved with capital investments), to ensure that these are comprehensible, professional and in line with applicable law. It must be established who has authorization to make and enforce decisions: Does final decision-making authority lie with the member or the investment manager of the family office? Even more rules are required if the family office includes an investment office authorized to act freely on the behalf of the customer. Please consult with a qualified compliance specialist about the specific legal standards for your jurisdiction.
- Family offices that serve solely to select external managers require **due diligence reviews:** How are potential providers selected? How will it be determined how many are needed? What facts from which sources must be audited, and how? Which questions must be answered by the providers, and how? Who will document the entire due diligence process and how? To counteract an improper favoring of friends and acquaintances, written rules should be formulated regarding impartial, professional behavior.
- The central task of a multi-generational single family office and its compliance rules are the long-term retention of knowledge regarding capital investments, decision-making processes and family-relevant facts. The rules and standards should include a system for **professional, long-term retention of contracts, files and documents** (account statements, balance sheets, shareholder decisions and corporate documents, documentation of fees and costs, email correspondence, family contracts such as wills, prenuptial agreements, living wills, powers of attorney, wealth management contracts, tendering documents and investment guidelines, contracts and instructions for the clients of the family office, meeting minutes, documents that served as the

(*continued*)

(continued)

basis for investment decisions, and tax documents). Electronic archiving systems can ensure the long-term availability of documents in easily sortable form. In particular, care must be taken to establish responsibility for files (record owners) and rules for the destruction of files. Because the family office will work with external service providers in many areas, the compliance rules and standards should also establish whether and which data retention obligations apply to partners (tax accountants, external reporting preparers).

The compliance rules and standards must also support tax and legal obligations on the part of the client. This includes the long-term retention of all receipts and contracts necessary for tax filings as well as all tax-relevant facts detailed in tax returns (denotation of all asset items, client income sources) and all necessary documents that are provided to the client's tax accountant.

The attitude of the employees is a crucial aspect of implementing an effective compliance framework. "The employees follow the lead of their managers. This is particularly true for small companies with executive structures that have grown organically over time, where the 'tone at the top' modeled by executives is personified, conveyed and lived out." (Boldt et al. 2013, p. 101)

The defined processes should be reviewed on a regular basis and adapted to current best practices and the needs of the family office. This helps ensure that the compliance will be enforced in an effective way. These ongoing adjustments and improvements are an important component of a family office's active quality management systems. "Compliance should be understood as a service unit, and this approach should be communicated and lived out regularly. The Compliance officer is both a consultant in questions related to establishment and organizational implementation, as well as for legally compliant processes and structures and any other concrete one-off compliance questions" (Boldt et al. 2013, p. 102).

To conduct these tasks, the family office requires qualified and dedicated employees and a functional technical infrastructure. Beyond personnel and operating expenses, additional costs can arise for independent tax assessments, tax consultations, independent legal assessments and portfolio management (portfolio costs, costs related to the purchase and sale of stocks, bonds, funds, real estate, etc.). As part of the structuring of the family office, it must be negotiated who will bear the costs for these services and, where necessary, how they will be allocated to the client.

12.4 Transparent Fees System for Financing

It is not recommended that a single family office be run as a profit center. Such a model ultimately encourages the single family office to charge the family unnecessarily higher fees, which is contrary to the interests of the family. Single family offices should charge their clients solely for costs that are actually accrued—potentially with a minor 'safety buffer' for future special services or projects. This stricture naturally does not apply to commercial multi family offices, which routinely endeavor to maximize profits and thereby provide their partners and shareholders with attractive dividends.

The costs for a family office integrated into a family business are often borne by the company (and hence proportionately by its shareholders). The owning family in this situation are only rarely directly billed for costs related to family office services. Single family offices that are not part of a business, as well as classic, non-commercial multi family offices, do charge their clients directly for services. In practice, three different methods are used to allocate costs to clients; it is possible to combine or vary between them, so long as they are handled in a comprehensible, fair and forward-looking manner:

- allocation based on fixed percentages
- allocation related to the share of assets under management
- allocation based on time and expense

12.4.1 Allocation Based on Fixed Percentages

Allocation based on fixed percentages is an appropriate method for smaller families. The principal (founder of the family office) generally assumes the lion's share of the costs (such as 55%), with each of the three children, for example, paying the remainder in equal amounts (in this case, 15% each of the costs). This system has the benefit of being eminently comprehensible. Because "small families" tend to make very similar or joint capital investment strategies, this form of allocation is also typically perceived by all as fair.

Over extended periods, however, the fixed percentage model can stagnate and lose acceptance, especially as the descendants develop separate lives and utilize the family office at differing degrees of intensity. There are several reasons for this: Personal preferences for capital investments, individual tax situations and the number of members of each "branch" can all diverge notably. Kirby Rosplock, a family office researcher and consultant, comments on this:

> Often, family offices were started by and financially supported by the senior family members. Over time there will be a generational change. Families who are experiencing a similar situation may want to consider a scaled fee sharing arrangement. (Rosplock 2014, p. 260)

12.4.2 Allocation in Relation to Share of Assets Under Management

When the client base develops as described above, the fees structure is often converted into a 'scaled fee sharing arrangement,' meaning fees are allocated based on the share of assets under management. Because the costs of providing consulting for a larger fortune are higher than for smaller fortunes, this form of allocation is often perceived as fair. Sandy Loder, founder of AH Loder Advisers, prefers: "… first method: asset-based fees. This is probably the most common method used for charging" (Archer and Hauser 2015, p. 69).

One variety of this involves a somewhat "overly high" percentage when calculating the allocations, but then capping the absolute total at some upper ceiling. The result is reasonable costs for smaller fortunes, as the costs of reporting on capital investment do not vary by the size of the invested capital. Those with larger fortunes are also spared from fees, preventing potential higher net worth customers from being scared off from joining. Allocation using cost ceilings are relatively forward-looking, because older generations in particular typically possess larger portfolios of assets and benefit from the cost ceilings. When a pool of wealth is divided among multiple heirs, the costs will initially be higher (because multiple customers require counselling), but the ceiling will only be triggered to a minor degree, if at all. The increased costs for the family office are then cancelled out by greater income.

Another variant of this allocation model specifies that certain capital investments not be included in the calculations, or only to a minor degree. Equity stakes in companies, fixed deposit accounts and owner-inhabited real estate might be excluded, as upkeep of these assets involves "no" expenditures. Money invested in ten "standard funds products" might be assessed at 50%, reflecting the cost efficiency at play through bundling. The remainder of the wealth is assessed at 100%. Customers often perceive this method as fair, although there is the risk that the family office will, for profit reasons, recommend investments that provide 100% fees, undermining trust through a creeping conflict of interest.

12.4.3 Cost Allocation Based on Time and Expenditures

Another possibility lies in setting family office fees on an individual service-by-service basis, charged either on a fixed or hourly rate. After all, some processes are more expensive and time-intensive than others, such as writing a will, which may require both external tax consultants and the time of the family office as well. Other family members may well wonder why they too are bearing an indirect share of those costs. Because this type of commission does not occur regularly and the consultation costs related to it can vary greatly, an hourly-based fee may be appropriate. Other services such as payroll for employees, the handling of private payment transactions and reporting services beyond the standard level may be better handled through supplemental monthly flat fees. These types of allocation are comprehensible and, compared with fixed fees, are often understood as more appropriate.

On the whole, it is recommended that the various different gradations of "ceilings" and rebates be kept relatively clean and simple. While it might seem that an extensive catalog with various precisely calibrated fees would seem fair, experience teaches that it instead encourages endless rounds of negotiations and eventually strife among the clients.

The fairest and most forward-looking system surely involves allocation based on time and expense. When a client asks for expanded services beyond those normally offered by the family office, the associated costs are then invoiced.

This form of billing corresponds with the methods used for decades by legal offices and tax consultants. Yet while the system is, objectively viewed, simple, fair and adaptable, the clients will not necessarily see it that way. In many cases they are unable to visualize how much time is required for preliminary and follow-up work on consulting services (and especially the costs of ongoing consultation). This can give rise to the constant, implicit accusation that the family office is not handling its responsibilities with sufficient efficiency.

Complicating this situation is the fact that the efficiency benefits associated with bundling of activities in this system can be difficult to evaluate. How should costs be split between multiple clients when it comes to the extremely labor-intensive due diligence process? The family office only performs the work once, but many clients can benefit from the insights it uncovers, now and later. Customers can get the impression that the family office's consulting service are only offered to accrue costs to the benefit of the family office. This attitude can lead clients to consult with the family office much less frequently, breaking down the basis for trust.

Costs for direct and active management of portfolios, family funds and investments in real estate or private equity can be assigned to the respective investments as block costs. They are then borne proportionally by all customers involved in the investment. In all cases, the costs must be billed in a clear and transparent manner and in explicit detail for all customers. Even so, this fee model runs the risk of leaving the family office exposed to accusations of conflicts of interest if there is a sense among clients that the fees are serving a commercial purpose.

To eliminate the perception of any conflict of interest, and ensure the neutrality of the consultations and an assessment of risk in line with the customer's own perspectives, no employee of the family office should receive bonuses or additional monetary remuneration for such activities. Such payments increase the temptation to recommend investments to clients because of the higher commissions they might earn. If the single family office is to be prevented from developing into a 'commercial organization' and maintain its mission of wealth management services focused at all time solely on the interests of the family members, then the cost allocation should be limited to repayment of demonstrable external costs.

In 2014, the German Central Bank issued an official statement on such practices: "Remuneration policies that focus on short-term parameters and only reward without properly punishing failure may tempt staff to lose sight of the factors that keep their company sustainably successful over the long term. Such remuneration policies are antithetical to adequate risk management. The financial market crisis has demonstrated that the 'moral hazard' created by misguided remuneration policies may put at risk not only the stability of individual enterprises, but also financial stability in general." (German Central Bank 2014).

12.4.4 Remuneration of Special Services for Individual Clients

In some cases, individual family members or, in a multi family office, individual families can repeatedly or routinely commission services that are not needed by other family members or families; examples include management of private vacation real estate for an individual family member, management of additional equity stakes in companies for a single shareholder, or management of highly unusual asset classes for one single family member. If these activities involve ongoing costs of a relevant volume, then consideration must be given as to whether the internal and external costs accrued in this manner should be charged 'on top' to the initiating party—not least to maintain some semblance of fairness. As Peter Schaubach, a professor specialized in family offices, determined in his book "Family Office in Private Wealth Management":

> When establishing the terms of payment, an analysis of the remuneration finds that 70% [of clients] prefer a base fee covering pre-defined services, with a surcharge applied for additional services (Schaubach 2011, p. 297).

It's important that the customer be informed, clearly and in advance, that requests for non-standard services will also incur additional personal fees. This can help cap rampant "side services" while covering the costs for personnel and infrastructure when such services are required. The benefit: The family office can continue to focus professionally and efficiently on its core competencies.

As already described, the fees for a single family offer should in particular 'only' serve to cover the costs accrued by the operation of the family office. For this reason, all family office services should regularly be audited for their efficiency. Are they necessary or just "nice to have"? For older family offices in particular, "concierge services" can be established over the course of time that were not part of the original vision and values, or which even run contrary to the long-term orientation of the family office. In many cases these are actually services for which the personnel of the family office are not qualified (and which are likely far overpriced). They usually would (and should) be handled more efficiently, effectively and affordably by other service providers.

Practical Tip: Fee Model Should Prevent Conflicts of Interest

The fee model for a single family office should, above all else, be simple and fair. Complex fee models lead to endless discussions among the clientele and ultimately resentment and dissatisfaction with exceptions and "special rules." This can devolve into dissatisfaction and skepticism toward the services themselves, and especially how they are billed. Whichever cost allocation model you choose, be sure that it promotes the central element of a single family office: freedom from conflicts of interest on the part of consultants. Awarding performance or sales-related commissions, "retrocessions" or portfolio commissions can all raise the specter of conflicts of interest and should be avoided. These same considerations apply when joining a multi family office as well—poorly designed fees structures can encourage "self-serving" advice. Be sure to ask about the fee model even at multi family offices and review whether the model promotes consultation that is free from conflict of interest.

12.5 Who Owns the Family Office?

Who holds ownership rights to the single family office? There are several possible options: The family office can belong to

- the family company,
- the clients of the family office,
- the management team, in part or whole, or
- a separate foundation or trust.

12.5.1 Dependent Department of the Company

A single family office that belongs to the family company starts out as a department of that company. In such a scenario, the principal's secretarial service handles the filing of personal contracts and receipts. Employees of the financial department manage the private accounts and portfolios "on the side," negotiate conditions and later also handle private real estate assets and other investments. Certain employees grow increasingly involved with wealth management, and eventually are solely dedicated to it. They form a single family office integrated into and formally owned by the family business.

This organizational form is not always a simple one for the affected employees. On the one hand, their job descriptions and employment contracts hold them responsible for the financial concerns of the company, and they report to the head of the financial department. On the other hand, they are subject to the ongoing instructions by the principal and other family members, instead of working in their ostensible areas of responsibility. They are obligated to confidentiality in their dealings with the family members, a troubling situation that can cause friction with their direct supervisors. Company management may also be uncomfortable with the charges and insurance requirements related to extremely sensitive (health related) matters on the part of the shareholder group, or with the private legal consultations related to "inappropriate" behavior by a shareholder.

12.5.2 Family Office as a Subsidiary

To get a clearer handle on its organizational structures and responsibilities, the "single family office" department is often spun off into its own company. This measure is a decisive step towards a comprehensive, independent single family office focused fully on the tasks of a family office and staffed with suitable employees. In this constellation, the new company is established as a subsidiary and remains closely tied to the parent company. The subsidiary can now hire employees for the family office and concentrate its full attention on that task.

The CEO and chairman of the family business and the director of the finance department continues to be responsible for the offloaded family office company. They can now harmonize the interests of the family company and the private asset investment of the shareholders and engage in comprehensive sharing of information about corporate and private topics. From the client standpoint, the bond to the company is enhanced through a deep relationship of trust to the outsourced family office.

One disadvantage with this construction is the joint liability through the family company and the family office—if the family company encounters economic difficulties, then the family office is also directly affected. Another potential disadvantage: the executives of the family office are neither a family officer nor capital market experts, and furthermore lack specialized expertise in private tax issues or questions related to will and testaments, living wills and lifestyle management. This makes it more difficult (if not impossible) for them to conduct their oversight obligations for the spun-off family office. Beyond this, "occupational injuries" resulting from the advice of the family office can have negative consequences for the reputation of the company executives and can trigger conflict or even claims for damages between shareholders and family companies.

> One of the unspoken risks of having a dedicated family office is the danger of falling into the 'family office trap', where a family accountant, former company secretary, or advisor takes on the responsibility for setting up and running a family office when the family's wealth is in the early stages of development, but stays on long after the job has outgrown his or her capabilities. Unfortunately, some long-standing family office managers hang on tenaciously to increasingly well-paid jobs (as the money grows) and resist accurate benchmarking or realistic reviews (as performance fades). Some of these underperforming family offices can do major harm to families and their wealth if trust systems are not properly set up or maintained, if sophisticated wealth management challenges are misunderstood or, in the worst case, if proximity to great family wealth leads to family staff members defrauding a family, or justifying in their own minds the acceptability of taking 'finder fees' of other inappropriate payments to build their own wealth. (Daniell and Hamilton 2010, p. 219)

For these reasons, internal "family offices" are often eventually spun off from the family company and an external single family office is founded. If it then remains exclusively in the ownership of the manager of the family office, then the family becomes a pure client. This step very often leads to highly professional family office structures. Because the interests of the employees (maximizing of profits and shareholder value) are not identical with those of the family shareholders (cost-conscious focus on the individual interests of the family shareholders), these structures typically develop into a classic multi family office in which the founding family only plays a subordinate role. In practice, after a certain period the founding family looks to create its own structures and so separates from the offloaded family office.

Another common development is that the shares are not held by the employees of the family office, but rather by the family itself. The clear division of the ownership relationships makes it possible to address the often varied competencies and responsibilities in detail without encountering the aforementioned problems. The family office in this constellation belongs to the family and thus in the long run represents a classic single family office. If the family is composed of various family branches and all are involved in the family office, then one often talks about a classic multi family office. If the office belongs to various families, then this develops into an additional form, the closed multi family office (see Figs. 3.1 and 3.3).

This family office ownership structure forces the participants to come to terms with appropriate expenditures and costs, a positive development from a commercial viewpoint. Costs are assigned directly, ensuring that clients of the family office have full price transparency. From an objective standpoint, this can and should lead to efficient design of the structures of the single family office, with a focus on services in core competencies best positioned to add strong value for the clients. This separation allows for a new corporate activity by the single family office outside the family company. It can also represent a "threat" to the financing of the family company and family cohesion. On the other hand, it allows the family members to take advantage of diversification and risk distribution, which reduces the dependency on the company, counteracts irrational fears that affect shareholder decision making and which often leads to professional, objective decisions in terms of the family company.

For family members accustomed to receiving the services for free, the direct allocation of costs can be upsetting and lead to an emotional distance from the family business. Both negatives should be actively addressed if these ownership models are pursued. One further disadvantage: the entry and departure of clients can put the value of the family office into question. As new clients are seeking to enter, the shareholders can require a suitable purchase price for their shares; when departing, the release of assets can be handled through a "dispute fund."

12.5.3 Association, Foundation, Trust

To avoid subjective questions and to bring an objective tone to entries and departures, the family office can be placed in the ownership of a club or foundation. Many families in Anglo-Saxon countries in particular have followed the trend of setting up a trust as a vehicle for ownership. These considerations are not possible for commercial multi family offices, of course. The use of an association as the legal form allows for a more active influence by the owners (members of the association), while foundations and trusts are fully independent legal persons without owners. Insofar as the family does not have fundamental rights of determination within the organs of the foundation or trust, this kind of structure can lead to sharply reduced entrepreneurial influence on one's "own single family office". Because these three structural choices are more exceptions than rules in much of the world, their organizational structure will not be explored in depth here.

12.5.4 Role of the Family Members

Regardless of the selected structure, family members are often actively integrated into the executive ranks of their single family office, and thus have a direct influence on a variety of decisions. In such cases the single family office is typically managed more entrepreneurially and represents a second company beyond the family business. This aspect is not present for multi family offices. In some cases, however, the opposite path is chosen and the family office is solely run by external employees—to take the load off the family members active in the family business or to ensure professionalism in advising and capital investments (presuming the family does not possess expertise in these areas).

In the scenario where the family is integrated, questions related to leadership succession take on a special relevance. In the second variant, where the family office is run exclusively by persons outside the family, it must also be determined how the clients and/or family members can be invited to take part in strategy decisions by the family office. In both cases an advisory council can help with the formulation of concepts.

12.6 Controlling and Consultation by the Advisory Council

An advisory council can function as a control instance and an advisor. If the advisory council is empaneled with family members from various "nuclear families" or "branches," then the strategies and activities of the family office can be conveyed effectively to a larger portion of the family. The name can vary by legal form and jurisdiction, such as "supervisory council" or "shareholder's council," but the role is the same. Family members selected to serve in the advisory council also represent important influencers in the effort to build trust in the single family office. Because the different "clans" within the family will feel directly represented by "their" advisory council member, the advisory council members are also key figures in promoting consensus throughout the entire family on the family office's strategies and proposals. This applies in particular to single multi family offices and classic multi family offices.

Their advisory function is even more crucial when the family office is exclusively run by directors outside the family. The members of the advisory council are important liaisons for communication between the executives and the family. The focus in this case is not on investment strategy and capital markets, which is more the responsibility of the investment council, another organ than can of course also include individual members of the family. The members of the advisory council instead bring to the discussion the concerns and desires of other family members (such as for new services), or report on their own past experiences with specific investments. Lisa Gray, a renowned family office consultant, in "The New Family Office": "The wealth management issues families' face today are the natural inheritance of the attitudes and actions of individual family members in the past" (Gray 2004, p. 114). And these experiences (whether positive or negative) can be discussed with the executives of the family office by family members on the advisory council—which in turn lends itself to a better overall understanding of client needs.

It is often easier for the (family) members of a single family office to use a relative as an "agent" to convey messages, such as questions about capital investments, advisory topics such as living wills or testaments or even considerations about privately used real estate or analyses of expenditures related to private hobbies.

Responsibilities of the Advisory Council

Single family offices run by non-family members use the advisory council as their interface with the interests of the owners. In this case, the advisory council members are focused on the long-term strategic orientation of the family office.

The responsibilities of an advisory council at a single family office encompass:

- Defining the **spectrum of services and long-term strategy** of the family office (including "Visions and Core Values").
- Participation in setting the **budget and cost structure forecast** for the family office. Those figures are then used to set the fee structure and levels.
- **Monitoring compliance** and receiving the report from the Compliance officer (and counteracting potential conflicts of interest at the single family office).
- Ensuring **transparent, efficient and complete communication** within the family office, as well as between the family office and its clients.
- Involving family members, especially the younger generation, in the work and orientation of the family office and ensuring that **the family identifies at an emotional level with the single family office,** not just its work (such as by organizing family activities and family continuing education).

Yet undoubtedly the most important task for the advisory council is the hiring of single family office employees. In any family office led by non-family members, the selection, support and advising of the director of the family office is its central task. The negotiated guidelines for executive succession form the strategic basis for this, especially if family members wish to join into the family office. The advisory council should also be involved in the selection of the reporting employees, managers of the various investment and tax issues and for the person responsible for handling payment transactions.

In this way, the advisory council contributes actively to the strength of the family office's pool of specialist knowledge and impacts the salary structure and totals (bearing in mind that salaries represent the largest cost block for any family office). The advisory council monitors the chemistry within the family office team, checks that the team is handling its responsibilities professionally, efficiently and at justifiable cost levels, and that the employees it has selected are a good fit for the family office clients and can establish a relationship of trust with them.

The advisory council takes an active influence on the spectrum of services and the cost structures for the family office and reviews all other classic shareholder functions. From a strictly legal standpoint, many of these decisions are subject to the vote of the shareholders. In this kind of constellation, the advisory council is often granted concrete decision-making authority to allow for a more intensive and regular exchange and to hedge against any unwanted emotional distance between the owner family and the family office. In that regard, the advisory council serves as a crucial emotional and factual liaison between the family office and the owner family.

In a multi family office, the advisory council is restricted solely to functional issues (specialist or investment councils). In this model it comprises representatives of the individual client families, serving in an especially crucial bridging function between the families/clients and the family office and its managers/third-party owners.

From Canada: "Financial investments, tax and estate planning and governance are only tools to help families achieve the things that are most important to them."

Interview with Tom McCullough

This interview touches on the distinctives of the Canadian family office market, finding talented staff, the benefits of MFOs and the non-financial goals behind good wealth management.

This interview was conducted by Peter Preller.

What's your background in the family office world?
Tom McCullough: My father built his wealth over the years through real estate investments. I worked for over 20 years in senior executive roles in wealth management at a high quality Canadian investment firm. As we began to talk about family succession planning, I realized that there was a gap in the market for families like ours. Many families of wealth had accountants, lawyers, investment managers and bankers, but they did not have anyone to create a central strategic plan, tie everything together, and to make sure that the plan actually happened. So I started Northwood Family Office in 2003, with my co-founder Scott Hayman, to try and address this gap in the market (and solve my own family's problems).

***Tom McCullough** is the co-founder, chairman and CEO of Northwood Family Office and a longtime advisor to families of significant wealth. Northwood is the leading multi-family office in Canada. Tom is also an adjunct professor at the University of Toronto's Rotman School of Management where he teaches the 'Management of Private Wealth,' and is co-author of Family Wealth Management (2013), and Wealth of Wisdom: 50 Questions Wealthy Families Ask, and Answers from the World's Top Family Wealth Experts (coming out late-2018), both published by John Wiley & Sons.*

The best analogy I know to describe what a family office does is that of an architect/general contractor. When you build or renovate a house, you need to hire plumbers, carpenters, and painters, but most people still want an architect/general contractor to organize the overall process and coordinate the other trades. A family office is similar to the general contractor, but instead of building a house, we are overseeing a family's integrated financial affairs. We coordinate all of the expert 'trades' (accountants, lawyers, investment managers) and make sure that the family's financial 'house' is in order.

Does the Canadian family office market differ greatly from the US one?
TM: In many ways, yes. Even though family offices have been around for over a century in the US, they're not nearly as well known or prevalent in Canada. Because of this, we thought there was a gap in the market and a real opportunity for us to develop a world class multi-family office in Canada.

Historically, the big six Canadian banks have dominated almost every aspect of the financial and wealth management in Canada—from brokerage to investment counselling right through to mortgages and mutual funds. In this concentrated market environment, independent firms can have a harder time emerging, whereas in the US the banking system is highly decentralized and independent firms are prevalent.

Did Canada's banks suffer a loss of trust during the great financial crisis?
TM: No, the Canadian banks were extremely strong during the 2008 crisis and actually were recognized globally for their stability during this time period. I would say that the level of trust in Canadian banks remained steady or even rose during the financial crisis.

Banks generally have a good reputation in this country. Everyone uses them, and they are viewed almost as national institutions. Most people also know that they are product sales organizations and are rarely the best fit for ultra high net worth clients, but it can take quite a long time for people to come to this realization, so many clients use them as a default.

What benefits do you see the family office experience offering over a bank?
TM: Our family office relationships start with a conversation. We sit down with each family and talk about their hopes, their goals, the resources they have at their disposal, and the constraints and challenges they face. We also undertake a full net-worth review, including an appraisal and analysis of all key financial documents, so we can get an accurate picture of the family's current situation. We then discuss what they are looking for from their family office and, together, we tailor a service plan that will work for them.

How are those plans put together?

TM: The services that we offer fall into four main categories:

First is integrated planning. This can include goal setting, cash flow planning, risk management, and tax and estate planning, among other topics. Our integrated approach helps clients see the big picture and allows us to manage all aspects of our clients' net worth. As a family office, our breadth and depth of experience in all key financial disciplines means we are uniquely able to pull all the pieces of the puzzle together.

I should also point out that we don't take away the job of the accountant or the lawyer that the family has historically worked with. These professionals still do their work (such as filing tax returns, drafting wills, and complex planning), and we work with them to make sure that each aspect of the family's financial affairs are coordinated.

Second is investment management. We don't select individual securities internally, but we do develop investment policy statements based on our client's goals and objectives. We identify appropriate asset classes for clients to invest in and research, retain and implement best in class investment management mandates. Once the client's investment portfolio is fully in place, we report on the performance of the portfolio on a quarterly basis and continue to monitor and evaluate all of the selected investment managers on an ongoing basis.

Third is administration and reporting. This means making sure the trains all run on time. It includes accurate and comprehensive quarterly reports of a client's full net worth and investment portfolio. It also includes a full range of administrative tasks, from ensuring trust resolutions are completed on an annual basis, to making sure that tax installments are paid on time. There are countless examples of tasks that fall into this category, but really it consists of making sure that nothing falls through the cracks of our client's financial lives.

The final area, and one that seems to be growing in importance for many of our clients, is family dynamics and governance. What I mean by this is all of the aspects of people's lives that are generally non-financial. This includes organizing and facilitating family meetings, setting up a family governance structure, and doing the ongoing work of managing family dynamics and making sure families are able to have productive conversations. In certain cases, it might even involve helping a family to draft a family constitution that is meant to serve as a guide to future generations. The education of the next generation and the task of preparing them for wealth inheritance is also growing in importance as more and more wealth begins to transfer to the next generation.

Is there a demand for concierge services?

TM: We don't offer traditional concierge services, such as travel bookings, personal shopping and household staff management. It's talked about all the time, because there's a narrative that a person de confidence looks after every little aspect of a family's life, but we have found there is limited demand for it amongst our client base. Having said that, we have provided hundreds of unique, bespoke services for clients over the past 15 years. We offer to help out wherever we can.

How do you find new employees and bind the talent you have or would like to have?

TM: It's very challenging to find the type of advisor that can manage all of the different kinds of work that we do for our client families. Our staff needs a wide range of knowledge, significant experience and the right temperament. As a result, finding and recruiting staff remains one of the most important challenges that we face.

Our approach has been to hire smart and credentialed younger professionals (CA, CFA, MBA, CFP), and then build up their integrated skill sets over time. This has worked well for us and it has created a very cohesive team with a long-term focus. When you have employees who are invested in the long-term success of the family office, it makes succession planning and continuity of service for our families much easier.

What would you say to a "next generation" member of a family office who says, "This is all fine and good, but I think I would like to found my own family office."

TM: I'd certainly encourage them to remember that running a family office is like running a business. Sometimes people think "I'll just hire a few people to help manage our affairs," but really you need to decide whether you want to spend time hiring and managing employees and dealing with HR related issues. I find that most people—maybe it's different for younger people, but certainly older people—have already done that in their careers and often don't want to go through the hassle again.

The second and bigger question is how much money do you have? Setting up your own single family office can be a very expensive proposition and you should make sure that you actually need one before undertaking this process. There are actually a lot of good arguments for using a multi-family office, beyond the lower cost and ease of management. Because they serve multiple families, MFOs see a wide variety of family situations, choices and issues. These learnings can benefit other families as well. MFO clients also benefit from the economies of scale and attendant cost savings that come from the combined asset pool of multiple families. I think every family should at least consider the MFO option before going down the path of building their own SFO. They should never come at this decision from the perspective of, "Asset managers and private banks didn't do a very good job, so my only other option is to set up my own SFO."

Do you see a trend here?
TM: I think there's an ongoing shift from SFO to MFO, primarily because of the cost savings from moving to an MFO, and also because of people's desire to be freed from the administrative tasks of running their own SFO. Some families will always want the control that comes with an SFO that works exclusively for one family, but I think the benefits (information sharing, economies of scale, and ease of management) still make MFOs the best options for most high net worth families considering a family office.

You offer "family dynamic services." How important are these?
TM: This has been a major growth area in our practice over the past five or ten years. Wealth typically adds complexity to family relationships, so ensuring good communication and decision making becomes essential. For instance, if we are trying to have a discussion with a family about their trusts, and two of the trustees aren't speaking to each other, then that is a family dynamics issue and we will work to solve it.

The same concept applies to asking a client: "What are the things that keep you up at night?" In some cases, it might be the condition of the market, but in other cases, it's that their son still lives in their basement and has trouble getting motivated. Another common concern is the effect that a large inheritance will have on a next generation family member's motivation and desire to find their own path in life.

These are the types of concerns that we hear from clients on a regular basis, so it is incumbent upon us to provide, or find, solutions for our families. In some cases we provide the advice and counsel ourselves. In other more severe cases, we bring in family psychologists, counsellors or communication specialists.

Does it make the family office function better?
TM: The best thing it does, in my opinion, is that it helps clients realize that most of the things that are important to them are not necessarily financial. Developing an investment strategy, tax and estate planning, and governance are only tools which can be used to help them achieve the things that are most important to them.

The work we do on family dynamics is central to our overall role as a family office. Most people would prioritize having strong healthy relationships with their family members over a higher investment return.

Even though the investment performance is important at the end of the day.

TM: Yes, it is critical. For most families, investments are what fund their goals and so good, risk-adjusted returns are extremely important. The problem is that most firms prioritize investments over all other aspects of what a family needs. I can understand why this happens. In fact, clients also want to talk about investments before anything else. At Northwood, we resist that temptation. Our process begins with fundamental questions like: "What is the money for?", "Who is it for?", "When will it be needed?" and "How high a priority is the particular goal?" Only once we have clear and detailed answers to these questions can we move onto the implementation stage of our process, including investments. These can be hard questions to answer, but it is worth the effort. They are the critical foundations of a goals-based wealth management philosophy and to making sure we help families accomplish what is most important to them.

Bibliography

Archer C, Hauser BR (2015) Family offices. Globe Business Publishing, London

Boldt T, Büll K, Voss M (2013) Die neue MaRisk-Compliance-Funktion – Ein Leitfaden für die Bankpraxis. Bank-Verlag, Cologne

Daniell M, Hamilton S (2010) Family legacy and leadership – preserving true family wealth in challenging times, 1st edn. Wiley, Singapore

German Federal Bank Bundesbank (2014) Auslegungshilfe zur Verordnung über die aufsichtsrechtlichen Anforderungen an Vergütungssysteme von Instituten. Frankfurt

Gray L (2004) The new family office – innovative strategies for consulting to the affluent. Linnius, London

Rosplock K (2014) The complete family office handbook – a guide for affluent families and the advisors who serve them. Wiley, Hoboken

Scharf P (2014) Compliance in Kredit- und Finanzdienstleistungsinstituten – Grundlagen der Compliance-Funktion. Abgrenzung zu den Grundsätzen ordnungsgemäßer Bankgeschäftsführung. Diplomica, Hamburg

Schaubach P (2011) Family Office im Privaten Wealth Management – Konzeption und empirische Untersuchung aus Sicht der Vermögensinhaber, 4. Aufl. Uhlenbruch, Bad Soden

Wilson RC (2014) The single family office: creating, operating & managing investments of a single family office, 1st edn. CreateSpace, Lexington

13

Leadership Structures in the Family Office

Christoph Weber

The size, composition and structure of the management team at a family office should reflect the office's size and the nature of the tasks it performs. In concrete terms, the management team should be assembled based on the number of families it serves and the volume of assets under management. The number of asset classes will also influence staffing decisions, as will the choice to include activities beyond pure asset management.

The bigger the combined wealth, the greater its complexity. Along the same lines, the demands placed on the management team's organizational structures rise as the size of the assets under management across all families grows in volume. For very large portfolios, the potential fees that can be earned by the management team allow for a comfortable range of possibilities for personnel costs.

The overall number of parties being served can also be expected to affect the breadth of requirements that the family office management team must master. Each family has its own distinct needs structure and will want to tailor its asset management to achieve its own goals. Asset allocation can differ greatly between different families, reflecting different attitudes toward performance, risk and individual asset classes.

Beyond this, latent conflicts of interest between the different families are a constant issue of concern, such as when the family office identifies an interesting investment whose volume is only sufficient for one family and must then decide which family will be presented with the investment opportunity. Management requires a particularly deft touch and effective communications skills in such situations.

B. Canessa et al., *The Family Office*, https://doi.org/10.1007/978-3-319-99085-9_13

The number of asset classes under management also determines the size of the family office: The managers at a family office who need to control only one single asset class are likely to face fewer stumbling blocks than those who offer a full-spectrum wealth management program that accounts for all asset classes.

Beyond pure asset management, the family office can also be assigned other tasks. The broader the offerings of the family office itself, the bigger it will become. Legal and tax consulting, mediation, coaching, succession planning, family governance consulting, support for family activities and continuing education of family members, organization of philanthropic engagement, convenience services—if this entire spectrum of themes is to be addressed within one family office, a pool of employees with different aptitudes and areas of knowledge is required.

13.1 Management Befitting the Requirements Profile of the Family Office

A highly professional family office requires not only a massive depth of expertise, but also a global perspective. This actually presents its own special problem, as it is difficult to find employees who are both talented generalists and experienced specialists in the various areas of responsibility.

Family offices that cover a broad palette of assets are better served by harnessing different experts for the individual asset classes, ideally managed by cross-disciplinary generalists with excellent leadership skills. Their positions correspond to that of a general director: a strong leader responsible for steering the different technical departments as well as delivering information in a form suitable for the specific client.

If the family office is also entrusted at a fundamental level with strategic consulting for the family and/or strategic development for its private assets, then this role takes on more of a Chief Operating Officer nature, reporting to a strategic-minded CEO. This figure, known as the Family Officer, must have a remarkable professional background and a firm bond of trust with the family.

The composition of the management team for the family office is determined not just by the volume of assets under management, but also by the degree to which the portfolio is diversified internationally. In some cases it may be advisable to open a branch in the country in which the office has a notable volume of its assets, or to enter a cooperative agreement with a local family office there.

If management is also responsible for a family's charitable foundation or offers extensive convenience services, then additional employees and managers are required to tend to these specific areas. Legal and tax advisors are often needed. An executive coach or mediator can help the family with the composition of a family codex, or in conducting seminars for the next generation.

Practical Tip: Factors that Impact the Size of the Family Office

The size of the family office will reflect the size of the family's portfolio, the number of assets requiring care, the number of family members and the spectrum of responsibilities beyond financial expected from the family office (such as tax and legal advice, family governance, philanthropy and convenience). These factors should all be taken into consideration when designing the management of the family office.

13.2 Management Structure of a Family Office

The following presents the potential management structure for a sample family office operating at a medium size level (€1 bn. of assets under management, distributed between ten families) with a full-spectrum approach to management (see Fig. 13.1). Four different levels of consultants can be observed:

Fig. 13.1 Sample executive organizational chart for a multi family office

- Strategic consultant (managing director of the family office, title: "Family Officer")
- Chief Operating Officer (COO)
- Departmental manager
- Additional specialists

The Family Officer

The Family Officer oversees a variety of consulting functions. As managing director, she represents the uppermost level of management in the family office. Her responsibilities include the strategic outlook as well as the commercial and personnel leadership of the company.

She should have an especially firm basis of trust with the family members she serves, drawing on her expertise, competency, years of professional experience and well-developed social tact. The Family Officer frequently slips into the role of family representative, both within the family office and in dealing with third parties. In return, the family expects an especially high level of responsibility, conscientiousness and identification with its goals. She is ready to fill the breach for the family with unflagging dedication, even in difficult situations. For this reason, she may even be called to duty as a mediator during internal family conflicts. Yet true commitment to the family is not enough; there must also be a sufficient level of self-confidence and an ability to act independently. This is essential to earn the respect of the family and their internal decision makers.

The central specialized responsibilities for the Family Officer include the development of a long-term and broad-based investment strategy for the family's private assets, discussing this strategy at regular intervals with the family and adjusting it to changing conditions. Collaborating with a Chief Operating Officer, she establishes a foundational investment strategy upon which business planning and investment guidelines for the overall asset portfolio can be created. She furthermore also determines when department leaders and external specialists such as mediators or coaches should be engaged.

On this basis, the Family Officer monitors the overall operative decision-making process within the family office. In an ideal situation, the family then gains a direct point of contact within their family office whom they trust unreservedly to maintain a complete overview over the asset portfolio and monitor and audit all ongoing activities within the family office. It is the Family Officer's task to validate that any and all measures are indeed compliant with the negotiated strategic approach.

Practical Tip: Skills Profile for a Family Officer

Any Family Officer you might consider hiring should possess the following knowledge, skills and experience.

Technical Aptitudes

- Generalist with above-average knowledge of all subject areas
- Global vision
- Ability to coordinate and channel technical talent
- Strategic vision
- Structured thinking
- Risk assessment, feel for tactical decision making
- Feel for market and overall economy

Personality Traits

- Service oriented
- Independent nature/strong character
- Sense of responsibility
- Conscientiousness
- Creativity
- Passion/enthusiasm
- Empathy
- Feel for the connections between people and their investments
- Discretion, honesty, trustworthiness

Chief Operating Officer

In a family office of the aforementioned size, each strategic consultant (Family Officer) should be provided with a Chief Operating Officer (COO). This employee is then responsible for coordinating, assessing and collating the deliverables from the individual departments and preparing them in an appropriate form for the Family Officer. He represents the second tier of the management structure and must possess personnel leadership skills as well as the ability to coordinate and integrate. He is also responsible for quality management in the reporting and financial planning as well as for the smooth progression of the working processes.

The COO should have a global vantage point but does not need detailed knowledge of the individual asset classes. He must however be in a position to understand the specialized input from the individual departments so as to assess that information and prepare proper decision-making documents for the Family Officer.

Departmental Manager

The manager of the individual departments is a well-established expert in the individual asset classes or technical field (law and taxes). For those in the securities field, this requires more than just a well-grounded training in the subject, familiarity with the various areas of capital investment and routine continuing education measures. Practical experience in operative investment management is a must. The family office will want to hire a securities investment manager with first-hand experience as a portfolio manager, and in particular how various investment instruments react through different phases of the exchange cycle. Such experience is irreplaceable for developing a fine sense of the workings of the capital investment market. This background alone lends this type of manager the gravitas needed to become a real sparring partner for the family's asset managers.

Whatever the depth of his technical expertise, the department manager must nevertheless avoid focusing too closely on just one field. He, together with his staff, form an important part of the overall family office team. Even if his contact to the client families is less intense compared to his interactions with the Family Officer and COO, he nevertheless must never lose sight of the family behind the numbers. The department leader must be aware that the family cannot be reduced to an asset class. As such, he is perpetually challenged to raise his eyes beyond the limitations of his own specific technical field. The department leader should also be a strong networker and have access to truly interesting investments that promise good yields.

Clarity in the Organizational Structure of a Family Office

The management structure of a multi family office brings with it distinctive requirements that reflect the diversity of the tasks required to support this kind of organization. It grows with the volume of assets under management, the number of client families, the spectrum of asset classes and the volume of supplemental services that the family office provides in addition to its classic responsibilities.

Depending on their position and function, the requirements for technical and social qualifications among individual employees can be extremely high. What's important is that the family can grasp the clearly delineated separations between responsibility for specific tasks and expertises and that it has at least one permanent contact who represents their interests with selflessness and dedication.

From the USA: "I think advisors have let the families down in the United States by saying 'We're financial advisors, we are not helping them on the family side.'"

Interview with Leslie Voth

This wide-ranging interview touches on the genesis of the multi-family office, promoting family cohesiveness and the qualities of effective family office advisors.

This interview was conducted by Peter Preller.

Did your company begin as a single or a multi-family office?

Leslie Voth: Our firm's roots are as a single family office that was established in 1923 by the Pitcairn family. The family patriarch, John Pitcairn, was a Scottish-born American industrialist who was a contemporary of John D. Rockefeller and Andrew Carnegie. He worked his way up through the ranks of the railroad industry, later becoming a serial entrepreneur and investor in real estate, oil and gas, and other private ventures. Most notably, he was the co-founder of Pittsburgh Plate Glass Company (today, known as PPG Industries).

John Pitcairn passed away in 1916 and without much structure around his wealth. His three sons, Raymond, Theodore and Harold, inherited a complex

---

Leslie C. Voth *is President and Chief Executive Officer of Pitcairn, a recognized global leader in the specialized multi-family office marketplace. Leslie's industry experience and invaluable insights have contributed to the success of both the firm and its clients.*

Leslie is directly responsible for overall corporate planning and strategic growth and oversees all client relationships. She has played a key role in Pitcairn's growth and expansion, spearheading development and implementation of an industry-leading 100% open architecture investment platform and developing a total wealth management strategy utilized by the firm's clients. She has pioneered the creation of multi-disciplinary teams to collaboratively meet the increasingly complex needs of the firm's clients.

pool of investments. At that time, each son had their own advisors and shared interests in the family business, trusts, and other investments. The eldest brother, Raymond, knowing there was a better way to manage their wealth and advisors, convinced his younger brothers to pool their assets and form a private holding company, today known as a family office.

So, this was a rudimentary family office?

LV: They didn't even know the words 'family office' back then, but they were really focused on: how do we continue to grow this wealth and sustain it. They saw value in bringing their own advisors under one roof to work together on behalf of the family.

That's the heart of the family office industry. Back then, the families who recognized the benefit of centralizing their resources found that they experienced better results, because things were better coordinated with respect to issues ranging from the family business to investments, legal and tax planning to personal spending needs. They really benefited from having a more diversified team around them that not only could do the work, but who could also understand all the moving pieces.

What happened as the family grew?

LV: The Pitcairn family office remained a single family office (SFO) for the next 60 years, planning for the third and fourth generations. By the 1980s, there were over 30 households to serve, which made the SFO feel more like a multi-family office.

Each household had different needs and objectives, but what held them together was the pooling of their investments in one entity that was managed in a cohesive way. They all benefitted from that. They had 60 years of terrific success.

Did they retain the legacy operating business?

LV: For some time, yes, but as the family grew, they needed more liquidity. So ultimately the Pitcairn family began to diversify away from that concentrated holding, eventually selling all of their stake in PPG in 1986. As a result, they liquidated the holding company, distributing the cash out to all the investors, trusts, partnerships, charities, and entities that they'd created.

So, there's the cash event. What next?

LV: The family recognized that there was a new business opportunity on the horizon. In 1987, they changed their legal structure and became a private trust company, regulated by the Commonwealth of Pennsylvania Department of Banking. This new legal structure would allow Pitcairn to provide family office services to other families.

And that was the genesis of the multi-family office?
LV: Yes, they spent some time trying to figure out the new business model. They decided that they would only offer investment services to the new families. But the new families that were coming to Pitcairn said: "We can get investment advice anywhere. What we can't get is this great planning that you've done for your family and the implementation of that."

They didn't know how to charge for these new services at first. There wasn't a lot of flat fee pricing at that time to compare with and for us to say, "For $200,000 a year, this service contract, we'll do the following things." That just wasn't something that was standard practice back then.

There was a lot of emphasis on investments initially. But as we've learned over time, investments are not the only thing these families need to do well to ensure that they successfully transfer wealth to the next generation.

And as the single family office transitioned to the multi-family office structure, some family members wanted to go their own way. The family leadership offered them the option to either remain with the family office or do their own thing.

What impact did this have?
LV: Over time, we've served fewer and fewer Pitcairn family members in the family office. We've found that as the wealth has moved to the fourth, fifth and, now sixth generations, not all family members want the full offerings of the family office and they prefer to do things more independently.

This wasn't part of the governance structure?
LV: It was new thinking, because back when they built the office, everybody did everything together and you were bound together legally. The idea of breaking that up, or changing it, wasn't really anticipated.

One of the things that I've learned from being the leader of this office is that families need to be flexible because things change, and the next generation may want to carve a different path. The previous generation may or may not even know what that next generation wants to do or not do with respect to the business, or the wealth, or the family office.

That's why it's so important to always include the next generation early enough to get their thoughts and desires on the table. As we moved through the Pitcairn family generationally, the firm learned a lot of these lessons. Giving family members the ability to leave the family office structure was a positive learning opportunity.

How do you manage the dynamics of keeping the family together? Each generation potentially has different views, different advisors and friends and different ideas.
LV: This is a really big philosophical issue that a family needs to consider. Some families are healthy and absolutely wired to stay together, and that's

how they think about it from the very beginning. Other families might not have the characteristics that lend themselves to making collective long-term decisions. That's where a lot of families lose momentum. Advisors need to be able to identify these issues and try to help the families work through it.

If your goal is to keep the family together, then you really need to spend time and effort and be very intentional about doing that. And I think advisors in the United States have let families down in that area. Many advisors draw a very, very strong line. They say, "We're financial advisors, we are not helping them on the family side, it's not our thing, we're not skilled at that. We're only going to run the money."

But if you look at it, it's the family issues that derail financial sustainability over time—advisors shouldn't become psychologists, but you have to be aware and be able to advise a family when they are having interpersonal issues.

Is it possible to promote 'effective behaviors' in this area?
LV: Sometimes we have this discussion with families directly, and they're open to that. Other times, we plant seeds and help them build out a multi-year strategy. It's very similar to what you would ask for a business transition: "What's your strategy for seeing this transition through?"

It takes a long time to make these transitions, or even to know what a successful transition looks like.

And what do you do in the meanwhile?
LV: We try to be more proactive—rather than wait until things aren't going well. It takes families a lot of time to be intentional about telling the next generation: "We want you to work side-by-side with us, we want you to learn what we're doing, to see how we make decisions. We want to invite you to come to this meeting with our advisors. We'd love for you to be part of that." Make it a normal routine.

Families that do that, that find structure, and are disciplined about doing that consistently are successful. It's all about achieving positive momentum into that next generation. We know because we've watched families lose momentum. They totally stall out and sometimes don't make progress for almost a whole generation.

How do you find talented employees, given that the FO sector is a colorful field with different knowledge—capital markets, legal, tax, personality?
LV: Over the years we've changed our view on this. We used to hire specialists—a lawyer, a tax specialist, etc. We built the teams with specialists, which was fine for doing the work and implementing the plans for families.

But specialists often don't make good relationship managers for multi-generational families. We found we needed more generalists, people with stronger communication skills and a desire to serve families. There's a service gene that has to be present. We can train other things around that.

That's fairly ambiguous. Is there something tangible you look for?
LV: We've started to train inside our talent pool, starting with our relationship management team. We've certainly hired from the outside, but we are very specific about what we're looking for. We want to find talent that can connect with families on a personal level, someone who demonstrates emotional intelligence. It's not just about the degrees and certifications. When the family needs support, you need to be able to recognize that and be able to help that family.

That's a certain skill that has really been lacking in many family offices. The advisors who are helping these families go through these transitions need to be smart individuals, but they don't need to be the smartest individual in the room. They have to be able to guide the family on their journey—set up the right agenda, facilitate conversations, facilitate conflict, and be organized to positively help that family move down the path.

14

Strengths, Weaknesses, Opportunities, Threats: Avoiding Traps, Preparing for the Future

Boris Canessa, Jens Escher, Alexander Koeberle-Schmid, Peter Preller, Christoph Weber, and Steven Sidore

"If you've seen one family office, you've seen … one family office."
—Source unknown

Celebrated Russian novelist Leo Tolstoy began his novel *Anna Karenina* with these famous words: "Happy families are all alike; every unhappy family is unhappy in its own way." Replace "family" and "families" with "family office(s)" and the core insight remains sound. Thriving organizations tend to follow many of the same principles as other successful organizations; the potential causes of failure, however, are virtually limitless.

This insight is important for understanding how to apply the overall teachings of this book. Each chapter is intended to provide a systematic exploration of one or more aspects of importance to the founding of a successful family office. We hoped to raise awareness of the wide range of potential issues that can make the difference between the success and failure of a family office, whatever its size and structure.

B. Canessa et al., *The Family Office*, https://doi.org/10.1007/978-3-319-99085-9_14

Issues that can make the difference between the success and failure of a family office include:

- The importance of selecting professional advisors with appropriate soft skills and who are free from conflicts of interest
- Potential friction points within high net worth families and especially involving the passing of power between generations
- The importance of transparency and reporting in all aspects of the business, from investment results and succession plans to philanthropy and the use of convenience services.

For each such issue or general theme, we have proposed a set of best practices or at least key considerations. In most cases, the interviews that supplement the various chapters also harmonize closely with this advice, albeit filtered through the speaker's own specific experience.

There is a danger to this systematic approach, however. Best practices are inherently general, whereas family offices are inherently specific. Indeed, no two family offices are quite alike, from member composition and asset base to risk thresholds and the specific financial needs of its shareholders. Relying on generalities can be dangerous; it can give rise to a false sense of overconfidence that issues have been resolved, and encourage blindness to the specific pitfalls of one's own situation until it is too late.

With this in mind, we endeavored to turn this weakness into a strength. We did so by posing two consistent questions during interviews:

- What are potential traps that people face when looking to found or sustain a family office?
- What lies ahead in the future for the family office?

Unlike in the authored sections and the main interviews, the desire here was not to achieve a systematic set of answers. The hope was instead to gather many specific, personal answers reflecting the lived experience of the interviewees, each of whom either works for or with, or is a shareholder in, a family office. Such insights are often contradictory, reflecting personal experience, local cultures, national environments and family situations.

We welcome diverse opinions, contradictions and all. Our hope is that these myriad insights, harnessed collectively, blossom into practical, rigorous wisdom that helps families get an early start on contemplating the issues that might well decide failure or success across generations.

14.1 Cohesiveness and Trust Within the Family: Contradictory Responses to the Same Trap

The issue of family governance looms large throughout this book. The topic is addressed at least tangentially in virtually every chapter and interview, including an entire chapter (Chap. 7) dedicated exclusively to core contemplations on the issue.

So when asked about the potential pitfalls, it is unsurprising that issues related to family governance were among the most frequently cited. The importance of trust within the family, the importance of maintaining the cohesiveness and identity of the family across growth and generations and the importance of open lines of communication were all mentioned repeatedly.

The crux of the problem is perhaps best summed up by a pair of family office shareholders, Nour Abou Adal & Maissa Abou Adal Ghanem of Lebanon:

> Cohesiveness is important. It means bringing everybody up to speed and on board. In a family—even if you're not involved in the day-to-day operations or if you're not in the BOD—as long as you have shares, as long as you have stakes in the business, you need to ensure that every member of the family has the same level of … not knowledge, but relevant information.
>
> It's important not to feel as a family member: 'Oh my God, we were put aside,' or 'they are cooking something up that I am not aware of.' There must be clear protocols, clear reporting processes and an authority matrix because otherwise you create a lot of complexities and a lot of frustration which will actually hinder your business.

Few of the interviewees would argue with this premise. How to actually achieve that cohesiveness is more a matter of debate. Klaus Kuder of Germany, whose firm advises family offices, frames it in simple yet general terms:

> Trite as it sounds, the family office must keep an open line to all participating family members, not just the patriarch of the family. The children may have other points of interest and expectations of the family office. These must absolutely be taken into account if each family member is to identify with the family office and if it is to enjoy the greatest degree of acceptance possible. This is especially important because the family office, if well managed, can make a significant long-term contribution to cohesiveness within the family.

Leslie Voth of the United States, CEO of one of the world's oldest family offices, sees precisely this dynamic as being one of the most difficult and requires sorting out from the beginning.

> I think many families run amazing businesses, but when it comes to the family office, they don't always apply the same principles to the strategic thinking and innovation that they need to. The family office is usually shaped around a very strong personality, and everyone around that person respects and knows how to work them. But when it comes to that next generation, the relationship dynamics are a lot more challenging.
>
> I'm thinking of one client. It is really sad, because the father died suddenly and his advisors were not prepared to deal with the next generation. It created a lot of friction within the family and even some legal actions.

The culprit, in Voth's view, is the limited perspective from which many families view their actions:

> I think what's so hard for families, and for family offices, is to think beyond the current generation. They're just not wired to do that automatically. None of us are, really. They think they have more control than they actually do. They really have to think about whether or not they are setting up the office in a way that supports multiple generations.
>
> In the US there are thousands of these smaller family offices, either embedded in a family business, or they're independent. Either way, the family office primarily serves the needs of one generation. And I think that's something to get clear on strategically. The question that has to be asked is, "Do we want to support that next generation? If the answer is yes, families need to think about when they are going to start bringing the next generation into the decision making and figure out how they are going to do that.

This problem was noted by many of the interviewees, but answers are at best difficult. Voth, for example, notes that planning is an issue on both ends. On one side, she bemoans a lack of planning:

> In the US, all over the world, we're getting calls from people literally in their 90s saying, "I might die." And they haven't done their planning. And they have this massive wealth structure, and they have advisors around them and trustees that are in their 80s. That doesn't work for the next generation.

And yet for Voth, too much planning can be damaging as well:

> There has to be a balance. If structures are too complex and there is too much specificity, these families can get overplanned and lock the next generation into a situation that they really aren't happy with.

Nicholas Warr, a legal advisor in the United Kingdom, also bemoans this lack of foresight:

> There is, in some of the less sophisticated topographies, the propensity to say, "I need a family office, therefore I'm going to go and hire a team of incredibly sophisticated and expensive investment professionals" without seeing how that all fits together.

Kuder, speaking in his capacity as an experienced advisor, recommends taking a highly organized approach to this planning. The hard work of cutting the planning down to just a few attainable goals bears tremendous dividends:

> Before it moves forward to founding, the family should be clear about what the family office is really responsible for. It should formulate between three to five objectives that the family office should achieve. It sounds simple, but it is not. You will quickly find that it is much simpler to put 20 to 30 wishes to paper that you would like to have the family office address. But in my view it is the wrong approach, because it will inevitably get bogged down. If you try to balance too many plates at once, it is highly likely that a few are going to fall and break. So while it is a simple piece of advice, it is also a crucial one.

Yet the Abou Adal sisters, members of a Lebanon-based family office serving 4 generations, call for just the opposite. For their family it was important to follow their own instincts and the overall process:

> When it comes to the family office structure, we're so happy that we did not just go along with advisors' recommendations and the best practices, but rather let it grow organically, as opposed to growing too fast or over-structuring too fast. This has been a relief so far, a liberating thing. One piece of advice: do not over-complicate the process and do what is right for your family enterprise!

The point here is not to argue the relative merits of these conflicting points of view. Kuder undoubtedly has seen successes and failures and can back them up with facts and figures; the Abou Adal sisters bear living testament to the potency of their own approach. The implementation of the principles explored in the various chapters of this book—that is: moving from theory into practice—is inherently a personal and specific affair. It is wise to respect the best practices that we lay out, but each family must acknowledge their own specific needs as well.

What ultimately matters, all agree, is an awareness of the issues, a genuine willingness to address the underlying issues from the start, and the sensitivity to appreciate and address different agendas by shareholders—either internally or with professional consultants at your side.

14.2 Looking Forward

14.2.1 The Future of the Family Office

This same openness to myriad possibilities should apply to any look forward as well.

Certainly some trends seem clearly ascendant. Many experts offered a bullish belief in further ceaseless rise of family office structures. They see clear indicators: Roughly 2.4 trillion US dollars are expected to be passed on to the next generation in the coming two decades. The wealth of the richest has grown by 17 percent (Source: "Billionaire Insights 2017," PwC and UBS), with especially powerful growth observed in China. In fact, 2017 saw more billionaires in Asia (637) than in the USA (563), the first time in documented history that this has occurred.

In this environment, there is a tremendous and growing need for highly professional asset management. Family offices will be in demand to provide support as a loyal partner and competent lobbyist—a trend that is likely to extend beyond the traditional markets of North America and Europe into Latin America, the Middle East and Asia.

Asked about the future of the family office, the interviewees primarily pointed at two concrete themes: the coming digitization and ESG/impact investment.

14.2.2 Digitization

The first theme, digitization, was largely predicted to supplement the work of current family office structures. In the words of Tom McCullough, a Family Officer in Canada, digitization will boost efficiency by automating some tasks:

> Digitization is already happening now. There's a lot more access to information on portals. I think that will continue. I can't picture how the 'robo' approach or artificial intelligence will affect our core advisory role with families, at least in the near term. So much of what we're doing is bringing judgment, wisdom and experience to clients to assist them with their very specific and unique concerns. Robo will be applicable when there are relatively simple tasks for a lot of people, but the core part of our work, our advice and counsel, is entirely customized and requires empathy and insight.
>
> There are many people worried about the incursion of robos, but it doesn't concern me much. I think technology will be a great tool for us to reduce some of

the back-office work and communication with clients and access to more flexible reporting for clients. So I think it's all positive.

Others see digitization as a tool to win acceptance among the younger ('digital native') generations. James Fleming, a Family Officer in the UK, expressed its promise thusly:

> In terms of channels to market, having an online capability where clients can access their portfolios throughout the internet is a given now. And it has to be. Now, we have not got that yet, but we are rapidly developing it and very soon we will have the facility for clients to view their entire portfolio through sitting at home on their PC.
>
> And I think that is something that we will develop further around information, so things such as podcasts, investment ideas and thought leadership piece, articles, etc. all of which are designed to connect with the clients using the digital channel are an enabler.

Fleming is also optimistic about technology's ability to supplement more than just simple tasks:

> These are very wealthy families and require a very high level of human intervention. That cannot be delivered by robots as yet.
>
> But where I see opportunities for say a business like us is gathering information, gathering knowledge, gathering research and investigating investment opportunities. That is where I think there will be a lot of development opportunities for us in the artificial intelligence world, in the facilitation of that research. I can see that happening in the retail market already, where AI is being utilized in that area.

And yet one of the figures most involved personally with the upcoming digitization, an IT consultant to an SFO who wished to remain anonymous, sees only limited benefits in this regard:

> Here we as a family office see a very clear distinction from other financial service providers. Our customers need only talk with us and they will be provided with precisely the information they are looking for at that moment. A customer with more than five accounts is not going to want to remotely check balance levels on their own.

Whether the family office will lead or follow in these trends remains to be seen. That their impact will eventually be felt, by contrast, seems clear.

14.2.3 ESG and Impact Investment

The second major point of prognostication involved Environmental, Social and Governance (ESG) and Impact Investment. While family offices often have a philanthropic element, and some even run or are associated with charitable family foundations, ESG/Impact Investment carves out a different space. It seeks to target investments toward good causes and other areas where the money will make a more immediate positive impact on the world. Like the idea that going green is not only doing good, but can inherently be a more profitable choice, ESG and Impact Investing are not charity per se, but rather a philosophy of activist investing.

The issue was perhaps most succinctly framed by McCullough, the Canadian Family Officer:

> Social and environmental investing is not requested by many of our clients, yet. But I believe it is a growth trend. I think of it in two or three different categories. On the one side is ESG, which I think will become absolutely standard fare in the next five years. It's just another way of doing an analysis. It's like Exxon, with their oil spill; if they had done better environmental governance, then shareholders would have lost less money. So I think that ESG is definitely coming.
>
> Second, Socially Responsible Investment (SRI), which is usually exclusion-oriented—"I don't want any carbon-based securities in my portfolio; we'll focus on wind and solar"—is also coming and I think it'll be done for money reasons (i.e. investment opportunity), not just social reasons.
>
> The third area is impact investing, which is finding investments that have more than just a financial bottom line. And I think that ends up being more in the venture type of category. We don't see a lot of demand from our families at this point, but I suspect it will come. The 'doing good' portion of family wealth is still firmly focused on charitable giving.
>
> ESG is definitely on the rise and will be integrated into the normal investment research process. SRI and impact are coming and that trend will accelerate as the next generation and women increasingly take control of the reins of the family investment portfolio. It may not be in 5 years, but maybe in 15 years it will be standard. I think it is important for all of us to be current and on the leading edge of this kind of work.

McCullough draws particular attention to the fact that these considerations do not emerge purely from a sense of conscience. They also make good business sense. As such, he sees them as clearly on the horizon.

Two elements of his observations are picked up elsewhere: the potential for this type of investment, but also the current lack of explicit demand for it. Larry Donckers, a family officer at an American single family office:

> I do keep it in mind because I hear about it so much. And I want to be ready when family members are interested and want more information. And I would say: of the dozen or so households we serve, there are several family members that are interested and go to workshops and sessions where they learn more about it.
>
> But it hasn't risen to the level where it's a family-wide mandate with x percent of the portfolio allocation. It is similar to our philanthropic efforts. We have not established a private foundation for the family yet, but individually, the family supports non-profit organizations and causes that they are passionate about and collectively, they provide support through the operating company, such as scholarships and community programs.
>
> But back to impact investing and ESG, we do have investments in the portfolio that would be considered in that category, but we do not segregate them internally for performance or evaluation at this point. In my view, the office is a reflection of the family members. We work to the speed, direction and course they set for us, so we have to be aware and knowledgeable of these different opportunities, such as ESG, to be responsive to their needs.

Simon Foster, CEO of a UK based family office for a Nigerian family described interest from his vantage point as well:

> ESG is vital to our investment philosophy and we try to achieve good balance across asset classes. In terms of appetite, we try and consider what we are as well. We have staunchly held beliefs, so we don't invest in any sin asset classes, things like gambling or arms dealership. We respect family values through that side of investing. We also actively ESG screen public market investments as part of the initial investment due diligence. ESG considerations also form a major part of our property investing. About 7 years ago we became a signatory to the UN Principles of Responsible Investing ("UNPRI"), so solid ESG permeates our activity.

Others saw interest as more muted. One consultant to family offices in Mexico viewed the entire field as somewhat fringe, with little general interest in ESG/impact banking. Clients might request that certain fields be avoided to respect their specific sensibilities but have little appetite otherwise for the field. This is especially true at the local level, since his clients tended not to be heavily invested in Mexico.

Others rejected the premise outright. One American family officer who requested anonymity reacted highly negatively to the label itself:

> We do not formally do "socially responsible" investing. Instead, we annually donate some of our profits to over 25 charitable organizations. So, we care about the community, helping the less privileged, the environment, etc, but it is not part of the portfolio. It is part of our charitable giving. Having said that, we look at cutting edge investment themes such as alternative energy, sustainable products, etc. If we think we will make money in these themes, we will invest. We are not going to put money in something just because it is "socially responsible." That is socialist and not a capitalist pursuit. We need a high probability of making a decent return first.

A German shareholder in a family office also dismissed the field as better served through a family office's philanthropic arm:

> While everybody is talking about this kind of thing, in practical terms I have yet to encounter any major single family office that has put Impact Investing or ESG at the center of its investment strategy. Our family regularly donates major sums to charitable organizations and also created a foundation. We use that as the hub for our charitable investments.

Here as with the family cohesiveness trap: the lesson is not that ESG/Impact Investment is or is not a good idea; time will tell if the sensibilities of the next generation make it a more prevalent theme. The lesson is that there are divergent, equally viable opinions even on the hot-button issues of the times.

14.3 Final Thoughts

Alan Greenspan, the former chairman of the US Federal Reserve, once quipped: "I guess I should warn you, if I turn out to be particularly clear, you've probably misunderstood what I've said." Like Mr. Greenspan, we caution against taking our general observations about the state of the family office market as concrete predictions of future performance. Our goal as authors was not to give specific advice on where to invest your money or who should inherit your company.

Quite the contrary. We have each learned an important lesson in our respective fields: the only certainty is uncertainty. Opinions and facts can and will change. Even reliable data is capable of contradicting itself, or of being too unclear to be of much use. Today's indicators may all point in one direction, but tomorrow's results may well go in the other. This is the nature of business and of life.

So how does one secure the important things in life? How can we organize the continuing success of a family-run business across generations and preserve prosperity and the family wealth for our children? The closest thing to an answer is no answer at all. It instead involves asking the smart questions that make it less likely that calamity will strike.

Throughout this book, we've encouraged you to be attentive to your situation, be honest in your self-reflections and above all else be thoroughly prepared. A family office serves as an extension, and even a multiplier, of this attitude. It is itself an inert tool and cannot guarantee success, but it can provide a broader base of wisdom, analysis and systematic rigor. It can reveal untapped economic potential, relieve stress by handling tax filings and create events and occasions for families to grow together. It can also identify and eliminate risks, both structural and acute. Above all else, it can work responsibly and free from conflict of interests to earn your trust and guard your flanks.

We encourage you to take the considerations we've covered in this book and transitioning them from the theoretical level to your own specific situation. Let these discussions, both with your family and your trusted advisors, guide the fundamental decision ahead: to found or join a family office, or to remain on the more classic wealth management path. Whatever you choose, we wish you luck and prosperity along your way.

Glossary[1]

Asset The building blocks of an individual or family's wealth. At its most basic, an asset is the cash value of anything that you can own. Note: this does not have to be a physical thing. If for example you author a song, the copyright for that song is also an asset.

In layman's terms, the opposite of an asset is a *Liability*.

As explained in Chap. 4, different assets and asset classes bring with them different levels of risk, which must be taken into account when structuring a portfolio of assets (See also: *Asset Allocation*, *Liquidity* and *Illiquidity*.)

Asset Allocation Asset allocation involves the various steps of choosing a portfolio's asset structure from the various asset classes, based on the family's level of wealth, life situation and risk appetite.

Asset allocation is typically broken down into three elements: the strategic, the tactical and the operative. Strategic asset allocation indicates which asset classes will be pursued over the long term. Decision-making at the tactical allocation level encompasses decisions in terms of weighting of those asset classes. The operative level then involves the actual purchase, sale or execution of the assets.

Asset Pooling The bundling together of a family's or families' wealth to achieve a greater critical mass of assets under management. This volume is important because the wealth manager can then attempt to leverage the economies of scale to negotiate better conditions on the market or even to qualify as an institutional investor, which opens the door to opportunities that might otherwise not be available.

[1] *While this book contains many obscure and difficult terms such as 'usufruct,' most can easily be cleared up with a dictionary. This abbreviated glossary contains solely key terms and concepts that the reader must grasp to understand its lessons.*

B. Canessa et al., *The Family Office*, https://doi.org/10.1007/978-3-319-99085-9

Basis Point In finance, basis points are used as a common unit of measurement for interest rates and other percentages. They indicate the percentage of change in a financial instrument, with one basis point is equal to 1/100th of 1%, or 0.01%, or 0.0001, and are used to denote the percentage change in a financial instrument. Within this system, 1% change = 100 basis points, while 0.01% = 1 basis point.

Bonds A bond is essentially a loan by the investor ('debtholder'), to be repaid after a defined period of time and at a negotiated interest rate, either fixed or variable. Bond is issued by entities, usually corporate or government, to raise money.

See also: *Security*.

Capital Capital is cash that is used to generate income or make an investment. Companies raise capital from investors by selling securities, and then typically use that money to expand their business. The platforms and institutions by which capital is raised are collectively known as the 'capital markets.'

Note that a corporation, as a legal person, can own its own capital separate and distinct from the owning family's wealth.

Closed Corporation Also known as "close corporation," "privately held company," "private company," "family corporation" or "incorporated partnership." All refer to a company whose shares are held by a small group of persons (such as a family) who are usually closely associated with the business. This legal form for a business often limits personal liability for the actions of the corporation without incurring many of the reporting requirements inherent to other limited liability forms of legal ownership.

Compliance Compliance is a branch of corporate governance that ensures the company and its employees observe internal policies and outside regulatory requirements. It is a crucial part of quality assurance and risk management, as it helps prevent the company and its employees from breaking laws and regulations (intentionally or unintentionally).

Concierge Services Non-financial private sphere services performed by the family office for individual owners. This can range from travel planning and minding houses or pets while the owners are away to choosing schools for the owners' children. Not all family offices offer concierge services, and fees models can vary greatly from family office to family office.

Conflict of Interest A conflict of interest arises when a person or corporation entrusted to perform a specific duty, typically advisory in nature, cannot execute that duty in an unbiased manner. This typically occurs if the advising person or firm has a vested interest in the outcome, such as a greater potential commission from recommending one product over another, regardless of whether that commission-bound product actually best serves the interests of the client. A family office should to the greatest extent possible be structured so as to be free from conflicts of interest.

Controlling In a business context, controlling is a managerial function that reviews all accounting-related activities. Among other key tasks, the controller is responsible for reviewing financial reporting.

Corporation One of the central concepts of modern business is the establishment of corporations as a "legal person" separate from the humans associated with it (such as its owners and employees). This "corporate personhood" conveys the entity with rights similar to those of a human individual (a 'natural person'), meaning the corporation can enter into contracts, sue or be sued, own assets and borrow or lend money.

When discussion corporations, it is important to clarify which version of the term is being used, as the term 'corporation' can mean different things in different places. In North America, for example, it usually describes large businesses or even business groups. In much of the rest of the world, that same concept is conveyed with the term 'company.' This book uses the North American definition.

Current Assets Current assets (AKA current accounts) are the value of all assets that can reasonably expect to be converted into cash within one year. All other assets are considered long-term assets. This value appears on the balance sheet and can be an important measure of *Liquidity*. See also: *Assets*.

Direct Investments Also known as 'foreign direct investment.' The investment is made in a business outside the investor's own country and is intended to acquire a controlling interest in that foreign business. Direct investment delivers capital funding in exchange for an equity interest without requiring the purchase of regular shares of a company's stock.

Distribution A distribution is a payment of stock, cash or physical products to a company's shareholders. This can also include capital gains from investment trusts, for example. In the context of this book, some wealth managers design portfolios whose quarterly or monthly distributions provide clients with their current income to cover ongoing costs. See also: *Dividends*.

Dividends A dividend is a distribution of a portion of a company's earnings paid to a class of its shareholders. In the context of this book, some wealth managers design portfolios whose quarterly or monthly distributions provide clients with their current income to cover their ongoing costs. See also: *Distribution*.

Due Diligence Due diligence is an important management function. It refers to the process of systematically reviewing facts—financial, legal, regulatory, political, etc.—about another person or entity before entering into an agreement with them. Due diligence is considered a crucial step in risk management.

Entrepreneurship Entrepreneurship at its most basic means founding a business to bring an idea to market, and assuming the risks and rewards associated with that venture. For the purposes of this book, it is presumed that the families of most of our readers will have earned their fortune through some original entrepreneurial act, as opposed to an inherited aristocratic fortune or wealth earned as an athletes or artists. Where this is the case, it often makes sense to join a multi family office whose clientele is also formed from entrepreneurial families.

Family Constitution A family constitution is a document that outlines how a family will govern itself. Beyond laying out expectations for behavior of the different family members, both on their own and in relation to one another, it should also be viewed as a shared statement regarding the universal questions at play in every family: power, money, love, personal fulfilment.

Family Governance Family Governance is a process that gives formal structure to the expectations and obligations of the members of the family. It typically includes policy rules regarding succession, decision paths in the family and notification chains in terms of information from the family office to the family, and defines the role, if any, of advisory councils, supervisory councils, family managers, family councils, investment councils or quorum requirements at shareholders meetings. It can also encompass conflict resolution, family activity, family education, and sometimes family philanthropy. Family governance is a crucial tool in promoting family unity and 'buy-in' to the family office.

Illiquid An asset is described as 'illiquid' if it cannot be easily sold or exchanged for cash without a substantial loss in value. In business, a company is called illiquid if does not have the cash necessary to meet its debt obligations. See also: *Liquidity*.

Impact Investment Impact investing inherently seeks to promote positive social or environmental effects in addition to financial gain. Unlike Socially Responsible Investing (SRI), which typically looks to 'do no harm,' impact investing actively seeks to make a positive impact through the act of investment, for example, in non-profits that benefit the community or in clean technology enterprises.

Limited Liability Company In a limited liability company (LLC), the members of the company cannot be held personally liable for the company's debts or liabilities. Limited liability companies function as hybrid entities combining the characteristics of a corporation and a partnership or sole proprietorship. Different countries and economic systems offer different versions of the LLC model.

Liquidity Liquidity describes the degree to which an asset or security can be quickly bought or sold in the market without affecting the asset's price. Cash is considered the most liquid asset. Other asset classes such as real estate and fine art are considered relatively illiquid.

A company is considered liquid if it has the cash to pay its debt obligations. See *Illiquid*.

Net Worth Net worth refers to the value of a person's assets (financial and non-financial), minus their liabilities. In the language of financial institutions, prospective family office founders are referred to as Ultra High Net Worth Individuals (UHNWI), often defined as having investable assets of at least $30 million.

Operating Company In the context of this book, distinction is made between an operating company, typically the legacy company with which the family earned its fortune, and the family office. The operating company earns income through the sale of goods or services; the family office is instead tasked with preserving and expanding the family's wealth through investments.

Partnership A partnership is a formal arrangement in which two or more parties cooperate to manage and operate a business. Various partnership arrangements are possible in which all partners might share liabilities and profits equally or some partners may have limited liability. Not every partner is necessarily involved in the management and day-to-day operations of the venture, such as in the case of a "silent partner." In some jurisdictions, partnerships enjoy favorable tax treatment relative to corporations.

Philanthropy Literally: 'the love of humanity.' In modern usage, a desire to improve the well-being of humankind, such as through charitable aid or donations. Many family offices have a philanthropic organ to give back to the communities that have contributed to their wealth.

Power of Attorney A Power of Attorney is a legal document giving one person the power to act on behalf another person. The person assigning power can choose to give comprehensive powers of representation or only limited powers, such as solely the authority to make medical decisions for the other party. Despite the name, the power of attorney can be assigned to anyone, such as a spouse or child, and not just a licensed attorney.

Prenuptial Agreement A prenuptial agreement is a contract that a couple enters into before marriage. While it can theoretically cover almost anything, most 'prenups' outline each party's responsibilities and financial assets in the event that the marriage dissolves. Because failed marriages can represent an existential threat to shared family wealth, many high net worth families require that their members enter into such agreements before wedding to reduce or eliminate exposure to splitting in a divorce or death-of-spouse situation.

Private Equity Private equity is capital that is not listed on a public exchange. Private equity investors typically form firms that then invest directly in other companies, instead of buying stock. Profits are then typically earned by increasing the purchased company's value and then reselling it.

Remuneration Purity For the purposes of a family office, this term refers to a model of financing whereby the family office operates solely on fees it earns from the owning family or families. This model is intended to reduce conflicts of interest. Commercial multi family offices in particular often draw on other potential income streams, such as commissions from recommending certain financial products, and hence can potentially be more susceptible to conflicts of interest.

Security A security is a tradable ("fungible") financial asset. In common usage it refers to any form of financial instrument, but its actual legal definition varies from jurisdiction to jurisdiction. Most typically it represents some form of investment (in a company via stock), collateral (a creditor relationship with a governmental body or a corporation through a bond from that entity), or a right to ownership (known as an option).

Shareholder Value 'Shareholder value' refers to an impetus, spoken or unspoken, by a company's management to generate a return on invested capital above the market average. If management successfully creates value over the long term, such as through sales growth, then share price will increase and the company can pay larger cash dividends to shareholders. The concept is sometimes criticized for encouraging short term results (and an immediate payout) at the cost of the long-term health of the company. Within the context of a commercial multi family office, shareholder value concerns ('earn more money from clients') can stand in direct conflict with the interests of the client family ('reduce costs and preserve wealth').

Sparring Partner One of the key precepts of due diligence is that ideas be reviewed from all angles. For reasons of corporate politics, it may be difficult for the team around the chief executive to offer honest criticism and ask hard questions about the boss's ideas. At the institutional level, it can help to have other structures in place to serve in this role of the 'sparring partner,' such as an independent advisory council or investment council. The name refers to the boxing partners used to train competitive boxers; they serve to challenge and hone the skills of the competitor by 'sparring' (practice fighting) at a highly competitive level.

Statutory Shares Many jurisdictions require that a portion of a deceased person's estate be distributed to the deceased's spouse or child, even if the deceased did not wish for them to receive a share, or specified a lesser amount. While the statutory share must be deduced from the total remaining inheritance for other beneficiaries, it does not otherwise change the terms of the testament. See *Testament.*

Stocks A stock is a type of security that signifies ownership in a corporation and represents a claim on part of the corporation's assets and earnings. See *Security.*

Succession Succession is the orderly passage of power, assets or other property from one entity to another, typically from generation to generation. This is related to, but not identical, to estate planning, which is more concerned with individual wealth and not larger structures.

Testament A last will and testament, known commonly simply as a 'testament' or 'will,' is a legal document that records a person's desires for their possessions after death. The estate's executor is tasked with carrying out those wishes where possible, but the desires of the deceased are not all-powerful. Applicable laws may invalidate some requests, especially where the disinheritance of spouses and children are involved. See: *Statutory Shares.*

Trust In common usage, 'trust' means good faith between individuals. In the financial world, however, it also refers to a fiduciary relationship between a trustor and another party, the trustee, on behalf of third party, the beneficiary. Trusts have the right to hold title to property or assets and provide legal protection for the trustor's assets. In a financial context, a trust can also be a type of closed-end fund established as a public limited company.

Bibliography

Archer C, Hauser BR (2015) Family offices. Globe Business Publishing, London
Boldt T, Büll K, Voss M (2013) Die neue MaRisk-Compliance-Funktion – Ein Leitfaden für die Bankpraxis. Bank-Verlag, Cologne
von Bechtolsheim C, Rhein A (2009) Management komplexer Familienvermögen – Organisation, Strategie, Umsetzung, 2nd edn. Gabler, Wiesbaden
Daniell M, Hamilton S (2010) Family legacy and leadership – preserving true family wealth in challenging times, 1st edn. Wiley, Singapore
Farkas-Richling D, Fischer TR, Richter A (eds) (2012) Private banking und family office, 2nd edn. Stuttgart, Schäffer-Poeschel
German Federal Bank Bundesbank (2014) Auslegungshilfe zur Verordnung über die aufsichtsrechtlichen Anforderungen an Vergütungssysteme von Instituten. Frankfurt
Gray L (2004) The new family office – innovative strategies for consulting to the affluent. Linnius, London
Koeberle-Schmid A, Unger M (2019) Nachfolge im Familienunternehmen. Beck Verlag, München
Koeberle-Schmid A, Kenyon-Rouvinez D, Poza E (2014) Governance in family enterprises. Palgrave Macmillan, Basingstoke, Hampshire
Moody N, Tasman-Jones J, Finnigan M (2015) Campden research/UBS – the global family office report 2015. London
Rosplock K (2014) The complete family office handbook – a guide for affluent families and the advisors who serve them. Wiley, Hoboken
Scharf P (2014) Compliance in Kredit- und Finanzdienstleistungsinstituten – Grundlagen der Compliance-Funktion. Abgrenzung zu den Grundsätzen ordnungsgemäßer Bankgeschäftsführung. Diplomica, Hamburg

B. Canessa et al., *The Family Office*, https://doi.org/10.1007/978-3-319-99085-9

Schaubach P (2011) Family Office im Privaten Wealth Management – Konzeption und empirische Untersuchung aus Sicht der Vermögensinhaber, 4. Aufl. Uhlenbruch, Bad Soden

Wilson RC (2012) The family office book – investing capital for the ultra-affluent, 1st edn. Wiley, Hoboken

Wilson RC (2014) The single family office: creating, operating & managing investments of a single family office, 1st edn. CreateSpace, Lexington

Index

B. Canessa et al., *The Family Office*, https://doi.org/10.1007/978-3-319-99085-9

Made in United States
Orlando, FL
05 July 2025

62647486R00171